17 Sept 2006

FREEDOM FROM WANT

Jenny —
We missed you in Honolulu.
Thanks for joining the struggle for
Freedom from Want.

Aloha, Jure

D1273154

Dr. Kent spoke at
ADA/FNCE 2006
in Honolulu, Hawai'i

For Jenny
From Marie

ADVANCING HUMAN RIGHTS

SUMNER B. TWISS, JOHN KELSAY, TERRY COONAN, SERIES EDITORS

FREEDOM
FROM WANT

The Human Right to Adequate Food

GEORGE KENT

FOREWORD BY JEAN ZIEGLER

GEORGETOWN UNIVERSITY PRESS WASHINGTON, D.C.

Georgetown University Press, Washington, D.C.
© 2005 by Georgetown University Press.
ALL RIGHTS RESERVED
Printed in the United States of America

10 9 8 7 6 5 4 3 2 1   2005

This book is printed on acid-free, recycled paper meeting
the requirements of the American National Standard for
Permanence in Paper for Printed Library Materials and
that of the Green Press Initiative.

Library of Congress Cataloging-in-Publication Data
Kent, George, 1939–
    Freedom from want : the human right
to adequate food / George Kent.
        p. cm. — (Advancing human rights series)
        Includes bibliographical references and index.
        ISBN 1-58901-055-8 (cloth : alk. paper) —
        ISBN 1-58901-056-6 (paper : alk. paper)
        1. Food supply. 2. Hunger. 3. Human rights.
    I. Title. II. Series.
        HD9000.5.K376 2005
        363.8—dc22

                                    2004025023

Design and composition by Jeff Clark
at Wilsted & Taylor Publishing Services

Dedicated to the hundreds of millions of people who suffer

because of what governments do, and fail to do.

Creo que el mundo es bello,

que la poesía es como el pan, de todos.

I believe the world is beautiful

and that poetry, like bread, is for everyone.

—MARTÍN ESPADA

Contents

PART III ■ APPLICATIONS

Tables and Figures

Tables

Figures

Foreword

We live in a world that is richer than ever before in history, yet 840 million people still suffer from hunger every day. There is already enough food in the world to feed the global population twice over, yet every seven seconds, a child dies from hunger or malnutrition-related diseases. This daily massacre of hunger is not a question of fate; it is the result of human decisions. Hunger, malnutrition, and chronic poverty still exist, not only in poor countries but also in some of the richest countries in the world. The divide between rich and poor, North and South, is growing every day. Yet, this could all be changed with political will and real action.

The right to adequate food is a human right for all people everywhere. The right to adequate food is laid out in the most important human rights document, the Universal Declaration of Human Rights, as well as the International Covenant on Economic, Social, and Cultural Rights. The right to food reflects President Franklin Roosevelt's declaration that "freedom from want" was one of the four fundamental freedoms that informed our original understanding of universal human rights.

George Kent's new book outlines the advances being made in our understanding of the right to adequate food. He explains and defines the right and appeals for an urgent recognition that the right to food is a human right. He shows how hunger and poverty are not simple, technical problems that can be addressed by raising agricultural production. Hunger and poverty are instead deeply political problems, rooted in the fact that many people do not have access to food because they do not have adequate control over local resources or decent opportunities to engage in meaningful, productive work. Kent argues that we must adopt a human rights approach to empower the world's poorest and to ensure the accountability of governments and other actors for their promises to eradicate hunger.

Human rights are primarily about human dignity. Kent explains that the right to adequate food is not about charity: It is the right to be able to feed yourself in dignity. Hunger will never be solved by charity or by food aid. It must be solved by creating the conditions in which all human beings can live a decent life, providing for themselves. The human right to adequate food is a practical goal, as well as a moral and legal obligation. It is not simply a theoretical or aspirational ideal. Understanding the right to food as a human right recognizes the imperative obligation to act. It requires all governments to work progressively toward the full eradication of hunger. If they fail to make progress, they can—and should—be held accountable by the people. The right to food is not merely a normative standard. Kent clarifies the need to establish specific institutional arrangements that will ensure accountability for the realization of human rights.

Many governments still resist the idea of accountability in the fight against hunger. Many make endless promises to eradicate hunger, yet resist the idea of the justiciability of the right to food. Kent shows that a number of governments still resist the very concept of human rights as including economic, social, and cultural rights, such as the human right to adequate food. He argues, for example, that the resistance of the government of the United States results from a systematic and sustained misunderstanding of the meaning of the right to adequate food. He also moves the human rights debate forward by challenging the view that human rights obligations stop at each country's borders. He argues that governments must recognize their human rights obligations not only to their own people but also to the citizens of other countries. In a globalized world of interdependent countries and in the common fight against hunger, the right to adequate food entails responsibilities and obligations of all of us to all of us.

Kent's important book is a part of a growing movement to construct a strong and coherent understanding of the right to food. Taking us through the history and politics of the human right to adequate food, he urgently calls for a true rights-based approach to development. He brings great insight to recent advances in our understanding of the right to adequate food, as well as other economic, social, and cultural rights. He also challenges the traditional boundaries of human rights and does not flinch from examining the political, economic, and ideological fault lines of the debate. It is a courageous book that shows us, as he says, that human rights are not only unashamedly utopian but are also eminently practical. Human rights can make a difference.

It is time to make the right to food a reality.

JEAN ZIEGLER
United Nations Special
Rapporteur on the
Right to Food

Acknowledgments

I would like to thank the many people who contributed to the preparation of this book, directly or indirectly, including many students, online and offline, who helped to make it work. I want to voice my special thanks to Asbjørn Eide, Wenche Barth Eide, Uwe Kracht, and Arne Oshaug for their support, assistance, and kind hospitality over these many years.

Introduction: Taking Rights Seriously

Each year, more than 10 million children die before their fifth birthdays, about half of them from causes associated with malnutrition. This is a silent holocaust, repeated year after year. Malnutrition leads to death, illness, and a significantly reduced quality of life for hundreds of millions of people. This book's central concern is that very many people do not get adequate food, in terms of quantity or in terms of quality.

A strong distinction is made here between this statement:

Everyone should have adequate food.

and this one:

Everyone has the right to adequate food.

The meaning of the human right to adequate food is to be found in the difference between these two claims. The second implies not only a normative claim (what ought to be the case) but also the idea that others have specific obligations to assure the realization of this right. It also implies the establishment of concrete institutional arrangements to ensure the realization of the right. This book explores the meaning of the claim that adequate food is a human right.

People have a right to adequate food, and to be free from hunger, as a matter of international law. The right is articulated in the Universal Declaration of Human Rights; the International Covenant on Economic, Social, and Cultural Rights; the Convention on the Rights of the Child; and several other international instruments. States and the governments that represent them, and other parties as well, have obligations to ensure that the right is realized. States that are parties to these agreements have made a commitment to ensure the realization of the right.

The purpose of this book is to help its readers understand the meaning of economic, social, and cultural rights through exploration of one of these rights, the human right to adequate food. It suggests how such individuals might formulate recommendations to adapt an agency's or a country's activities to conform more closely to the human rights framework, and thus contribute more effectively to the realization of human rights. Thus, it should be of value to:

- the director of a nutrition program within a country,
- the director of a food program in an international agency,
- an executive in a ministry of agriculture or ministry of health who is responsible for food and nutrition,

- a member of a nation's legislature,
- a nongovernmental organization concerned with food issues,
- a specialist working on socioeconomic and legal aspects of national development, and
- ordinary people concerned with their own and their community's well-being.

This book can be used to introduce human rights as a new and different approach to dealing with social issues. At a deeper level, its purpose is to help expand the base of shared understandings of human rights in general and the human right to adequate food in particular. Human rights work is, in part, the effort to reconcile differences in understandings of the meanings of specific rights. This book can be used as a basis for dialogue on human rights that cuts across cultures, classes, and contexts.

Protein-energy malnutrition, the major nutrition problem throughout the world, is used here to illustrate the meaning and application of the human right to adequate food, but this human right is much broader than that. It applies in rich as well as in poor countries. It is relevant not only for the poor in rich countries, but also for the middle class and the rich, and it is concerned not only with the hunger of the poor but also with the ways in which middle- and upper-class diets may lead to obesity, heart disease, cancer, and other food-related ailments. The human right to adequate food is relevant to school meals and to prison food. The management of micronutrient deficiencies such as iron-deficiency anemia, iodine deficiency, and vitamin A deficiency should be guided by the human rights approach, whether in rich countries or poor countries. Good drinking water, which is essential to the human diet, should be regarded as part of the human right to adequate food. Food safety also is an essential element of the human right to adequate food.

This book comprises seventeen chapters. This introduction previews the entire book. Chapter 1 introduces the major technical and social dimensions of food and nutrition issues. It does not discuss human rights. Chapter 2 describes the international human rights system in broad terms. Chapter 3 describes the role of food in human rights law, and also in international humanitarian law.

Part II begins with chapter 4, which argues that the three key elements of any rights system are

A. The *rights holders* and their rights;
B. The *duty bearers* and their obligations corresponding to the rights of the rights holders; and
C. The *agents of accountability*, and the procedures through which they assure that the duty bearers meet their obligations to the rights holders. The accountability mechanisms include, in particular, the remedies available to the rights holders themselves.

National, international, or other rights systems may be viewed as specific forms of this generic type. These three key elements of rights systems are analyzed in turn in chapters 5, 6, and 7.

Part III considers various applications of the human right to adequate food. It begins with reviews of that right in three selected countries, India, Brazil, and the United States. Chapters 11, 12, and 13 then examine several issues common to all countries: feeding infants, feeding infants of HIV-positive mothers, and water.

Although chapters 8 through 13 look primarily at the ways in which the human right to adequate food works within countries, the remaining chapters explore the ways in which the right works, or should work, on a global basis. Chapter 14 is on the implications of the human right to adequate food for international trade, especially trade in food products. Chapter 15, on refugees, explores the obligations of the international community for that distinctive category of people who, by definition, are no longer under the protection of their home states.

The broader issue of the obligations of the international community to needy people throughout the world is considered in chapter 16. The premise of these chapters is that the human right to adequate food, like other human rights, should be viewed as truly *inter*-national in character, implying *inter*-national obligations.

The concluding chapter highlights the need for understanding human rights and the corresponding obligations as being global in scope and not limited by national borders. It argues that there is a need for democratic global governance if human rights are to be realized everywhere.

The chapters in part III describe a variety of concrete applications of the human right to adequate food. The literature provide additional illustrations, such as the case studies on Burma (Burmese Border Consortium 2003), New York (New York City Welfare Reform and Human Rights Documentation Project 2000), the Philippines (Regalado 2000), India (Dev 2003), Zimbabwe (Human Rights Watch 2003; Amnesty International 2004), and indigenous peoples (International Indian Treaty Council 2002), and also reports of the United Nations special rapporteur on the right to food (e.g., United Nations, Economic and Social Council 2003a, 2003b) listed in the references at the end of this book. The chapter on food in the South African Human Rights Commission's annual *Economic and Social Rights Report* provides accounts of the status of the human right to adequate food in that country (South African Human Rights Commission 2002, 2003). There is a case study on Russia (United Nations, Economic and Social Council 1995) that should be read together with a commentary from the Foodfirst Information and Action Network (1997). The Food and Agriculture Organization of the United Nations has issued case studies on the right to food in Brazil, Canada, India, South Africa, and Uganda (available at http://www.fao.org/righttofood/en/23419/highlight_51629en.html; for an overview of these studies, see http://www.fao.org/DOCREP/MEETING/008/J2475E.HTM).

One central message in this analysis is that you do not solve the hunger problem by feeding people—that only perpetuates it. The problems of hunger and malnutrition can be solved only by ensuring that people can live in dignity by having decent opportunities to provide for themselves.

The human right to adequate food and all other human rights imply strong obligations on the part of national governments to their own people. However, if the obligations were limited to those of one's own national government, the idea of global human rights would be little more than a cruel joke. Human rights do not end at national borders, and neither do the corresponding obligations. Thus, the second major message here is that all of us have obligations in some measure to ensure the realization of all human rights for all people. A child may have the misfortune of being born in a poor country, but that child is not born in a poor world. The world as a whole has the capacity to sharply reduce global hunger and malnutrition. It is obligated to do that.

PART I Foundations

CHAPTER 1

Food and Nutrition

Malnutrition

Hundreds of millions of people around the world do not get enough to eat, and for many more millions, the quality of their food is not adequate to maintain basic health. One cannot escape the finding of the United Nations' special rapporteur on the right to food: "In the world today, it is an affront to human dignity to see how many people starve to death, or live a life not worthy of the name, in conditions of squalor and unable to escape, with minds and bodies that are not whole" (United Nations, Economic and Social Council 2002a, 9).

Nutrition is a process through which living organisms use food to maintain life, growth, and normal functions. Malnutrition results when this process goes wrong, whether because of problems on the intake side or because of problems in processing the intake.

Protein-energy malnutrition (PEM), sometimes described as protein-calorie malnutrition, is one of the most widespread forms of malnutrition. It is so prevalent that in the absence of other specifications, references to malnutrition are generally understood to indicate PEM. Kwashiorkor and marasmus are intense forms of PEM. At times, the term *undernutrition* is used to designate PEM.

PEM is usually due to a lack of energy foods rather than to a lack of protein intake. The symptoms of the protein deficit often observed in cases of severe malnutrition result from the fact that the protein that is obtained is diverted to fulfilling immediate energy needs, and thus is not available for the body building and maintenance functions normally fulfilled by protein. If energy supplies are adequate, the protein remains available for its body-building and maintenance functions, a phenomenon described as *protein sparing* (McLaren 1974).

The United Nations System Standing Committee on Nutrition (SCN)—formerly known as the United Nations Administrative Committee on Coordination/Sub-Committee on Coordination (ACC/SCN)—is responsible for coordinating nutrition-related activities among the UN agencies. The independent Commission on the Nutrition Challenges of the 21st Century appointed by the SCN submitted a report titled *Ending Malnutrition by 2020: An Agenda for Change in the Millennium* that identified eight major issues:

EIGHT MAJOR NUTRITIONAL CHALLENGES

1. *Low birth weights.* Some 30 million infants are born each year in developing countries with low birth weight, representing about 24% of all

newborns in these countries. Population-wide interventions aimed at preventing fetal growth retardation are urgently needed.

2. *Childhood undernutrition underestimated.* There are still more than 150 million underweight preschool children worldwide, and more than 200 million are stunted. This underweight and stunting is the tip of the iceberg. Suboptimal growth may affect many more. Stunting is linked to mental impairment. At current rates of improvement about 1 billion children will be growing up by 2020 with impaired mental development.

3. *Undernourished adults.* High proportions of Asian and African mothers are undernourished: this is exacerbated by seasonal food shortages, especially in Africa. About 243 million adults in developing countries are severely undernourished, judged by a body mass index of less than 17 kg/m^2. This type of adult undernutrition may impair work capacity and lower resistance to infection.

4. *Pandemic anaemia.* Anaemia during infancy, made worse by maternal undernutrition, causes poor brain development. Anaemia is also very prevalent in school children and adolescents. Maternal anaemia is pandemic, over 80% in some countries, and is associated with very high rates of maternal death.

5. *Extensive persisting vitamin A deficiency.* Severe vitamin A deficiency is on the decline in all regions. However, subclinical vitamin A deficiency still affects between 140 to 250 million preschool children in developing countries, and is associated with high rates of morbidity and mortality.

6. *Adult chronic diseases accentuated by early undernutrition.* Evidence from both developing and industrialised countries links maternal and early childhood undernutrition to increased susceptibility in adult life to noncommunicable diseases such as adult-onset diabetes, heart disease and hypertension. These diet-related noncommunicable diseases—including cancers—are already major public health challenges for developing countries.

7. *Obesity rates escalating.* Overweight and obesity are rapidly growing in all regions, affecting children and adults alike. These problems are now so common in some developing countries that they are beginning to replace more traditional public health concerns such as undernutrition and infectious disease. Obesity is a risk factor for a number of non-communicable diseases, adult-onset diabetes in particular.

8. *Sustaining iodization programs.* Efforts are needed to sustain the remarkable progress made in the past decade towards universal salt iodization and elimination of iodine deficiency disorders. Monitoring systems, quality control, and sound legislation are key priorities, as well as improving outreach to isolated communities. (United Nations System Standing Committee on Nutrition 2000, 8)

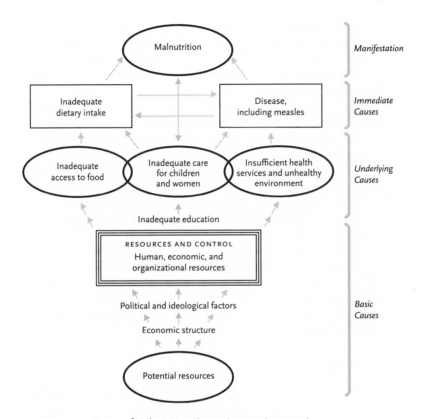

Figure 1.1. Causes of Malnutrition. *Source*: Jonsson (1997, 377).

Causes of Malnutrition

There are many different ways of conceptualizing the relationships between malnutrition and its causes. UNICEF's approach, which is represented in figure 1.1, has been adopted by many UN agencies and other groups in analyzing the broader context of malnutrition.

The UNICEF framework considers causes of malnutrition at different levels, distinguishing among the *immediate, underlying,* and *basic* causes. For simplicity's sake, figure 1.1 shows many one-way arrows, and it may suggest that the different causes operate independently of one another. Often, however, the causes of malnutrition impinge on and reinforce one another. For example, disease can prevent a household or society from mobilizing needed resources.

Immediate Causes

The immediate causes of malnutrition are inadequate or improper dietary intake and disease. The two are closely linked because bad diets can increase vulnerability to disease, and many diseases are accompanied by fever with loss of appetite and reduced absorption. Even with good food coming in, exposure to infections or to infestation by parasites may result in the nutrients being run right out through diarrhea or diverted to parasites. Disease often increases the body's food requirements.

Often, young children are malnourished despite the availability of food, especially if their caretakers do not have sufficient time to feed them frequently enough. If they are offered only one or two meals a day, the small stomach capacity of children can prevent them from eating enough to meet their needs. This is especially critical where the staple is maize or a starchy root like cassava. Unless special precautions are taken, cooking porridge or *stappe* causes the maize or cassava to bind water, swelling it, and produces meals with low energy and nutrient density. Children who depend on such foods must be fed frequently during the day or they will not get enough.

When children die at an early age, the cause is usually not malnutrition alone but a combination of malnutrition and disease. Thus, though food is necessary, it is not by itself sufficient for ensuring good nutritional status. Environmental hygiene and general health status play major roles in assuring good nutrient utilization. The immediate causes can be understood as the *clinical* causes of malnutrition.

Underlying Causes

The major underlying cause of malnutrition is *food insecurity*, which is discussed later in this chapter in the section titled "Food and Nutrition Security." Insufficient and unstable access to adequate household food supplies constitutes the major underlying cause of malnutrition. A number of factors all work together to produce malnutrition: the food insecurity of the household, combined with skewed distribution within the family (usually in favor of the male head of household), inadequate care of vulnerable groups (children, women, the elderly), limited prenatal and postnatal care, improper weaning practices, lack of immunizations, inadequate access to basic health services, an unhealthy environment, women's heavy work burdens, and poor water supplies.

Feeding with breast milk substitutes clearly illustrates how malnutrition can arise from provision of the wrong kind of food, especially when it is combined with bad sanitation. The promotion of infant formula is especially pernicious in underdeveloped countries where sanitation is poor, literacy levels are low, and people are extremely poor. As a result, infants in these countries who are fed with formula have much higher mortality rates than breast-fed infants. The health effects of formula feeding have been less severe in rich countries, but it is clear that morbidity and mortality levels are higher among formula-fed infants, even in rich countries (Chen and Rogan 2004).

Feeding patterns and the choice of foods used to complement breast milk are critical. At times, children are given inappropriate foods such as tea. Some traditional beliefs regarding appropriate foods and feeding patterns can result in deficient diets for pregnant or lactating women or children.

Nutrition status is determined not only by food supply and good health services (including a healthy environment) but also by the quality of care, "the provision in the household and the community of time, attention and support to meet the physical, mental and social needs of the growing child and other family members" (Gillespie and Mason 1990). The care element has been subjected to systematic analysis (Engle, Menon, and Haddad 1999; Haddad and Oshaug 1999; Longhurst and Tomkins 1995; United Nations Development Program 1999, chap. 3). It is now widely accepted that food, health, and care are the three pillars of good nutrition. These are the underlying or *household*-level factors that determine nutrition status.

Basic Causes

The basic causes of malnutrition can be divided into three broad categories. First, there may be problems relating to *human resources*, having to do with inadequate knowledge, inadequate skills, or inadequate time. Second, there may be problems relating to *economic resources*, referring to inadequate assets in terms of money income, land, or other factors. Third, there may be inadequate *organizational resources*, such as inadequate schools, health care programs, or water supply systems. The basic causes can be understood as relating to *societal* causes of malnutrition.

Conventionally, explanations of malnutrition have centered on the clinical and household levels, but an understanding is needed at the societal level as well. The endless marginalization of the poor certainly is one of the basic causes of malnutrition in the world (Kent 1984, 1995; Drèze and Sen 1989; Sen 1981).

Amartya Sen and Jean Drèze argue that hunger is due primarily to a failure of entitlements rather than, say, to inadequate agricultural productivity or excessive population growth:

> What we can eat depends on what food we are able to acquire. . . . The set of alternative bundles of commodities over which a person can establish such command will be referred to as this person's "entitlement." If a group of people fail to establish their entitlement over an adequate amount of food, they have to go hungry. (Drèze and Sen 1989, 9, 22)

This approach avoids "the simplicity of focusing on the ratio of food to population [that] has persistently played an obscuring role over centuries, and continues to plague policy discussions today much as it has deranged anti-famine policies in the past." This approach requires a shift in thinking from *what exists* to *who can command what* (Eide 1995, 95).

Food analysts distinguish between the *availability* of food, which refers to the overall quantities and types of foods in any particular place, and food's *accessibility*, which refers to the ability of individuals to obtain that food. Even when food is available, many people may not have enough money to make a legitimate claim on it. Many famines have occurred in places where overall food supplies have been more than adequate.

Thus, at its root, the issue is not simply about the access to food as such; it is also about access to the means of production and to decent opportunities for doing productive work. Sen's analysis was anticipated by Edgar Owens, who argued that "creating economic and social rights for the world's small farmers, is the first step in enabling countries to feed their own people. Where these rights have been created and small farmers have access to production resources, public organizations, and law, very high farm productivity has been achieved (Owens 1987, 51). The importance of clear claims to ownership of the means of production is emphasized in the analyses of Hernando De Soto (2000).

It is important to know not only what resources exist but also who has what sorts of control over resources. This in turn leads to questions regarding the way in which the local community and society as a whole are governed. More democratic societies are likely to be associated with a more equitable distribution of resources, and thus with less malnutrition.

It follows from this approach that strengthening entitlements can help to remedy the hunger problem. Some analysts implicitly assume that this can be done only by increasing the household's capacity to produce or purchase food. However, it is now widely recognized that, under some conditions, people also should have a claim on the resources of their societies on the basis of their needs. They should have claims not only on food but also on care and health services, and other factors essential to an adequate standard of living. The meaning of entitlements is discussed more fully in chapter 5.

Growth Measurement

Assessments of protein-energy malnutrition are commonly based on anthropometric (body) measures. Measurements may be made of height, weight, or arm circumference, for example, and the results compared with appropriate norms. For a time, the Gomez scale of expected weight (or height) for age was used. The extent of malnutrition was assessed in terms of the ratio of a child's weight to the expected weight for healthy children of the same age and gender, expressed as a percentage. Thus a child between 60 and 75 percent of the standard weight for his or her age would be said to be moderately malnourished. The preference now is to make the assessment in terms of the number of statistical standard deviations below the expected weight (or height). A child more than 2 standard deviations below the standard is described as undernourished. Work is now under way to improve the charts describing the standard weights and heights for children of different ages (Garza and De Onis 1999; Fomon 2004).

In adults, assessments are sometimes made in terms of the body mass index (BMI), calculated as the individual's weight in kilograms divided by the square of the individual's height in meters. Adults whose BMI is very low are thin and possibly undernourished. Though a BMI of 18.5 has sometimes been used as the standard, the exact cutoff point that should be used to categorize an individual as undernourished remains a matter of debate. Other anthropometric measures of nutrition status are sometimes used as well. For rapid assessments, as in emergency situations, the mid-upper-arm circumference is frequently used.

Most malnutrition, especially malnutrition among children, is not caused by food shortages in the household. Often, feeding programs fail to have any significant effect on children's nutritional status. One review of the effects of feeding programs on the growth of children showed that overall anthropometric improvement was quite small (Beaton and Ghassemi 1982). As these researchers speculated, much of the food may have failed to get to the targeted individuals, with the result that their dietary intake actually did not improve very much.

A more fundamental reason may have been that food supply was not really a major problem to begin with, and the observed growth retardation could have been addressed more effectively with other kinds of programs, perhaps emphasizing immunizations, sanitation, or improved child care. The feeding programs may have not only reached the wrong individuals but may have also been altogether the wrong choice of remedy.

Some of these concerns about the ineffectiveness of feeding programs, which were voiced in the 1980s, have by now been allayed, especially with regard to the treatment of severe acute malnutrition. Therapeutic feeding programs have become much more effective, at least in the short term, because of their careful consideration of mineral and vitamin deficiencies and electrolyte imbalances.

Anthropometric measures do not assess nutrition status directly; they assess developmental impairment or growth failure, the most extensive public health problem among children in developing countries. This problem results from the complex interaction of nutritional, biological, and social factors. Rates of physical growth and achieved body size have been accepted as markers of this syndrome. Growth failure may be partly due to dietary adequacy, but there can be other causes as well. Different forms of growth failure can be described in these terms:

- *underweight* or *overweight*, for deviations of body weight from expected weight-for-age;
- *wasted* or *obese*, for deviations of body weight from expected weight-for-height; or
- *stunted*, for deviations of height below expected height for age.

Growth retardation, whether in the form of wasting, stunting, or under-weight, often is a sign of malnutrition, but sometimes it might result from other causes. Thus children who show growth retardation should be clinically exam-ined to characterize their conditions more precisely. For our purposes, however, the degree of growth retardation generally can be taken as a reasonable indicator of the extent of malnutrition.

If the objective is to identify individual children in need of attention, it is most useful to assess the extent to which children are *wasted*, that is, the extent to which they have low weight for their height. Many children who are *underweight*—that is, who have low weight for their age—may have "scars" of past malnutrition and not signs of current problems ("wounds"). *Stunting*, in which children are short for their age, is due more to past than to current problems.

Growth failure is most active between six and twenty-four months of age, which is thus the main window of opportunity for prevention. Actions targeted to children beyond two years of age will not be very useful in reversing their growth retardation, because their low weight or height is likely to have originated in their first two years of life.

This has important implications for public policy. Some nutrition programs concerned with protein-energy malnutrition as indicated by low weight or low height may be misdirected in terms of their intended coverage. School lunch pro-grams, for example, are not likely to be of much use for reversing growth retar-dation. Rather than selectively targeting underweight or underheight individuals among older children, it may be more efficient and effective to focus the resources on all children up to two years of age. This conforms to findings that public ex-penditure on children generally yields far better results when focused on very small children (Carnegie Task Force on Meeting the Needs of Young Children 1994).

Numbers of Malnourished People

According to the Food and Agriculture Organization of the United Nations' (FAO's) *Sixth World Food Survey* of 1997, "The number of people with inadequate access to food declined from 918 million in 1969–71 to 906 million in 1979–81 and further to 841 million in 1990–92. Nevertheless, this number was still very high in 1990–92, as one out of five people in the developing world faced food in-adequacy" (Food and Agriculture Organization 1997, v–vi).

Overall, there has been little improvement. The FAO's *The State of Food Inse-curity in the World 2002* said, "the latest estimates indicate that some 840 million people were undernourished in 1998–2000" and "literally millions of people, including 6 million children under the age of five, die each year as a result of hunger" (Food and Agriculture Organization 2002d, 1).

The FAO's *The State of Food Insecurity in the World 2003* delivered bad news, telling us that "the number of undernourished people in the developing world is no longer falling but climbing. During the first half of the 1990s, the number of chronically hungry people decreased by 37 million. Since 1995–1997, however, the number has increased by over 18 million" (Food and Agriculture Organization 2003, 4).

In 2004, the United Nations System Standing Committee on Nutrition showed that the situation in Sub-Saharan Africa, in particular, was bad and becoming worse, with Eastern Africa experiencing large increases in the numbers of underweight children (United Nations System Standing Committee on Nutrition 2004, 7). As we will see in chapter 10 on the United States, there is considerable malnutrition in rich countries as well as in poor ones. But some rich countries are reluctant to acknowledge that reality.

Malnutrition and Mortality

The preceding section discussed the causes of malnutrition. Here we consider some of its consequences. Malnutrition is strongly linked to many different forms of disease, and thus to death. It also inhibits mental and physical development, especially when children suffer from it. Malnutrition in childhood can affect not only the individual's development as an adult but also the health and well-being of the affected individual's children and even grandchildren.

The most dramatic impact of malnutrition is on mortality. Most deaths related to malnutrition do not result from flagrant starvation but from the ways in which malnutrition weakens the human body and increases its susceptibility to disease. Malnutrition is best understood as a risk factor rather than as a direct cause of death. This is why the major international data-gathering agencies—the World Health Organization, FAO, and UNICEF—normally do not provide estimates of the numbers of people who die from malnutrition each year. They cannot do this because the system for coding causes of death used in most of the world, based on the International Classification of Diseases, views malnutrition as a risk factor, not as a direct cause of death.

The Burden of Disease Unit at Harvard University has developed analytical techniques to assess the impact of risk factors on mortality. Among the ten major risk factors it has examined (malnutrition, poor sanitation, unsafe sex, tobacco use, alcohol use, occupational hazards, hypertension, physical inactivity, illicit drug use, and air pollution), malnutrition is by far the most serious cause of death. As indicated in figure 1.2, of the approximately 50 million total deaths in 1990, roughly 5,881,000—about 11.7 percent of the total deaths—were associated with malnutrition (Burden of Disease Unit 1996).

More recent studies show that "undernutrition has remained the single leading global cause of health loss." More precisely, the "leading causes of burden of disease in all high-mortality developing regions were childhood and maternal undernutrition—including underweight," causing an estimated 14.9 percent of the

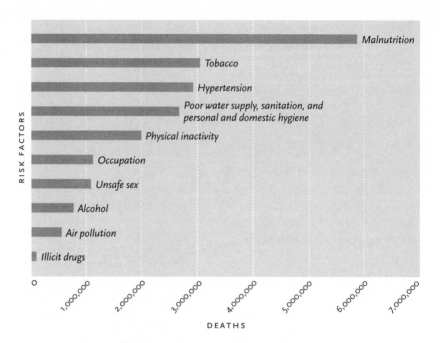

Figure 1.2. Contribution of Various Risk Factors to Deaths in 1990.
Source: Burden of Disease Unit (1996, 2).

overall burden of disease, more than any other factor examined (Ezzati et al. 2002, 1355; Ezzati et al. 2003).

The linkage between malnutrition and mortality is especially strong in young children. In 1994, UNICEF estimated that "about 55% of the 13 million under-five deaths in the world each year are the deaths of children who were malnourished. And of those 7 million nutrition-related deaths, some 80% are the deaths of children who were only mildly or moderately malnourished" (Jonsson 1994, 7). These are nutrition-*related* deaths, but they are not due entirely to malnutrition. This account was based largely on a study by David Pelletier and his colleagues. It showed that in the data for fifty-three developing countries, more than half the child deaths were attributable to malnutrition's potentiating effects (Pelletier et al. 1995). There is a strong association between protein-energy malnutrition and children's mortality. One can say that the biggest risk factor of all is being a child, especially being a child in a poor country.

Children who are severely malnourished in terms of anthropometric measures are more likely to die. For children who are mildly or moderately malnourished, however, the prospects are not so grim. In the United States, there is little linkage between malnutrition and children's mortality because the malnutrition is rarely severe.

The point that children who are severely malnourished are more likely to die may appear to contradict the finding in Pelletier's study that, of the child deaths associated with malnutrition, most of these were attributable to mild-to-moderate as opposed to severe malnutrition. The explanation is that worldwide there are far more children who are mildly or moderately malnourished than there are children who are severely malnourished. Thus, even though the odds of dying for a mildly or moderately malnourished child are much lower than the odds for a severely malnourished child, there will be more deaths of mildly and moderately malnourished children associated with malnutrition simply because there are so many more such children.

It takes much more effort to save children who are severely malnourished than to save those who are mildly or moderately malnourished. This has important implications for policy. If we are concerned with saving lives, in the face of scarce resources, it may be wise to focus efforts on those who are mildly or moderately malnourished, rather than on those who are severely malnourished.

Comparative Mortality

In the preceding section, we showed that, according to the Burden of Disease Unit at Harvard University, in 1990 malnutrition led to almost 6 million deaths a year, more than 10 percent of all deaths. To get more perspective on the relative importance of malnutrition, it may be useful to extend that analysis and compare the impact of malnutrition with that of other causes of death.

Table 1.1 gives the factors that are identified as *direct causes* of death by the World Health Organization in accordance with the International Classification of Diseases. The data given in the table cover the leading causes of death in developed and developing countries (Murray and Lopez 1996, 465–68, table 6i). These are distinguished from the indirect causes, or *risk factors*, analyzed by the Harvard group (Burden of Disease Unit 1996, 28).

The numbers in table 1.1. must be interpreted with caution. More comprehensive categories (e.g., respiratory infection) necessarily have larger numbers than more specific subordinate categories (e.g., pneumonia). For technical details, the table's source documents should be consulted.

The preceding section showed that malnutrition is an important indirect cause of death. Table 1.1 shows that it remains among the most important causes, even when compared with direct causes.

These figures can be compared with the mortality associated with other kinds of factors. War was estimated to cause about 502,000 deaths worldwide in 1990 (Murray and Lopez 1996). While HIV was estimated to cause about 312,000 deaths in 1990, in the period 1981–2001 the average death rate due to HIV/AIDS worldwide was about 1.1 million a year. The International Federation of the Red Cross estimates that disasters, excluding war, cause about 150,000 deaths per year (International Federation of the Red Cross and Red Crescent Societies

TABLE 1.1. FACTORS CONTRIBUTING TO MORTALITY, 1990

Factor	Deaths
*Ischaemic heart disease	6,260,000
#Malnutrition	5,881,000
*Cerebrovascular disease	4,381,000
*Lower respiratory infections	4,299,000
#Tobacco	3,038,000
*Diarrheal diseases	2,946,000
#Hypertension	2,918,000
#Poor water supply, sanitation, and personal and domestic hygiene	2,668,000
*Perinatal conditions	2,443,000
*Chronic obstructive pulmonary disease	2,211,000
#Physical inactivity	1,991,000
*Tuberculosis	1,960,000
*Self-inflicted injuries	1,851,000
#Occupation	1,129,000
#Unsafe sex	1,095,000
*Measles	1,058,000
*Road traffic accidents	999,000
*Trachea, bronchus, and lung cancer	945,000
*Malaria	856,000
#Alcohol	774,000
*Stomach cancer	752,000
*Diabetes mellitus	571,000
#Air pollution	568,000
*Colon and rectum cancers	472,000
*HIV	312,000
#Illicit drugs	100,000
Global total, 1990	50,446,000

Note: The factors marked with an asterisk are identified as *direct causes* of death by the World Health Organization in accordance with the guidelines in the International Classification of Diseases. The data given here cover the leading causes of death in developed and in developing countries (Murray and Lopez 1996, 465–68, table 6i). These are distinguished from the indirect causes, or *risk factors*, analyzed by the Harvard group, marked here with the "#" symbol (Burden of Disease Unit 1996, 28). *Source:* Burden of Disease Unit (1996, 28).

1996b, 24). But Reuters, apparently using a narrower definition, estimated that natural disasters killed only 25,000 people worldwide in 2001 (Dahinten 2001). UNICEF estimated that about 12,700,000 children died before their fifth birthday in 1990. Thus we see that, as suggested in the preceding section, childhood may be the worst risk factor of all.

A Worldwatch Institute study called attention to the fact that in the twentieth century, 10 million people died as a result of natural catastrophes (Abramovitz 2001). More than that number of children died before their fifth birthday in *every single year* of the twentieth century. Moreover, in terms of available technologies, these deaths were far more predictable and preventable than the disaster-related deaths. Estimates of the number of child deaths for various years are provided in table 1.2. As was pointed out above, UNICEF estimates that approximately half of these children's deaths were associated with malnutrition (Jonsson 1994; Pelletier et al. 1995).

The data presented so far in this section on the effects of malnutrition on mortality have been global. Similar analyses can be made on a regional basis. In some parts of the world, malnutrition accounts for a far larger proportion of deaths

TABLE 1.2. ESTIMATED NUMBER OF DEATHS OF
CHILDREN UNDER FIVE YEARS OF AGE, 1960–2003

Year	Deaths
1960	18,900,000
1970	17,400,000
1980	14,700,000
1990	12,700,000
1991	12,821,000
1992	13,191,000
1993	13,272,000
1994	12,588,000
1995	12,465,000
1996	11,694,000
1997	11,574,000
1998	11,140,000
1999	10,630,000
2000	10,929,000
2001	10,803,000
2002	10,889,000
2003	10,643,000

Source: United Nations Children's Fund, *State of the World's Children*, annual.

TABLE 1.3. DEATHS ATTRIBUTABLE TO MALNUTRITION, 1990

Region	Number	Percent
Established market economies	0	0
Formerly socialist economies of Europe	0	0
India	1,722,000	18.4
China	278,000	3.1
Other Asia and islands	679,000	12.3
Sub-Saharan Africa	2,619,000	31.9
Latin America and the Caribbean	135,000	4.5
Middle Eastern Crescent	447,000	9.8
World	5,881,000	11.7

Source: Murray and Lopez (1996, table 6.3).

than the global figures would suggest. Table 1.3 shows the Burden of Disease Unit's estimates of the number and the proportion of deaths associated with malnutrition in the world's regions.

These data show the remarkable variation among regions in the impact of malnutrition on mortality. For the world as a whole, malnutrition was estimated to account for about 11.7 percent of all deaths, but 14.9 percent in developing regions. In Sub-Saharan Africa, malnutrition accounts for almost a third of all deaths.

The findings of the Burden of Disease Unit were updated and confirmed in the World Health Organization's *World Health Report 2002: Reducing Risks, Promoting Healthy Life*. Globally, underweight is by far the most serious of the twenty risk factors examined. The study showed that in the high-mortality developing countries, "about one-sixth of the entire disease burden is attributed to underweight, with a substantial additional proportion attributable to micronutrient deficiencies." It also pointed out that "underweight and micronutrient deficiency-related burden clearly affect children almost exclusively." However, other diet-related risks are "almost equally distributed among adults above and below the age of 60 years" Overall, the World Health Organization study found that "about one-fifth of the global disease burden can be attributed to the joint effects of protein-energy or micronutrient deficiency. In addition, almost as much burden again can be attributed to risk factors that have substantial dietary determinants—high blood pressure, cholesterol, overweight and low fruit and vegetable intake" (World Health Organization 2002, 83–85).

Food and Nutrition Security

Words like "hunger" and "starvation" have a strong emotional impact but are rarely used as technical terms by specialists in the field. There are no measures and no published data on starvation as such. The experts prefer to use terms such as "food insecurity" and "malnutrition." According to the FAO,

> Food security exists when all people, at all times, have physical, social and economic access to sufficient, safe and nutritious food to meet their dietary needs and food preferences for an active and healthy life. (FIVIMS 2004, 1)

Food security is concerned with questions relating to the food supply, but nutrition status depends not only on suitable food but also on good basic health services and, particularly for children, adequate care. Malnutrition generally results not from a lack of food in the community but from the skewed distribution of the food that is available. That skewing results because some people are too poor or too powerless to make an adequate claim on the food that is available.

The U.S. Department of Agriculture also has taken initiatives to map food insecurity (U.S. Department of Agriculture 1999, chap. 6). In its review of the food security situation around the world published in late 2000, the department projected that per capita food consumption for sixty-seven low-income countries would increase in the following decade (U.S. Department of Agriculture 2000a). It also projected that the number of people who fail to meet their nutritional requirements would decline from 774 million in 2000 to 694 million in 2010. It expected that an increasingly large share of the food insecure would be located in Sub-Saharan Africa. In this region, per capita consumption was expected to decline, partly as a result of reduced production due to widespread HIV/AIDS.

The FAO equates food insecurity with the more popular concept of hunger (Food and Agriculture Organization 1999b, 6). It also distinguishes between undernourishment and *undernutrition*. Undernourishment refers to an inadequate supply of food and is assessed by estimating food supplies. Undernutrition, however, refers to the physiological consequences, and is assessed on the basis of anthropometric measures, that is, people's weights and heights (Food and Agriculture Organization 1999b, 6). Referring back to figure 1.1, we recall that nutrition status, as an outcome, results not only from the quality of food but also from the qualities of care and health services, as inputs. Food status is one major factor determining nutrition status. The other two major factors are care and health services. Thus, we can say that *nutrition status depends on food status, care status, and health status.*

There is now increasing attention to the concept of *nutrition security*. This term has been defined as the "appropriate quantity and combination of inputs such as food, nutrition and health services, and caretaker's time needed to ensure an active and healthy life at all times for all people" (Haddad, Kennedy, and Sullivan 1994, 329).

Food security focuses on the food component of nutrition security. Thus, food security and nutrition security are different. The FAO's *Sixth World Food Survey* showed that while food inadequacy is more prevalent in Sub-Saharan Africa than in South Asia, the incidence of malnutrition (or, more precisely, undernutrition) based on anthropometric measures is higher in South Asia. The study suggests that the discrepancy is largely due to differences in disease patterns. Most life-threatening malnutrition occurs among children, but children do not require very large amounts of food. There can be widespread malnutrition in a population even while food security measures indicate that the food situation is relatively good. Millions of children worldwide die each year as a result of diarrhea, for example, but this has little to do with the level of food supply in their communities or even in their households.

Human security has many different aspects or dimensions. Food security is one component of nutrition security, together with health security and care security. Nutrition security, in turn, is one component of the broader concept of *livelihood security*. The livelihood security approach uses the idea of entitlements that was discussed earlier in this chapter:

> Livelihoods can be seen to consist of a range of on-farm and off-farm activities that together provide a variety of procurement strategies for food and cash. Thus, each household can have several possible sources of entitlement which constitute its livelihood. These entitlements are based on a household's endowments, and its position in the legal, political, and social fabric of society. (Frankenberger and McCaston 1999, 206)

A postmodern perspective on food security offered by one of the key analysts proposed to unpack the convergence on the understanding of food security that was achieved with such struggle (Maxwell 1996). The issue remains unsettled, perhaps usefully so.

The literature often fails to make a clear distinction between *status* and *security*. The understanding proposed here is based on the idea that, in its most general form, security means freedom from fear of harm. Particular kinds of security refer to freedom from fear of particular kinds of harm. Thus, physical security refers to freedom from fear of physical harm, environmental security means freedom from fear of environmental harm, and so on. In this understanding, *status* refers to current conditions, while *security* refers to anticipated conditions.

It would have been useful if the FAO consistently used the term food *inadequacy*, rather than food *insecurity*, to describe the condition of inadequate food supplies when it is assessing conditions that are current at a given point in time, not conditions that are anticipated from that moment in time. This terminology would make it easier to distinguish between food status and food security.

Just as we can say that nutrition status depends on food status, care status, and health status, we can also say that *nutrition* security depends on *food* security, *care* security, and *health* security.

The distinction between nutrition status and nutrition security is particularly useful when one assesses different kinds of interventions intended to respond to nutrition problems. Straightforward feeding programs may be very helpful in improving people's current nutrition status. However, they do nothing to improve their nutrition security. Such interventions respond to symptoms rather than to the underlying sources of the problem. Indeed, if people come to depend on such feeding programs, these programs may in fact weaken their nutrition security. In a perverse way, feeding programs, by responding only to symptoms, may actually help to sustain problems rather than end them. You do not solve the hunger problem by feeding people.

Improving nutrition security would require introducing some sort of change in local social and institutional arrangements, or providing training or tools or some other resources that could change things over the long run. Nutrition interventions should be assessed not so much on the basis of their immediate impact but on the effects that they are likely to have over the long run, long after the interventions have ended.

The difference between nutrition status and nutrition security may seem slight, but the significance is that the security concept takes account of the institutional measures that come into play. To illustrate, you are interested not only in whether your house is currently on fire but also in whether there are adequate institutional arrangements to put out a fire if one occurs. Or to offer a more appropriate illustration, if you have washed up on a desert island and just eaten your last can of beans, your nutrition *status* may be all right but your nutrition *security* is bleak.

Varieties of Government Action

National governments can do many different things that influence the food and nutrition situation within their countries—for better or worse. In many cases, there are programs explicitly designed to improve the nutrition status of particular segments of the population, such as school meal programs, child feeding programs, subsidies on staple foods, breast-feeding support programs, and nutrition education programs. In addition, the government's agricultural policy, fiscal policy, land tenure policy, and so on are likely to have substantial effects on the food and nutrition situation.

Of course, many other actors in the society, apart from government, can have significant effects. Decisions made by food producers, processors, and marketers will have a great impact. Labor unions may be influential. In some cases, church groups or other nongovernmental organizations may establish feeding programs for vulnerable groups. Here, however, our special concern is with the actions of government.

The core assumption is that in well-functioning societies, normally individuals, in the context of their families and communities, will provide adequate food for themselves. The government's task is not to feed people but to make sure that people live in circumstances in which they can provide for themselves. Of course, there will always be situations in which some people are not able to provide for themselves and help is needed. The things that governments can do to strengthen food and nutrition security may be usefully divided into four broad categories: respect, protect, facilitate, and provide.

First, governments can *respect* people's efforts to feed themselves and not interfere with their efforts to do so. In some cases, governments fail to show this respect by, say, taking away land they had historically used to produce their own food or by blocking their access to that land.

Second, governments can *protect* people's efforts to feed themselves. The need for protection comes up when, say, marauders steal farmers' crops before they can be harvested.

Third, governments can *facilitate* people's efforts to feed themselves. Governments can provide extension services, sound currencies, market information, and a variety of other services that make it easier for people to feed themselves. Governments may help to improve the number and quality of employment opportunities, and thus indirectly help people to provide food for themselves.

Fourth, in some circumstances, governments may *provide* for people's needs by supplying food directly, through programs such as school meals, emergency shelters, and subsidized staple foods.

In brief, your government *respects* your efforts to get what you need by not interfering with you; it *protects* you from others who might get in the way of your getting what you need; it *facilitates* helping you get what you need; and in some cases, it *provides* what you need directly.

In any country, it is possible to identify a variety of things that the government *can do* with regard to respecting, protecting, facilitating, and fulfilling food and nutrition needs. One can also identify those things that it actually *does*. We can discuss what government *ought to do* from a moral perspective. Later, in chapter 6, we will discuss what the government *must do* from the perspective of the human right to adequate food.

This section has focused on government action because our main concern is with human rights, and thus with the behavior of national governments in relation to people under their jurisdiction. Nevertheless, these categories describing different types of action may also be applied to the activities of other kinds of agencies, such as nongovernmental organizations and international agencies. In offering food and nutrition services, all of them can *respect, protect, facilitate,* and *provide.*

CHAPTER 2

The International Human Rights System

Historical Foundations

The distinct rights of some classes of individuals have been recognized at least as far back as the Code of Hammurabi, about 1780 B.C. These early rights were mainly claims of some individuals against other individuals, such as claims against dishonest merchants. Individuals could make very few claims against government. For much of human history, it was accepted that the power of emperors and kings was nearly absolute, at least with respect to secular issues.

In time, it was argued that—in recognition of the interests of the monarch's subjects—the powers of the sovereign ought to be limited. The claims of these countervailing interests were articulated in the Magna Carta, arguably the first major rights document. Barons and churchmen in England drew up this "great charter." They forced the tyrannical King John to affix his seal to it at a meadow along the Thames, called Runnymede, on June 15, 1215. It was based on the Charter of Liberties issued by Henry I more than a hundred years earlier.

Like many later rights documents, the Magna Carta was not fully implemented. Indeed, King John recruited a new army and sought to destroy the barons who had forced it on him. Moreover, the Magna Carta's reach was quite limited. It sought to protect only the established rights of feudal lords and church dignitaries; it did not challenge the institutions of serfdom. It was only much later that the Magna Carta came to be seen as the first assertion of the rights of subjects against the king.

The Magna Carta represented constraint on the sovereign from within the sovereign's jurisdiction. Sovereigns were not constrained from without. International law did not apply to individuals but only to states. There was no international protection for the rights of individuals at all.

The modern nation-state system had its beginnings in the Treaty of Westphalia of 1648. Its core principles were that states were sovereign in that they had no ruling bodies above them, and no state was permitted to interfere in the internal affairs of any other. Within states, people lived at the mercy of their rulers, their sovereigns.

In 1776, the Declaration of Independence, marking the revolution of the American colonies against the tyranny of King George III, launched another major rights movement. It was consolidated in the Bill of Rights, which was added in 1791 to the U.S. Constitution of 1787. These first ten amendments spelled out the basic rights of citizens of the new United States. (The text of the U.S.

Constitution is at http://www.ncmd.uscourts.gov/const.htm; that for the Bill of Rights is at http://www.ncmd.uscourts.gov/bor.htm.) The French Revolution led to the Declaration of the Rights of Man and of the Citizen, approved by the new French National Assembly on August 4, 1789.

These efforts advanced the cause of rights within particular nations but were not bases for international agreement or action. Thus they were not about human rights as that term is now understood. As explained in chapter 5, by definition the term *human rights* is understood to refer to those rights that are universal. All persons have all human rights simply by virtue of being human. On this basis, those rights that are recognized only in one country cannot be viewed as human rights. They are sometimes described as civil rights.

Human rights, understood as claims for universal recognition of rights, arguably began with the antislavery movement in the nineteenth century. That movement led to the signing at Brussels in 1890 of a multilateral treaty prohibiting the international slave trade. The Anti-Slavery Society, now Anti-Slavery International, headquartered in London, is the oldest human rights organization in the world.

Early in the twentieth century, labor rights came to be recognized, partly to resist the growing attractiveness of Marxism. The International Labor Organization was created soon after World War I, and it helped to create a number of international agreements for the protection of workers.

The modern era of human rights began with the signing of the Charter of the United Nations in 1945 and the adoption of the Universal Declaration of Human Rights by the UN General Assembly in 1948. A good chronology of developments in the field of human rights since World War II may be found on the website of the Office of the UN High Commissioner for Human Rights (http://www.un-hchr.ch/chrono.htm).

This chapter provides only a brief overview of the international human rights system. Although there are many texts on human rights that provide a good overview of the system, a good place to start is *Human Rights: A Basic Handbook for UN Staff* (United Nations, Office of the High Commissioner for Human Rights 2001).

International Humanitarian Law

It is important to distinguish international human rights law from international humanitarian law. International humanitarian law is the branch of international law that is concerned with humanitarian action related to armed conflict situations. Its origins can be traced back to a Swiss businessman, Henri Dunant, who was appalled at the neglect of casualties in the 1859 Battle of Solferino, in what is now Italy. He started what were to become the national Red Cross societies. These agencies provided services for sick and wounded soldiers, and also lobbied for new international agreements regarding the care of soldiers. As a result, the first Geneva Convention for Victims of War was concluded in 1864.

During decades of negotiation, the principles for care not only of soldiers but also of civilians were steadily refined. The four Geneva conventions of 1949 are the major sources of the law of armed conflict. They are the Convention Relative to the Protection of Civilian Persons in Time of War; the Convention for the Amelioration of the Condition of the Wounded and Sick in Armed Forces in the Field; the Convention for the Amelioration of the Condition of Wounded, Sick, and Shipwrecked Members of Armed Forces at Sea; and the Convention Relative to the Treatment of Prisoners of War. Although these four conventions apply primarily to situations of international conflict, they have a Common Article 3 that extends their application to situations of internal (noninternational) conflict.

After negotiations at the Geneva Conference on the Reaffirmation and Development of International Humanitarian Law beginning in 1974, two supplements, Protocols Additional to the Geneva Conventions of 1949, were adopted in 1977. Protocol I applies to international armed conflicts, and Protocol II applies to noninternational armed conflicts. The four Geneva conventions of 1949 together with these two protocols constitute the core of international humanitarian law. Most states have by now become parties to the Geneva conventions and the two protocols.

Apart from the primary parties, the ratifying nation-states, there is a single distinct agent, the International Committee of the Red Cross (ICRC), which has the responsibility to implement international humanitarian law. Indeed, the ICRC initially drafted the 1949 conventions. Its mission statement says:

> The International Committee of the Red Cross (ICRC) is an impartial, neutral and independent organization whose exclusively humanitarian mission is to protect the lives and dignity of victims of war and internal violence and to provide them with assistance. It directs and coordinates the international relief activities conducted by the Movement in situations of conflict. It also endeavours to prevent suffering by promoting and strengthening humanitarian law and universal humanitarian principles.

The ICRC's potentials are limited because of the inherent difficulties of dealing with armed conflict, especially when it involves major powers. Nevertheless, the ICRC generally commands great respect for its work.

The Geneva conventions can be accessed through the website of the Office of the UN High Commissioner for Human Rights (http://www.ohchr.org), but international humanitarian law is not human rights law. With few exceptions, international human rights law is applicable not only in peacetime but also in situations of armed conflict and other public emergencies. Its provisions with regard to the human right to adequate food apply in armed conflict situations as well as in peacetime.

International humanitarian law includes some special provisions related to food in conflict situations. The Protocol Additional to the Geneva Conventions of August 12, 1949, and relating to the Protection of Victims of Non-International Armed Conflicts (Protocol II), says in article 14:

> Starvation of civilians as a method of combat is prohibited. It is therefore prohibited to attack, destroy, remove or render useless, for that purpose, objects indispensable to the survival of the civilian population, such as foodstuffs, agricultural areas for the production of foodstuffs, crops, livestock, drinking water installations and supplies and irrigation works.

Although they are separate, international human rights law and international humanitarian law are strongly linked, and both require attention in situations of armed conflict.

The International Bill of Human Rights

By the middle of the twentieth century, the extremes of despotism and tyranny in many countries of the world had become intolerable. The horrors of Nazi Germany, in particular, elicited a demand for new kinds of policy to apply not only to Germany but to all countries. The international community began speaking out and acting in support of human rights. In the Charter of the United Nations, adopted in 1945, nations pledged to take action to achieve "universal respect for, and observance of, human rights and fundamental freedoms for all without distinction as to race, sex, language or religion."

The key event launching the postwar human rights movement, however, was the approval, with no dissenting votes, by the United Nations General Assembly of the Universal Declaration of Human Rights on December 10, 1948 (Glendon 2001). Eight countries—Saudi Arabia, South Africa, and the Soviet Union and three of its allies—abstained. By 1993, seven of them had renounced their 1948 abstentions. Only Saudi Arabia remains openly opposed to the declaration (Weiss, Forsythe, and Coate 1994, 116), apparently because of its resistance to the idea of the equality of women. December 10 is now recognized as global human rights day.

After this declaration was made, international human rights agreements proliferated rapidly, and many new organizations, both governmental and nongovernmental, arose to make sure that these rights were realized. Human rights became a major subject in global discourse.

Most of the norms in the declaration were given binding effect in the International Covenant on Civil and Political Rights and the International Covenant on Economic, Social, and Cultural Rights. There are also two Optional Protocols to the International Covenant on Civil and Political Rights. The purpose of the first is to allow the Human Rights Committee (the UN treaty body overseeing implementation of that covenant) to receive complaints from individuals. The two covenants and the first protocol were adopted in 1966 and entered into force in 1976. The second protocol, aimed at the abolition of the death penalty, was adopted by the UN General Assembly on December 15, 1989, and came into force on July 11, 1991.

The declaration together with the two covenants and the two protocols are commonly recognized as the International Bill of Human Rights. Some feel that the bill should be understood to also include the Charter of the United Nations, particularly the preamble and articles 1, 55, and 56 (Shue 1996, 181). Most states are parties to the two covenants.

Article 28 of the International Covenant on Civil and Political Rights provides for the creation of a Human Rights Committee to receive reports from states parties on the actions they take to implement the covenant. For those states that accept it, the first Optional Protocol allows the committee to receive "communications from individuals claiming to be victims of violations of any of the rights set forth in the Covenant." In such cases the committee, having very limited powers, would act not as a court but more as a mediation service. Despite this limitation, this protocol represents an enormous step away from Westphalia principles and traditional understandings of the scope of international law in that it allows individual persons, and not just nation-states, to have direct access to an agency of international law.

There have been numerous declarations, proclamations, and resolutions asserting human rights in different issue areas. However, they do not require formal signature and ratification, and they do not have the status and binding character of international conventions. Seven of the major international human rights conventions now available for signature and ratification are listed in table 2.1. These seven are distinctive because they have actively functioning treaty bodies in the United Nations associated with them.

There are many other international human rights conventions, but having no actively functioning treaty bodies, many of them are generally ignored. A thorough list of international human rights agreements, including not only conventions but also declarations and other sorts of documents, may be found on the website of the Office of the UN High Commissioner for Human Rights (http://www.unhchr.ch/html/intlinst.htm). The website also provides a list describing the ratification status of the major treaties.

Human rights are sometimes grouped into three broad clusters. First-generation rights are civil and political rights. These are the types of rights found in the International Covenant on Civil and Political Rights and in the U.S. Constitution's Bill of Rights. Second-generation rights are socioeconomic rights, such as those articulated in the International Covenant on Economic, Social, and Cultural Rights. Third-generation rights, or solidarity rights, are the rights of groups rather than individual persons. The rights to development, peace, environment, and communication are regarded as solidarity rights because they are associated with the community rather than with individual persons. The UN's 1984 Decla-

TABLE 2.1. SEVEN MAJOR TREATIES AND TREATY BODIES

Treaty	Date Adopted by UN; Date Entered into Force	Committee; Date of First Meeting; No. of Members	Meeting Site	Authorized to Handle Individual Complaints?
International Covenant on Civil and Political Rights	December 16, 1966; March 23, 1976	Human Rights Committee (HRC); 1976; 18	Geneva	Yes
International Covenant on Economic, Social, and Cultural Rights	December 16, 1966; January 3, 1976	Committee on Economic, Social, and Cultural Rights (CESCR); 1985; 18	Geneva	No
International Convention on the Elimination of All Forms of Racial Discrimination	December 21, 1965; January 4, 1969	Committee on the Elimination of Racial Discrimination (CERD); 1970; 18	Geneva	Yes
Convention on the Elimination of All Forms of Discrimination Against Women	December 18, 1979; September 3, 1981	Committee on the Elimination of Discrimination Against Women (CEDAW); 1982; 23	Vienna to 1993; New York since 1993	Yes
Convention Against Torture and Other Cruel, Inhuman, or Degrading Treatment or Punishment	December 10, 1984; June 26, 1987	Committee Against Torture (CAT); 1988; 10	Geneva	Yes
Convention on the Rights of the Child	November 20, 1989; September 2, 1990	Committee on the Rights of the Child (CRC); 1991; 10 initially, 14 after 41 ratifications, and 18 since 2002	Geneva	No
International Convention on the Protection of the Rights of All Migrant Workers and Members of Their Families	December 1990; July 1, 2003	Committee on the Protection of the Rights of All Migrant Workers and Members of Their Families; 2003; 10	Geneva	Yes

ration on the Right to Peace, its 1986 Declaration on the Right to Development, and the draft Declaration on the Rights of Indigenous Peoples fit this category. There is some resistance to the idea of group rights, especially from the U.S. government, but it is strongly favored by many non-western governments.

At times, first-generation rights have been called negative rights on the ground that they are intended to block governments from taking actions that interfere with rights such as freedom of thought, speech, religion, privacy, and assembly. Second-generation socioeconomic rights have been thought to be different because they require positive action by government. Now, however, most leading human rights scholars reject this distinction because the realization of both kinds of rights requires positive action by government. This is discussed again in chapter 6.

Even the division of human rights into three clusters or generations may not be warranted (Eide 2001, 9–10). It is now widely accepted that all human rights are intimately interconnected, as recognized in paragraph 5 of the Vienna Declaration and Program of Action, set out at the conclusion of the World Conference on Human Rights held in Vienna in June 1993:

> All human rights are universal, indivisible and interdependent and interrelated. The international community must treat human rights globally in a fair and equal manner, on the same footing, and with the same emphasis. While the significance of national and regional particularities and various historical, cultural and religious backgrounds must be borne in mind, it is the duty of States, regardless of their political, economic and cultural systems, to promote and protect all human rights and fundamental freedoms. (United Nations, Office of the High Commissioner for Human Rights 1993)

Mary Robinson, the former United Nations high commissioner for human rights, sometimes listed the rights in alphabetical order—civil, cultural, economic, social, and political—to make the point that the traditional groupings are quite arbitrary. Though human rights are all of equal status, there is nothing to prevent prioritization among alternative courses of action in the concrete local situation. Governments or nongovernmental actors may focus on improvements in food or clothing or housing, depending on which seems most urgent and most likely to be improvable. To draw an analogy, when you build a house, you build the foundation before you build the walls or the roof, not because one part is intrinsically more important than another, but because at a given moment in time it is the sensible priority for action.

Children's Rights

There are specific international agreements regarding the human rights of different categories of individuals, such as women, refugees, and children. Consider, for example, the evolution of the rights of children. Both governmental and civil society (i.e., nongovernmental) agencies offer many different kinds of services to address children's concerns, and many of them have been very effective. However, the coverage is often uneven, largely a matter of charity and chance. There is now an evolving understanding that if children everywhere are to be treated well, there must be recognition that they have specific rights to good treatment. Thus there is now a vigorous movement to recognize and ensure the realization of children's rights.

Children's rights have been addressed in many different international instruments. On February 23, 1923, the General Council of the Union for Child Welfare adopted the Declaration of Geneva on the rights of the child. On September 26, 1924, it was adopted by the League of Nations as the Geneva Declaration on the Rights of the Child. It was then revised and became the basis of the Declaration of the Rights of the Child, which was adopted unanimously by the United Nations General Assembly in 1959. The declaration enumerates ten principles regarding the rights of the child. As a nonbinding declaration, it does not establish any institutional arrangements to ensure the implementation of those principles.

The Universal Declaration of Human Rights, the International Covenant on Civil and Political Rights, and the International Covenant on Economic, Social, and Cultural Rights apply to all persons. The covenants include a few specific references to children. Nevertheless—largely as a result of an initiative from Poland—it was agreed that it was necessary for the international community to articulate children's rights more directly and systematically.

After ten years of hard negotiations in a working group of the Commission on Human Rights, on November 20, 1989, the United Nations General Assembly adopted the new Convention on the Rights of the Child by consensus. It came into force on September 2, 1990, when it was ratified by the twentieth nation. Weaving together the scattered threads of earlier international statements of the rights of children, the convention's articles cover civil, political, economic, social, and cultural rights. It includes not only basic survival requirements such as food, clean water, and health care, but also rights of protection against abuse, neglect, and exploitation, and the right to education and to participation in social, religious, political, and economic activities. By 2001, all countries except Somalia and the United States had ratified or otherwise acceded to the Convention on the Rights of the Child.

The convention is a comprehensive legal instrument, legally binding on all nations that ratify it. The articles specify what states parties are obligated to do under different conditions. National governments that agree to be bound by the convention have the major responsibility for its implementation. To provide added international pressure for responsible implementation, article 43 calls for the creation of a Committee on the Rights of the Child. It consists of experts whose main functions are to receive and transmit reports on the status of children's rights. Article 44 requires states parties to submit "reports on the measures they have adopted which give effect to the rights recognized herein and on the progress made on the enjoyment of those rights." Article 46 entitles UNICEF and other agencies to work with the committee within the scope of their mandates. The committee originally was comprised of ten experts, but because of its heavy workload, an amendment to the convention that entered into force on November 18, 2002, raised the number of members to eighteen.

Regional Human Rights Agreements

The agreements discussed just above are international in the sense of being global in coverage. There are also several international human rights agreements that are regional in coverage, in Europe, in the Americas, and in Africa. There is no regional human rights agreement in Asia. In Europe, the Council of Europe was established soon after World War II to resist the remnants of fascism. It drew up the European Convention on Human Rights and Fundamental Freedoms, which was opened for signature and ratification in 1950 and came into force in 1953. The convention deals only with civil and political rights, not with economic, social, and cultural rights. All the states belonging to the council agreed to have the European Commission of Human Rights, set up in 1954, hear complaints, whether from state governments or from individuals. The European Court of Human Rights was established in 1959. The court interprets the convention and rules on the legality of state action under the convention. Eleven protocols to the convention have been adopted. The European Court of Human Rights is separate from the European Court of Justice.

Under the original arrangement, the commission would try to work out a negotiated agreement on an issue, and if it was unable to do that, the petition would be taken to the European Court of Human Rights. However, the backlog of cases in both the commission and the court led to a restructuring. Under Protocol No. 11, which came into force on October 31, 1998, the commission was abolished. The old court was abolished as well, and a new European Court of Human Rights came into operation on November 1, 1998 (Merrills and Robertson 2001).

To complement the European Convention on Human Rights and Fundamental Freedoms, the Council of Europe drafted a European Social Charter to cover economic and social rights. It was opened for signature on October 18, 1961, and came into force on February 26, 1965. An Additional Protocol, adding certain rights, entered into force on September 4, 1992, but few states have ratified it. There have been several other additions to the charter since then.

In 1987, the Council of Europe concluded the European Convention for the Prevention of Torture and Inhuman or Degrading Treatment or Punishment. It entered into force in 1989. The council expanded in 1990 to include the states of Eastern Europe. All are now parties to the convention, and they are thus committed to following the procedures and rulings of the commission and the court.

Although it does not have the status of a treaty, the Final Act of the Conference on Security and Cooperation in Europe, which was signed in Helsinki on August 1, 1975, has made an important contribution to the advancement of human rights in Europe. The Final Act consists of three parts, or "baskets." Basket III, on "Cooperation in Humanitarian and Other Fields," articulated major guiding principles regarding human rights. The signatories now constitute the Organization for Security and Cooperation in Europe.

The American Convention on Human Rights entered into force in 1972. It has been ratified by most members of the Organization of American States, but not by the United States.

In 1981, the Organization of African Unity, now called the African Union, adopted the African Charter on Human and People's Rights, also known as the Banjul Charter (http://www1.umn.edu/humanrts/instree/ratz1afchar.htm). The commission established by the charter began its work in 1987.

Regional human rights agreements are important because they reflect particular regional cultural perspectives with regard to the means for realizing human rights. They also can be important bases for developing innovative institutional arrangements for ensuring the realization of human rights.

Human Rights Agencies

Human rights generally belong to individual persons, although in some cases rights are associated with groups of individuals. The obligations associated with particular human rights rest primarily with national governments. Others have some obligations as well. For example, individuals should not interfere with other individuals' human rights. It is the national government's responsibility to see that they do not.

Governance in the world is exercised mainly through nested layers of government, ranging from villages and townships through cities, counties, provinces, and nation-states, and—at the global level—the nascent governance administered through the international community, primarily the United Nations. Because it is "states parties" that sign and ratify human rights agreements, these nation-states, and the governments that represent them, have the primary responsibility for implementing these agreements.

From a strictly legal perspective, only states can violate international human rights law directly, because only states are parties to the international human rights agreements. However, implementing legislation at the national level may explicitly spell out obligations of other parties in the nation's jurisdiction. Thus, private citizens and nongovernmental organizations that violate this national legislation would, indirectly, also be violating the norms of international human rights. Even where there is no explicit legal assignment of responsibility, parties have a moral responsibility to uphold human rights.

Although national governments have the primary responsibility to implement human rights agreements, other bodies within nations, both governmental and nongovernmental, also play a supporting role. For example, when the national government commits the nation-state to implement particular human rights, responsibility for implementation may devolve to other levels of government such as provincial, county, or municipal governments. Civil society organizations may be assigned some responsibility either for implementing rights directly or for monitoring the government's performance in implementing rights. Most civil society organizations concerned with human rights operate within single countries, but some are international in their coverage. In chapter 7, the section titled "National and Local Human Rights Agencies" discusses several different kinds of bodies within national governments that have special responsibilities with regard to human rights.

At the global level, the major international bodies involved in human rights are the United Nations agencies described in the two following sections. Several other international bodies also play roles in relation to human rights as part of their broader mandates. These include regional bodies dedicated to carrying out the regional human rights agreements described in the preceding section. Several international nongovernmental organizations (or, in the emerging terminology, international civil society organizations), such as Amnesty International and Human Rights Watch, are actively involved.

Many different bodies in the United Nations system play a role with regard to human rights. There are two major groups: those that have been created, directly or indirectly, on the basis of the Charter of the United Nations; and those that have been created by, or in connection with, specific international treaties. Figure 2.1 shows the relationships among the UN's human rights bodies.

The dark areas indicate six principal organs of the United Nations, whereas the light ones indicate bodies or programs serviced by the Office of the UN High Commissioner for Human Rights. If this figure is accessed on the UNHCHR website (see the figure source note for the figure's site address), clicking on the titles of specific bodies will lead to additional information on them.

Apart from these bodies, many of the UN specialized agencies, financial institutions, and funds play important roles in the realization of human rights. These include agencies such as the World Bank, the Food and Agriculture Organization of the United Nations, the World Health Organization, the United Nations Children's Fund, the United Nations Development Program, and the United Nations Fund for Population Activities.

The UN system is financed through regular assessments and voluntary contributions from member states. The annual budget of the United Nations for the

Structure of the United Nations Human Rights Bodies and Mechanisms

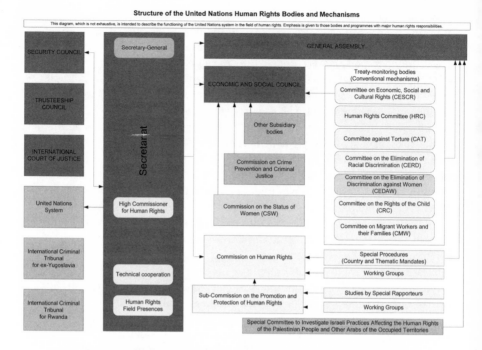

Figure 2.1. Human Rights Bodies in the United Nations. *Source*: Website of
the Office of the United Nations High Commissioner for Human Rights,
http://www.unhchr.ch/hsostr.htm. Copyright 1997, Office of the United Nations
High Commissioner for Human Rights, Geneva. Used by permission.

period 2002–3 was about $2.6 billion, or about $1.3 billion a year. In 2001 the
Office of the High Commissioner for Human Rights received $21.4 million from
the regular UN budget, and $31.4 million from voluntary contributions (United
Nations, Office of the High Commissioner for Human Rights 2002). Thus, with
the Office of the High Commissioner for Human Rights getting less than 2 percent of the United Nations' already-meager regular budget, our expectations of
that office must remain modest. The total budget of the Office of the High Commissioner for Human Rights, at about $50 million a year, is about 0.014 percent
of the $355.5 billion defense budget adopted by the United States alone in Octo-
ber 2002. It is evident that the national governments of the world do not give the
pursuit of human rights a very high priority. This is not an accident or oversight.
Few nations of the world are receptive to the idea of having their performance
monitored and critically assessed by an outside agency.

United Nations Charter Bodies

Several bodies within the United Nations have major responsibilities related to human rights: the General Assembly, the Economic and Social Council, the Commission on Human Rights, the Commission on the Status of Women, the Center for Human Rights, and the Office of the High Commissioner for Human Rights.

Security Council

The Security Council has played a role in relation to human rights in places like Bosnia, Cambodia, Iraq, and Somalia. However, to some observers, it has played only a reluctant and indirect role. As Philip Alston sees it, "The Council has a long history of refusing to consider itself as an organ for the promotion of respect for human rights, except in so far as a given situation constitutes a threat to international peace and security" (Alston 1992a, 9).

The General Assembly

The General Assembly is especially important because it is the most representative decision-making body in the United Nations, with all members having the right to vote. Thus it has served as a major forum for discussion, and it has also served as the site for the preparation and adoption of numerous major international human rights agreements. Most human rights issues are referred to the assembly's Third Committee, which is responsible for social, humanitarian, and cultural matters. The General Assembly has several subsidiary bodies concerned with human rights, including

- the Special Committee with Regard to the Implementation of the Declaration on the Granting of Independence to Colonial Countries and Peoples (known as the Special Committee on Decolonization),
- the United Nations Council for Namibia,
- the Special Committee Against Apartheid,
- the Special Committee to Investigate Israeli Practices Affecting the Human Rights of the Population of the Occupied Territories, and
- the Committee on the Exercise of the Inalienable Rights of the Palestinian People.

The Economic and Social Council

In its first decades, the United Nations' concern for human rights was focused in the Third Committee. However, because of frequent political stalemates in that committee, some human rights action shifted to the Economic and Social

Council (ECOSOC) and its subsidiary organs. ECOSOC's members are elected by the General Assembly.

Under article 62 of the Charter of the United Nations, ECOSOC may make recommendations with regard to international economic, social, cultural, educational, health, and related matters to the General Assembly, to the members of the United Nations, and to the specialized agencies, and in particular, according to paragraph 2, "It may make recommendations for the purpose of promoting respect for, and observance of, human rights and fundamental freedoms for all." It may draft conventions on these issues for submission to the General Assembly, and, under article 68, it may "set up commissions . . . for the promotion of human rights." To help it deal with human rights issues, ECOSOC established the Commission on Human Rights and the Commission on the Status of Women. The Commission on Human Rights, in turn, established the Sub-Commission on Prevention of Discrimination and the Protection of Minorities. These subsidiary bodies of ECOSOC are described in the following three subsections.

The Commission on Human Rights

The Commission on Human Rights, established by ECOSOC in 1946, has become the hub of United Nations activity with regard to human rights. The commission reports through ECOSOC to the General Assembly. The commission has established a number of subsidiary bodies, including the Sub-Commission on Prevention of Discrimination and Protection of Minorities, and Working Groups and special rapporteurs focused on particular human rights issues. The Commission on Human Rights should not be confused with the Human Rights Committee, the treaty body for the International Covenant on Civil and Political Rights.

An important factor in the commission's work has been ECOSOC's Resolution 1503, passed in 1970, which allows suborgans of ECOSOC to deal with "communications" (petitions, complaints) alleging violations of human rights from private individuals and nongovernmental organizations. Complaints must suggest "a consistent pattern of gross and reliably attested violations of human rights and fundamental freedoms." This means that the commission cannot deal with isolated violations of human rights. It offers no redress to individual victims.

The 1503 procedure is confidential, which means that those charged are protected from adverse publicity during the investigation. However, each year the commission chair does announce the names of the countries that were considered under the 1503 procedure. The commission may release its evidence and its views on the allegations when investigations are completed, but so far it has not done so.

The Sub-Commission

When the Commission on Human Rights in 1947 established the Sub-Commission on Prevention of Discrimination and Protection of Minorities, the Sub-Commission's main mission was to recommend standards to be adopted for the prevention of discrimination and the protection of minorities. However, its mission has expanded considerably since then, partly because it has been able to function quite independently. The Sub-Commission now has twenty-six "independent experts" as members, elected by the Commission (its current members are listed at http://www.unhchr.ch/html/menu2/2/subcmem.htm).

The Sub-Commission has created four subsidiary bodies: the Working Group on Communications, the Working Group on Slavery, the Working Group on Indigenous Populations, and the Working Group on Minorities. The Working Group on Communications examines communications that are received alleging violations of human rights. These communications may come not only from individuals but also from nongovernmental organizations. If they appear to reveal consistent patterns of gross violations, they are brought to the attention of the corresponding working group of the Commission on Human Rights, and ultimately to the commission in plenary. To reflect the Sub-Commission's broad agenda, on July 27, 1999, ECOSOC changed its name to the Sub-Commission on the Promotion and Protection of Human Rights.

The Commission on the Status of Women

The Commission on the Status of Women was established by ECOSOC in 1946 to prepare reports and recommendations on women's rights. This commission is different from the Committee on the Elimination of Discrimination Against Women, which is the treaty body for the Convention on the Elimination of All Forms of Discrimination Against Women.

The Office of the High Commissioner for Human Rights

In 1982, Ireland sponsored a resolution in the Third Committee of the General Assembly that authorized a study to consider the creation of a high commissioner for human rights. Yet it was not until December 1993 that the General Assembly agreed to create this position. The first appointee, José Ayala Lasso of Ecuador, took up the post in 1994. Subsequently, Mary Robinson, the former president of Ireland, was appointed in 1997, and Sergio Vieira de Mello of Brazil was appointed in 2002. In May 2003, de Mello was asked by Secretary-General Kofi Annan to take a four-month leave of absence from his position as high commissioner to serve in Iraq as Annan's special representative. Tragically, he was killed in Iraq on August 19, 2003. Bertrand Ramcharan, who had been de Mello's deputy, took over as acting high commissioner for human rights. In February

2004, the UN General Assembly approved the appointment of Louise Arbour as the high commissioner for human rights. Arbour has served as a Canadian Supreme Court justice and as prosecutor in the war crimes tribunals for the former Yugoslavia and for Rwanda.

Other UN Bodies

Many other bodies within the United Nations also have human rights on their agenda, and there is a web of complex interrelationships among them. It is easy to suggest that human rights activities in the United Nations should be tidied up, with clearer missions and better organization. However, the arrangements cannot be compared with that of, say, a corporation, in which the directors can simply redesign the operations under their command. These United Nations bodies have accumulated more than half a century of experience in response to a broad array of different and often conflicting forces. United Nations operations in human rights are not yet based on a singular well-defined mission under a singular authoritative command structure.

United Nations Treaty Bodies

As indicated earlier in this chapter, the two UN covenants and five other international human rights treaties have corresponding treaty bodies (committees) in the United Nations. The treaties established six of these, but the Committee on Economic, Social, and Cultural Rights was established by ECOSOC. Operating procedures vary among the seven committees, but they have certain common features. All are composed of independent experts rather than individuals representing particular governments. However, the distinction is sometimes blurred (March and Olsen 1989, 30).

The committees' central function is to monitor the situation within nations to try to ensure that national governments effectively implement their obligations under the treaties they have signed and ratified. This is done largely on the basis of reports the committees receive from the states parties to the conventions in accordance with procedures outlined in the conventions. The committees may also receive information from other sources, such as United Nations specialized agencies or civil society organizations, and they may, to a limited extent, make inquiries of their own. The treaty bodies are authorized to gather information, and they are also authorized to express their views and state their findings.

As indicated in the last column of table 2.1, the Human Rights Committee (HRC) may consider complaints from individuals. The committee accepts complaints from individuals in states that are parties to the first Optional Protocol to the International Covenant on Civil and Political Rights.

The Committee on Economic, Social, and Cultural Rights (CESCR) and the Committee on the Rights of the Child have no procedures enabling them to respond to individual petitions. Efforts are under way to implement an Optional Protocol to the International Covenant on Economic, Social, and Cultural Rights that would allow the CESCR to consider petitions from individuals.

The Committee on the Elimination of Discrimination Against Women is now also able to accept complains from individuals. An Optional Protocol for that purpose was adopted by the UN General Assembly in 1999 and entered into force in 2000.

The Committee on Elimination of All Forms of Racial Discrimination (CERD) and the Committee Against Torture (CAT) can deal with complaints from individuals alleging violations of their rights under the relevant treaty. The Committee on the Protection of the Rights of All Migrant Workers and Members of Their Families may accept complaints from individuals if the relevant state party agrees to it, and if the complaint has not been examined in another international context. There are procedures allowing for interstate (as distinguished from individual) complaints in HRC, CERD, and CAT, but they have not been used.

The governments that sign and ratify (or otherwise accede to) the international human rights agreements are responsible for carrying them out. The committees' task is to ensure that the states parties are held accountable for fulfilling their commitments under the treaties. The treaty bodies are not tribunals, but committees that try to help the states, through constructive dialogue, to abide by the obligations they had undertaken on ratifying the agreements (Kornblum 1995, 52).

The committees are sometimes described as implementation mechanisms, but that is a mistake since the primary agents for implementation of the conventions are the states parties, not the treaty bodies. They are sometimes described as oversight or supervisory bodies, but that too is misleading because these terms suggest that the committees have authority over the states parties in the way that a supervisor might have authority over employees. The states parties are not subordinate to the treaty bodies. The treaty bodies may make suggestions, but they do not have the authority to direct the states parties to take any particular action.

Civil Society Organizations

There are many bodies concerned with human rights, at the global level, regionally, and within nations. National governments and the international agencies created and operated by their member governments are described as governmental organizations. The others are described as civil society organizations (CSO's). These have been called nongovernmental organizations (NGO's), but there is now an increasing consensus that they should be known by what they are, not by what they are not. Corporations are not governmental organizations, but they are generally not included in the CSO category. International ones are often called multinational or transnational corporations.

The International Committee of the Red Cross, which has a special responsibility for implementing international humanitarian law, does not fit the usual categories. Although it is a nongovernmental organization, it has some powers that approach those of governments. And although it operates internationally, it is not truly international because the committee members are all Swiss. However, its staff is international.

Several different kinds of international nongovernmental organizations have significant influence on human rights, for good or ill. There are international industry-related groups, sometimes described as international business organizations, whose interests are generally quite different from those of the public-interest international nongovernmental organizations. Some NGO's are so closely affiliated with governments that they are disparagingly described as government-oriented NGO's, or GONGO's. When we speak of nongovernmental organizations in this text, we are generally referring to public-interest international human rights advocacy organizations.

CSO's working on food issues can be sorted out in many different ways. Some are more concerned with direct service delivery, and some focus more on advocacy. Some are explicitly human rights oriented, while others are not. There are many human rights advocacy bodies within nations, such as the American Civil Liberties Union. The Union of International Associations (http://www.uia.org) maintains an online yearbook of international organizations.

The United Nations has a Non-Governmental Liaison Service (NGL's), "an interagency unit of the United Nations system which promotes cooperation between the UN system and non-governmental organizations on economic and social development issues." With offices in both New York and Geneva, NGLS is part of the UN system, and thus is not itself an NGO or CSO.

Some CSO's serve as bridges between international government agencies and other CSO's. For example, there is an NGO Committee on UNICEF that helps to link NGO's (CSO's) concerned with children with UNICEF's activities. Some umbrella groups of this sort focus on human rights. There is an NGO Group for the Convention on the Rights of the Child. It meets regularly in Geneva and works to facilitate the implementation of the Convention on the Rights of Child. It has various subgroups, including, for example, the Sub-Group on Sexual Exploitation of Children.

Informal Civil Society

Some observers speak as if civil society were constituted entirely of civil society organizations. This can lead to the neglect of the social functions of the population as a whole. Through voting, social movements, writing letters to newspapers, holding neighborhood discussions, contributing money and energy to some causes and not to others, and many other day-to-day activities, ordinary people can play major roles in shaping their societies. The term *informal civil society* can be used to designate this sector.

The active functioning of informal civil society is essential to the realization of human rights. Individuals have their rights fulfilled not as passive objects benefiting from governmental largesse but as active subjects, fully participating in establishing the public agenda and in crafting proposals and final decisions. Thus, the realization of human rights implies the existence of democracy. There must be real democracy, going beyond the mere mechanics of voting and representation, and including active public participation and broad sharing of power.

As we will see in chapter 9, the movement in support of the human right to adequate food in Brazil was based on a clear understanding of the central role of civil society, in both its informal and its organized manifestations:

> A strong government–civil society partnership is essential for a human rights approach to food and nutritional security. The formation of this partnership may require: (i) for social movements to play a facilitating role in mobilising all sectors (rather than a confrontational role); (ii) for government leaders to be sensitive to social demands and to open up negotiating spaces; and (iii) for all segments of society to understand that social problems, such as hunger, and the establishment of a democratic society are linked, and that only in partnership can social problems be resolved, and not just by the State. The partnership implies equality of status, and finding complementarities in relative strengths of action. (Valente et al. 1999, 4)

Human rights do not come simply as a gift from above but as a result of political struggle. Civil society, both informal and organized, plays a central role in social mobilization, providing the public support that is needed in the transition to governance based on human rights.

After human rights–based governance is established, civil society continues to play key roles in shaping legislation and other forms of policymaking, but the roles played after that transition might be quite different. It is not so much a matter of challenging the fundamental legitimacy of established power but rather of working with it to protect and strengthen the culture of human rights. The relationship of civil society with government becomes more collaborative than confrontational.

Neil Stammers has shown the importance of social movements in forcing the transition to human rights–based governance. He points out that the human rights literature is preoccupied with international public law and technical issues such as monitoring and enforcement, and that it fails to recognize the role of social movements in the construction of human rights (Stammers 1999).

Human rights movements can be used to sustain particular forms of power, by providing a kind of sustaining legitimation. To illustrate, natural rights came to be used to impede further change when "the original and largely bourgeois proponents of natural rights gradually moved out of political opposition and into control" (Donnelly 1989, 29). Stammers (1999) shows that social movements often construct human rights as challenges to power. Thus, depending on the circumstances, human rights can be either a conservative or a radical political force (Galtung 1994).

How, then, can we understand why human rights work has a power-sustaining impact in some settings but a power-challenging impact in others? Stammers puts his answer in the form of a question:

> If it is indeed the case that it is in their institutionalized/legal form that ideas and practices in respect of human rights are most likely to sustain relations and structure of power, is it also the case that it is in their pre-institutionalised, non-legal forms that we can see claims for human rights most evidently challenging relations and structures of power? (Stammers 1999, 997–98)

Thus:

> Social movements construct claims for human rights as part of their challenge to the status quo. To the extent that social movements succeed in facilitating change, new relations and structures of power will then typically become institutionalised and culturally sedimented within a transformed social order. In other words, political, economic and cultural forms come to reflect and sustain that balance of relations and structures of power both instrumentally and expressively and do so, partly, through existing discourses on human rights.(Stammers 1999, 998)

Social movements can help to create democratic societies based on legally codified human rights. However, after that transition, social movements of another form are needed to continue the task of ensuring that existing rights are fully honored and that new and more fully elaborated rights become codified. The transition to a culture based on human rights may sometimes involve a transformational crisis. However, after that transformation, the refinement and realization of human rights is an ongoing process that requires continuous effort.

CHAPTER 3

Adequate Food Is a Human Right

Economic, Social, and Cultural Rights

Although human rights are indivisible, there has in fact been a historical cleavage by virtue of the partition established by the two covenants, one for civil and political rights and the other for economic, social, and cultural rights. Since the adoption of the Universal Declaration of Human Rights, human rights advocates have focused most of their energy on civil and political rights. Now, in the second half-century of post–World War II human rights advocacy, economic, social, and cultural rights are gaining increasing attention.

There has been extensive debate over whether the two groups of rights are really significantly different. Our view is that they are not different in any important way: All rights involve questions of justiciability, entitlement, resources, and so on. All involve government obligations to respect, protect, facilitate, and fulfill, though perhaps to different degrees. However, there are differences. As Eide, Krause, and Rosas point out:

> Taking economic, social and cultural rights seriously implies at the same time a commitment to social integration, solidarity and equality, including tackling the question of income distribution. Economic, social and cultural rights include a major concern with the protection of vulnerable groups, such as the poor, the handicapped and indigenous peoples. (Eide, Krause, and Rosas 2001, 5)

Economic, social, and cultural rights include the right to an adequate standard of living. Article 25, paragraph 1, of the Universal Declaration of Human Rights says:

> Everyone has the right to a standard of living adequate for the health and well-being of himself and of his family, including food, clothing, housing and medical care and necessary social services, and the right to security in the event of unemployment, sickness, disability, widowhood, old age or other lack of livelihood in circumstances beyond his control.

This was elaborated in article 11 of the International Covenant on Economic, Social, and Cultural Rights. Paragraph 1 says:

The States Parties to the present Covenant recognize the right of everyone to an adequate standard of living for himself and his family, including adequate food, clothing and housing, and to the continuous improvement of living conditions.

Thus, the call is not simply for adequate food but more broadly for an *adequate standard of living*. Article 11 of the covenant is explicit about food, clothing, and housing, but it also implies adequate health, education, and other requirements that are addressed in other parts of the covenant and other human rights instruments. Though this book focuses on food, we have much to learn from the work that has emerged on health, education, housing, and other issues relating to an adequate standard of living (e.g., see Hunt 1998; Kothari 1997; Leary 1994; Leckie 1989; Toebes 1998).

Individuals and organizations working to end hunger and malnutrition sometimes use the slogan "Food First." The concept expresses their feelings that the food issue should be given high priority. However, it should be recognized that food and nutrition constitute just one of the dimensions of adequate livelihood, and it would be inappropriate to argue that nutrition is more important than, say, housing or education. All aspects of livelihood are interrelated and need to be kept in balance (Eide 2001, 135).

The point may be clarified by posing a question: Can the human right to adequate food be fulfilled by an authoritarian regime? It is certainly possible to ensure that individuals' biological nutritional needs are fulfilled through authoritarian measures. Even chained prisoners can have their minimum required daily allowances of nutrients delivered to them. But fulfilling one's *need* for food in the biological sense is different from fulfilling one's *human right* to food. It is true that many human needs can be met by authoritarian powers without consulting with the people. Certainly, one can provide food for individuals that will meet their basic nutrient requirements, as in a prison or an army. However, if people have no chance to influence what and how they are being fed, if they are fed prepackaged rations or capsules or are fed from a trough, their right to adequate food is not being met, even if they get all the nutrients their bodies need. Serving pork to a Muslim prisoner would violate his human rights, even if it contained the nutrients he needed.

Human rights are mainly about upholding human dignity, not about meeting physiological needs. Dignity does not come from being fed. It comes from providing for oneself. In any well-structured society, the objective is to move toward conditions under which all people can provide for themselves.

One of the major critiques of humanitarian assistance programs has been that "aid processes treat lives to be saved as bare life, not as lives with a political voice" (Edkins 2000, xvi). The human rights approach responds directly to this concern. One can ensure that people are treated like dignified human beings, rather than like animals on a feedlot, by making sure that they have some say in how they are being treated. This is why, in a human rights system, the people *must* have some institutionalized remedies available to them that they can call upon if they feel they are not being treated properly. There must be some meaningful action they can take if they feel their rights are not being acknowledged.

Saying that people must have actions they can take is another way of saying that they must be free to participate in shaping the conditions in which they live. This refers not only to the quality of relationships between individuals and their governments but also to the quality of their relationships with one another. Human rights are not only about the potentialities of isolated individuals. People must be recognized as social beings with a need and a right to share in shaping not only their individual futures but also the futures of their communities. At one level, human rights may appear to be individualistic, but it should be recognized that the basis of the realization of individual human rights is the quality of our social relationships (Fields 2003). This is the essence of democracy.

On the basis of this formulation, democracy is required for the realization of the human right to adequate food and all other human rights. The fulfillment of human rights requires a democratic social order. A democratic social order is one in which individuals can play an active role in shaping the conditions under which they live. Democracy is about participation.

Limitations in available resources necessarily limit achievements with regard to the standard of living, but nevertheless, there is the requirement of continuous improvement. This point is elaborated in two important collective efforts to interpret economic, social, and cultural rights. The Principles on the Implementation of the International Covenant on Economic, Social, and Cultural Rights were formulated by a conference of experts held in Limburg, the Netherlands, in 1986. This statement came to be known simply as the Limburg Principles (United Nations 1986). The issues were revisited in 1997 at a conference at Maastricht University in The Netherlands. The result was a new statement, the Maastricht Guidelines on Violations of Economic, Social and Cultural Rights (*Human Rights Quarterly* 1998; also see Dankwa, Flinterman, and Leckie 1998), that further clarified the nature and scope of economic, social, and cultural rights.

Just as the human right to adequate food must be seen in the context of the right to adequate livelihood, that cluster of rights must in turn be viewed in the broader context of all human rights. Livelihoods may be adequate in terms of specific measures of income, health care, housing, and the like, but this must not be achieved through means that violate other human rights. Human rights are indivisible.

Food in International Human Rights Law

Historically, national and international responses to problems of malnutrition have been based on compassion and the recognition that reducing malnutrition can be of considerable benefit to the society as a whole. These responses have ranged from small local feeding programs to large-scale international actions involving the United Nations Children's Fund, the World Bank, the World Food Program, and many nongovernmental organizations. Now, however, there is increasing recognition that adequate food is a human right, and thus there is a legal *obligation* to ensure that all people get adequate food.

As indicated in the preceding section, the articulation of the human right to adequate food in modern international human rights law arises in the context of the broader human right to an adequate standard of living. The Universal Declaration of Human Rights of 1948 asserts in article 25(1) that "everyone has the right to a standard of living adequate for the health and well-being of himself and his family, including food."

In the International Covenant on Civil and Political Rights, which came into force in 1976, article 1, paragraph 2, says, "In no case may a people be deprived of its own means of subsistence." In addition, article 6 says, "Every human being has the inherent right to life." This clearly implies the right to adequate food and other necessities for sustaining life.

The human right to adequate food was affirmed explicitly in two major binding international agreements. In the International Covenant on Economic, Social, and Cultural Rights (which came into force in 1976), article 11 says that "[t]he States Parties to the present Covenant recognize the right of everyone to an adequate standard of living for himself and his family, including adequate food, clothing, and housing" and also recognizes "the fundamental right of everyone to be free from hunger."

In the Convention on the Rights of the Child (which came into force in 1990), two articles address the issue of nutrition. Article 24 says that "States Parties recognize the right of the child to the enjoyment of the highest attainable standard of health" (paragraph 1) and shall take appropriate measures "to combat disease and malnutrition ... through the provision of adequate nutritious foods, clean drinking water, and health care" (paragraph 2c). Article 24 also says that states parties shall take appropriate measures "[t]o ensure that all segments of society, in particular parents and children, are informed, have access to education and are supported in the use of basic knowledge of child health and nutrition [and] the advantages of breastfeeding." Article 27 says in paragraph 3 that states parties "shall in case of need provide material assistance and support programmes, particularly with regard to nutrition, clothing, and housing."

Even if the human right to adequate food had not been stated directly, it would be strongly implied in other provisions, such as those asserting the right to life and health, or the Convention on the Rights of the Child's requirement (in article 24, paragraph 2a) that states parties shall "take appropriate measures to diminish infant and child mortality." The human right to adequate food has been reaffirmed at the international level in many different settings.

Henry Shue (1996) defines basic rights as those necessary for the enjoyment of all other rights. In these terms, there can be no question that the human right to adequate food is a basic right.

The foundations for the human right to adequate food lie in the Universal Declaration of Human Rights and the binding international human rights instruments in which it is explicitly mentioned, primarily the International Covenant on Economic, Social, and Cultural Rights and the Convention on the Rights of the Child. Other binding international human rights agreements, such as the Convention on the Elimination of All Forms of Discrimination Against Women, contribute to the articulation of relevant rights. The Food and Agriculture Organization of the United Nations (1999a) has identified a large number of authoritative international instruments that address the human right to adequate food. Apart from these developments in formal international law, the international community has taken major initiatives to spell out commonly agreed standards with regard to food and nutrition, as described in the section titled "Global Declarations and Commitments" later in this chapter.

On reviewing the hunger data, Philip Alston and Katarina Tomaševski observed that "these statistics make hunger by far the most flagrant and widespread of all serious human rights abuses." Alston added that "the right to food has been endorsed more often and with greater unanimity and urgency than most other human rights, while at the same time being violated more comprehensively and systematically than probably any other right" (Alston and Tomaševski 1984, 7, 9). There is no need to propose the human right to adequate food; it is already well established in international law. The task now is to ensure the universal recognition and realization of that right.

Food in International Humanitarian Law

Food plays a special role in international humanitarian law, that part of international law that is particularly concerned with conflict situations, as described in chapter 2. In the statement *The Right to Food* made to the un's Commission on Human Rights in April 2001, the International Committee of the Red Cross described the major relevant rules:

- International humanitarian law expressly prohibits starvation of civilians as a method of combat in both international and noninternational armed conflict. This prohibition is violated not only when lack of food or denial of access to it causes death, but also when the population suffers hunger because of deprivation of food sources or supplies.
- It should be noted that intentional starvation of civilians as a method of warfare is a war crime when committed in international armed conflict under the 1998 Rome Statute establishing a permanent Interna-

tional Criminal Court. Intentional starvation of civilians is a serious
violation of international humanitarian law when committed in internal armed conflict as well.

- In elaboration of the prohibition of starvation, international humanitarian law specifically prohibits attacking, destroying, removing, or
  rendering useless objects indispensable to the survival of the civilian
  population. Such objects include foodstuffs, agricultural areas for the
  production of foodstuffs, crops, livestock, drinking water installations,
  drinking water supplies, and irrigation works.
- It is fairly obvious that population displacement is a major cause of
  hunger and starvation in war. International humanitarian law prohibits the forced displacement of civilians unless their security or
  imperative military reasons so demand in both international and
  non-international armed conflict. Forced movement of civilians is
  a war crime in both types of conflict under the Rome Statute.
- Last, but by no means least, international humanitarian law contains
  specific rules on assistance to civilian populations in armed conflict
  situations. Parties to an armed conflict must allow humanitarian
  and impartial relief operations—including those aimed at providing
  food—when supplies essential for the civilian population are lacking.
  (International Committee of the Red Cross 2001)

The representative of the International Committee of the Red Cross pointed
out that "the strength of humanitarian law lies also in the fact that its prescrip-
tions must be applied immediately, rather than progressively, that it unequivo-
cally binds both state and non-state actors and that it permits no derogations
whatsoever." Strictly speaking, the rules related to food in international humanitarian law are not cast as human rights; rather, they complement the human right
to adequate food in international human rights law (Pejic 2001).

Global Declarations and Commitments

Alongside the developments in international law described in the preceding sections, numerous conferences and nonbinding international declarations
and resolutions have helped to shape the emerging international consensus on
norms regarding the human right to adequate food. On March 14, 1963, a Special Assembly on Man's Right to Freedom from Hunger met in Rome and issued
a *Manifesto* asserting that freedom from hunger is a fundamental right. However,
the idea was not elaborated (Krishnaswamy 1963).

In 1974, the World Food Conference issued a Universal Declaration on the
Eradication of Hunger and Malnutrition. It asserted that "[e]very man, woman
and child has the inalienable right to be free from hunger and malnutrition in order to develop fully and maintain their physical and mental faculties." That dec-

laration was endorsed by the United Nations General Assembly in Resolution 3348 of December 17, 1974.

From time to time, rules related to the food needs of special populations, such as refugees or prisoners, have been set out. For example, article 20 of the *Standard Minimum Rules for the Treatment of Prisoners* (United Nations, Economic and Social Council 1977), which is on food, says:

> (1) Every prisoner shall be provided by the administration at the usual hours with food of nutritional value adequate for health and strength, of wholesome quality and well prepared and served. (2) Drinking water shall be available to every prisoner whenever he needs it.

There is widespread violation of the right to adequate food of prisoners, in developed as well as in developing countries. In Japan, for example, it was reported that "many foreign inmates complain that the quantity of food is insufficient and that they are constantly hungry. Prisoners may not purchase or be given supplementary food" (U.S. Department of State 1999, 3).

In response to concerns about inappropriate marketing and promotion, the International Code of Marketing of Breastmilk Substitutes was adopted by the World Health Assembly in 1981 (World Health Organization 1981). The assembly has approved a series of resolutions in subsequent years to further clarify and strengthen the code.

In November 1984, the World Food Assembly, comprised primarily of representatives of nongovernmental organizations, met in Rome. Its purpose was to call attention to the fact that the promise made at the 1974 World Food Conference that "within a decade no child will go to bed hungry" had not been fulfilled. Its final statement asserted that "the hungry millions are being denied the most basic human right—the right to food." In 1986, Howard University in Washington conducted a conference on food and the law that examined the right to food from a variety of perspectives (*Howard Law Journal* 1987).

On August 1, 1990, the Innocenti Declaration on the Protection, Promotion, and Support of Breastfeeding (http://www.elogica.com.br/waba/inno.htm) was adopted by participants at a meeting on breast-feeding held at the International Child Development Center in Florence. The declaration stated a variety of specific global goals, including the goal that "all women should be enabled to practice exclusive breast-feeding and all infants should be fed exclusively on breastmilk from birth to 4–6 months of age." In 1991, the UNICEF Executive Board passed a resolution (1991/22) saying that the Innocenti Declaration would serve as the "basis for UNICEF policies and actions in support of infant and young child feeding." In May 1996, the World Health Assembly passed a resolution on Infant and Young Child Nutrition (WHA49.15) in which it confirmed its support for the Innocenti Declaration.

At the World Summit for Children held at the United Nations in New York in September 1990, most heads of state signed the Plan of Action for Implementing the World Declaration on the Survival, Protection, and Development of Children. Among the major goals specified in the plan was: "Between 1990 and the year 2000, reduction of severe and moderate malnutrition among under-5 children by half." This was elaborated in eight Supporting Goals. These goals have been endorsed repeatedly, both before and after the World Summit for Children, by many international bodies, including the World Health Assembly in 1990, the UNICEF Board Session of 1990, and the United Nations Conference on Environment and Development in 1992. The constitution of the World Health Organization says that "the enjoyment of the highest attainable standard of health is one of the fundamental rights of every human being," clearly implying the human right to adequate food (Brundtland 2000).

An International Conference on Nutrition, organized by the Food and Agriculture Organization of the United Nations and the World Health Organization, was held in Rome in December 1992. The idea of the human right to adequate food was frequently endorsed. In his address opening the conference, Pope John Paul II said:

It is up to you to reaffirm in a new way each individual's fundamental and inalienable right to nutrition. The Universal Declaration of Human Rights had already asserted the right to sufficient food. What we must now do is ensure that this right is applied and that everyone has access to food, food security, a healthy diet and nutrition education.

In the conference's concluding World Declaration on Nutrition, the nations of the world agreed that "access to nutritionally adequate and safe food is a right of each individual." The conference also endorsed the nutrition goals set out at the 1990 World Summit for Children, and it added the goals of ending famine and famine-related deaths, and ending starvation and nutritional deficiency diseases in communities afflicted by disasters. The goals set out at the 1990 and 1992 conferences have been supported by many nations in the National Programs of Action they prepared in fulfillment of their commitments at the World Summit for Children.

In July 1996, as part of the preparatory work for the World Food Summit, a meeting on "The Fundamental Human Right to Food" was called by the president of Venezuela and held in Caracas. The Caracas statement called for the development of a Code of Conduct that would clarify the content of the right to food and provide guidance regarding its realization. This statement helped to highlight the importance of the right to food at the World Food Summit.

In November 1996, the World Food Summit concluded with agreement on the *Rome Declaration on World Food Security and World Food Summit Plan of Action* (Food and Agriculture Organization 1996). The first paragraph declared: "We, the Heads of State and Government, or our representatives, gathered at the World Food Summit at the invitation of the Food and Agriculture Organization of the United Nations, reaffirm the right of everyone to have access to safe and nutritious food, consistent with the right to adequate food and the fundamental right of everyone to be free from hunger." The summit called for further specification of the meaning of the right to food, through a process described in the following section.

The 1996 *Rome Declaration* said: "We pledge our political will and our common and national commitment to achieving food security for all and to an ongoing effort to eradicate hunger in all countries, with an immediate view to reducing the number of undernourished people to half their present level no later than 2015." This was repeated in paragraph 7 of the Plan of Action. However, apart from a minor mention in paragraph 60, the thirty pages of commitments, objectives, and actions that followed made no further reference to this specific time frame.

In the late 1990s, work on the human right to adequate food centered on a mandate from the World Food Summit held in Rome in 1996. In the summit's concluding Plan of Action, objective 7.4 called upon

the UN High Commissioner for Human Rights, in consultation with relevant treaty bodies, and in collaboration with relevant specialized agencies and programmes of the UN system and appropriate inter-governmental mechanisms, to better define the rights related to food in Article 11 of the Covenant and to propose ways to implement and realize these rights. (Food and Agriculture Organization 1996)

Several different initiatives were taken to respond to this call, including supportive resolutions from the Commission on Human Rights; a Day of Discussion on Right to Food held by the UN Committee on Economic, Social, and Cultural Rights; and Expert Consultations on the human right to adequate food held in Geneva, Rome, and Bonn. In April 1999, the United Nations System Standing Committee on Nutrition (then known as the United Nations Administrative Committee on Coordination / Sub-Committee on Nutrition) focused its annual meeting on the human right to adequate food. In May 1999, the United Nations Committee on Economic, Social, and Cultural Rights released its landmark *General Comment 12* on the right to adequate food, which is described in the following section.

All these efforts were given further impetus at the Millennium Summit of the United Nations in 2000. The eight Millennium Development Goals, supported by all 189 nations at the summit, were led off by goal 1, to eradicate extreme poverty and hunger. The final report of the Millennium Task Force on Hunger (accessible at http://www.unmillenniumproject.org/reports/reports2.htm) argues that developed countries should contribute more generously to development in poor countries. It does not argue that they have any legal obligation to do so.

General Comment 12

The United Nations human rights treaty bodies elaborate the major treaties through their responses to national reports and through the issuance of *General Comments* or *General Recommendations* on particular themes. In 2003, the United Nations prepared a compilation of all *General Comments* and *General Recommendations* from all the treaty bodies up to that time in a single document running over 300 pages (United Nations, International Human Rights Instruments 2003). The individual documents are available at the website of the Office of the UN High Commissioner for Human Rights (http://www.ohchr.org). The advocacy organization Human Strategies for Human Rights also provides ready access to the individual *General Comments* through its website (http://www.hshr.org/generalcommentsintroduction.html).

The *General Comments* of particular interest here are those provided by the Committee on Economic, Social, and Cultural Rights. Chapter 12 of the present volume, for example, mentions *General Comment 14*, on the right to the highest attainable standard of health (United Nations, Economic and Social Council 2000). Chapter 13 reviews *General Comment 15*, on the human right to water (United Nations, Economic and Social Council 2002b). Of immediate interest here is the fact that on May 12, 1999, the UN's Committee on Economic, Social, and Cultural Rights released *General Comment 12 (Twentieth session, 1999): The Right to Adequate Food (Art. 11)* (United Nations, Economic and Social Council 1999d). This statement constitutes a definitive contribution to international jurisprudence. Though it is only eight pages long, it warrants careful review. A few highlights are mentioned here. Its paragraph 6 presents the core definition:

> The right to adequate food is realized when every man, woman and child, alone or in community with others, has physical and economic access at all times to adequate food or means for its procurement.

The paragraph goes on to emphasize that the right to adequate food "must not be interpreted in a narrow or restrictive sense which equates it with a minimum package of calories, proteins and other specific nutrients." In other words, as pointed out in the first section of this chapter, simply delivering prepackaged meals in the way one might deliver feed pellets to livestock cannot fulfill the right. That sort of approach would be incompatible with human dignity. Delivering such meals may be sensible in a short-term emergency, but it cannot be the means for realizing the human right to adequate food over the long run.

General Comment 12's paragraph 1 begins by citing the foundation of the legally binding human right to adequate food in article 11 of the International Covenant on Economic, Social, and Cultural Rights. It draws a distinction between the reference in the first paragraph of that article to an adequate standard of living, including adequate food, and the second paragraph of that article, which calls for ensuring "the fundamental right to freedom from hunger and malnutrition." *General Comment 12* indicates that "more immediate and urgent steps may be needed to ensure" the fundamental right to freedom from hunger and malnutrition. Thus, hunger and malnutrition signify more acute, more urgent problems than are indicated by inadequate food in itself. The distinction is addressed again in *General Comment 12*'s paragraph 6 (emphasis in original):

> The *right to adequate food* will have to be realized progressively. However, States have a core obligation to take the necessary action to mitigate and alleviate hunger as provided for in paragraph 2 of article 11, even in times of natural or other disasters.

It is important to distinguish the broad concern with food supplies from the immediate need to deal with hunger and malnutrition. As Rolf Künnemann explains it, "The human rights standard recognized by the right to adequate food is access to adequate food. For the right to freedom from hunger, it is the absence of hunger or malnutrition" (Künnemann 2002, 165). The access or food supplies approach focuses attention on what is in the family's or the nation's cupboard, while the concern with hunger and malnutrition focuses attention on the conditions of people's bodies.

General Comment 12's paragraph 4 highlights the linkage of the human right to adequate food to "the inherent dignity of the human person" and points out that it is indispensable for the realization of other human rights. It is also inseparable from social justice. Paragraph 5 observes that "fundamentally, the roots of the problem of hunger and malnutrition are not lack of food but lack of *access to* available food, inter alia because of poverty, by large segments of the world's population." This sentence might have been clearer if the phrase "lack of food" was followed with something like "in the community." The reference here is to the fundamental distinction between *availability* (Is there food around?) and *access* (Can you make a claim on that food?).

General Comment 12, paragraph 7, explains that *adequacy* means that account must be taken of what is appropriate under given circumstances. Food *security* implies food being accessible for both present and future generations. *Sustainability* is related to long-term availability and accessibility. Thus, as explained in paragraph 8, the core content of the right to adequate food implies that

> the availability of food in a quantity and quality sufficient to satisfy the dietary needs of individuals, free from adverse substances, and acceptable within a given culture; the accessibility of such food in ways that are sustainable and that do not interfere with the enjoyment of other human rights.

These terms are then explained further in paragraphs 9 through 13 of *General Comment 12*. Paragraph 14 summarizes the obligations of States as follows:

> Every State is obliged to ensure for everyone under its jurisdiction access to the minimum essential food which is sufficient, nutritionally adequate and safe, to ensure their freedom from hunger.

The obligation applies to everyone under the state's jurisdiction. Thus, it is not permissible to exclude immigrants or refugees, even if they are in the country illegally. The obligation cannot be limited only to citizens, or only to particular ethnic groups. If a group of people is under military occupation, the obligation extends to them as well.

Paragraph 15 of *General Comment 12* draws out the different kinds or levels of obligations of the state. These obligations may be sorted into categories, as follows:

- *respect*—"The obligation to *respect* existing access to adequate food requires states parties not to take any measures that result in preventing such access."
- *protect*—"The obligation to *protect* requires measures by the State to ensure that enterprises or individuals do not deprive individuals of their access to adequate food."
- *fulfil (facilitate)*—"The obligation to *fulfil (facilitate)* means the State must pro-actively engage in activities intended to strengthen people's access to and utilization of resources and means to ensure their livelihood, including food security."
- *fulfil (provide)*—"Finally, whenever an individual or group is unable, for reasons beyond their control, to enjoy the right to adequate food by the means at their disposal, States have the obligation to *fulfil (provide)* that right directly. This obligation also applies for persons who are victims of natural or other disasters."

The levels of obligations will be discussed further in chapter 6. *General Comment 12* should be consulted for its analyses on these and other themes, including the issues of implementation at the national level, framework legislation, monitoring, remedies and accountability, international obligations, and so on.

The Special Rapporteur

In 1983, the UN's Economic and Social Council appointed its first special rapporteur on the right to food, Asbjørn Eide of Norway. His report, *The Right to Adequate Food as a Human Right* (Eide 1989), was approved by the Commission on Human Rights in 1987. As a result of subsequent developments, especially at the World Food Summit of 1996, in September 2000 the UN's Commission on Human Rights decided to appoint another special rapporteur on the right to food. The task was given to Jean Ziegler of Switzerland. In Resolution 2000/10, the commission specified that the mandate of the Special Rapporteur is to

- receive information and highlight violations of the right to food;
- cooperate with UN agencies, international organizations and [nongovernmental organizations] to put the right to food into practice around the world; and
- identify emerging issues related to the right to food.

In Resolution 2001/25, the commission also asked him to

- look at the question of drinking water and its relation to the right to food;
- contribute to the review of the implementation of the World Food Summit 1996 Declaration and Plan of Action; and
- adopt a gender perspective in his work.

The special rapporteur makes annual reports on his work to the Commission on Human Rights in Geneva each April and, at the request of the commission, he or she also makes an annual report to the UN General Assembly in November each year. In 2002, for example, the special rapporteur's recommendations for immediately reducing hunger and malnutrition included placing emphasis on nutrition education, universal school lunches, breast-feeding, family gardens, and so on. He urged national governments to develop national legislation to protect the right to food in accordance with *General Comment 12*, and he called for respect for international humanitarian law, especially as it relates to food.

He also recommended that the negotiations on agriculture and other issues at the World Trade Organization should take food security into particular account, and he said that it should be ensured that trade rules do not conflict with international human rights law. He called for a review of international trade obligations to ensure that they do not conflict with the right to food.

The special rapporteur also undertakes country missions to look at the situations of the right to food in different countries across the world (cf. United Nations, Economic and Social Council 2003a, 2003b). These missions focus on examining progress in realizing the right to food over time, monitoring the situation of vulnerable groups, and monitoring compliance with the obligations relating to the human right to adequate food.

In his more general reports, the special rapporteur addresses issues such as gender discrimination, trade liberalization, genetically modified food, food sovereignty, armed conflict, nutrition, and justiciability. His reports may be accessed at the website of the Office of the UN High Commissioner for Human Rights (http://www.unhchr.ch/html/menu2/7/b/mfood.htm) and at his own website (http://www.righttofood.org/).

The Voluntary Guidelines

As indicated earlier in this chapter, the World Food Summit of 1996 was not the first global gathering to recognize the human right to adequate food, but it was the first to set out a process for clarifying and implementing that right. Subsequent international consultations on the theme, the publication of *General Comment 12* in 1999, the appointment of a special rapporteur on the right to food in 2000, and the FAO's sponsorship of a series of case studies all helped to build consensus on the meaning of the right.

There was a follow-up to the World Food Summit of 1996, called the World Food Summit: five years later, which was actually held in 2002 because of the events of September 11, 2001. This second summit produced a final declaration that called for the creation of an International Alliance Against Hunger. Paragraph 10 called upon the FAO Council to establish

an Intergovernmental Working Group, with the participation of stakeholders, in the context of the [World Food Summit] follow-up, to elaborate, in a period of two years, a set of voluntary guidelines to support Member States' efforts to achieve the progressive realisation of the right to adequate food in the context of national food security; we ask the FAO, in close collaboration with relevant treaty bodies, agencies and programmes of the UN System, to assist the Intergovernmental Working Group, which shall report on its work to the Committee on World Food Security. (Food and Agriculture Organization 2002a)

This was a disappointment to many because the idea of voluntary guidelines replaced the idea of creating a code of conduct on the right to adequate food. This appeared to be a move away from acknowledging any sort of firm obligation on the part of the international community with regard to the human right to adequate food. Norway explained:

Norway would have preferred the expression code of conduct instead of voluntary guidelines because it is clearer and more definite. However, we hope that this will set in motion a process that will lead to a useful instrument that would have the same function as a code of conduct on the right to adequate food, and in fact lead to such a code in the future. (Food and Agriculture Organization 2002b, 1)

This contrasted sharply with the position taken by the United States on paragraph 10, as will be described in chapter 10.

The Intergovernmental Working Group functioned as a subgroup of FAO's Committee on Food Security. In two years of hard discussion, some governments pressed for keeping the guidelines in the form of soft recommendations, while some, supported by a group of nongovernmental organizations led by FIAN (FoodFirst Information and Action Network, based in Heidelberg, Germany, with website at http://www.fian.org/fian/index.php), put more emphasis on the need to recognize firm obligations. In the final compromise, the obligations under international human rights law remain in place, and the guidelines show that governments have some choices regarding the means through which they are fulfilled.

The Intergovernmental Working Group approved its final text on September 23, 2004, and obtained approval later on the same day by the Committee on World Food Security. (The text is available at ftp://ftp.fao.org/unfao/bodies/council/cli27/J3345e1.pdf.) It was adopted by the FAO Council, the executive governing body of FAO, on November 23, 2004 (FAO 2004).

This process of clarification will go on, in some form. As in any other area of human rights, there is a need for never-ending work to build consensus on the meaning of the human right to adequate food.

PART II Human Rights Systems

CHAPTER 4

Human Rights, Governance, and Law

Human Rights and Governance

One of the major functions of human rights is to guide governance at local, national, and international levels. Human rights restrain and give direction to the exercise of governance. In *Webster's Third New International Dictionary*, one of the definitions of "governor" is "an attachment to a machine (as in a gasoline or steam engine) designed to afford automatic control or limitation of speed or power: esp : such an attachment actuated by the centrifugal force of whirling weights opposed by gravity or by springs." With reference to the governor sketched on p. 64, Robert Thurston, in *A History of the Growth of the Steam Engine*, explained:

> The speed of the engine varying, that of the spindle changed correspondingly, and the faster the balls were swung the farther they separated. When the engine's speed decreased ... they fall back toward the spindle. ... The arms carrying the balls ... are pinned to rods ... closing and opening the throttle valve, and thus adjusting the supply of steam in such a way as to preserve a nearly fixed speed of engine. (Thurston 1878, III, 23)

Thus, a governor is a control system, a means for keeping on target in pursuit of a particular goal. The goal could be a particular speed, in the case of a steam engine, or a particular temperature, in the case of a furnace. A home heating system is based on having the homeowner set the thermostat for the desired temperature. The thermostat's mechanism then "reads" the current room temperature and compares it with the desired temperature. If the room temperature is too low, it switches on the heater. When the desired temperature is reached, the heater is turned off. This is a kind of self-regulation, in contrast to, say, an open fireplace that has to be tended manually.

Often, regulation must be based on human rather than mechanical control devices. Most vehicles are navigated by regular course corrections made by a driver. When you drive a car or sail a boat, you do not just point it and start it. You have to pay attention and make constant adjustments to keep the vehicle headed toward your destination. There must be constant corrections for deviations from the path toward the goal.

In society, we normally think of government as an instrument for controlling and regulating the people. However, there is also a need to govern governments; that is, there is a need to restrain and to give direction to the exercise of governance. In a properly functioning democracy, with active and independent mass

63

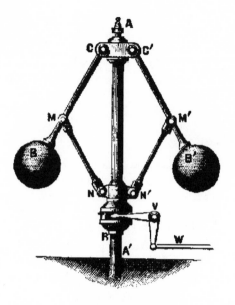

Figure 4.1. Mechanical Governor. *Source*: This diagram of the mechanical governor is from Robert Thurston's *A History of the Growth of the Steam Engine*, published in 1878. The complete text can be accessed at http://www.history.rochester.edu/steam/thurston/1878.

media, the public is able to hold its government to account and keep its government's behavior within an acceptable range. Where there are no such constraints, governments act with impunity and may quite literally go out of control. Of course, in real (rather than ideal) situations, the most influential segment of the population has the greatest impact on the government, and governments are less responsive to those who are politically weak. For these reasons, well-articulated, effective rights are needed to guide and direct the government.

Many governments have policies saying, for example, that there is to be freedom of speech, social security, and many other good things. Some of these things may even be promised in the nation's constitution. We know that there are many cases in which governments go off course and fail to deliver on their promises. However, in nations where there are comprehensive and effective human rights, specific mechanisms call the government to account, making course corrections.

The most fundamental of these mechanisms of accountability is for rights holders themselves to have effective remedies through which they can complain and have the government's behavior corrected. *Where there are no effective remedies, there are no effective rights.* In a well-developed legal system of rights, there are three major roles to be fulfilled: the *rights holders*, the *duty bearers*, and the *agents of accountability*. The task of the agents of accountability is to make sure that those who have the duty carry out their obligations to those who have the rights. To describe a rights system, we need to know the identities and also the functions of those who carry out these roles. We also want to know the mechanisms or structures through which these functions are to be carried out. Thus, we want to know:

A. the nature of the *rights holders* and their rights;
B. the nature of the *duty bearers* and their obligations corresponding to the rights of the rights holders; and
C. the nature of the *agents of accountability*, and the procedures through which they assure that the duty bearers meet their obligations to the rights holders. The accountability mechanisms include, in particular, the remedies available to the rights holders themselves.

These are the three core components, the "ABCs," of any legal system of rights. The three are examined in detail in chapters 5, 6, and 7.

Some parties may carry out several roles. Those who are rights holders generally also have duties, and conversely, those who have duties also have rights. Nevertheless, though those who carry out the roles may overlap in different ways, it is useful to draw out these distinctions among the different types of roles.

One can have systems of rights and duties not only in nations but also in many other settings. For example, patients in a hospital or inmates in a prison can have particular rights. Responsibility for implementation would then rest not with a government but with the institution's administration.

Although there are many different legal systems involving a wide variety of rights and duties, the universal human rights system is distinctive in that it deals with rights that are—or should be—enjoyed by all individuals simply by virtue of their being human. There are exceptions to this universality. For example, there are rights that are universal only in the sense that they apply to all members of a category, such as women, children, refugees, and migrant workers. Also, some specific rights may be curtailed through due process of law, as in the case of convicted prisoners.

There is no government at the global level, but only looser mechanisms, composed primarily of the United Nations system, that can be described as constituting the international community. The primary responsibility for the implementation of human rights rests with the states. Their governments have many tasks to perform, such as promoting economic progress, maintaining domestic peace and security, ensuring that all people are properly integrated into the society, and ensuring national security in relation to other states. In performing their tasks, governments must be restrained and guided by universal human rights.

Although national governments have the primary obligations for the realization of human rights, other bodies, including the international community, have obligations as well. The obligations of the international community are discussed further in chapters 14 through 17.

All elements of the international community—including UN agencies, international financial institutions, transnational corporations, and international nongovernmental organizations—have obligations with regard to human rights. Even if the obligations are not yet spelled out in legal form, they have strong moral obligations to uphold human rights.

Some of the agencies comprising the international community have distinct roles in holding national governments accountable. The major agencies playing this role are the United Nations human rights bodies, described in chapter 2. On a more informal basis, international nongovernmental human rights organizations such as Amnesty International and Human Rights Watch also serve as agents of accountability at the global level.

National governments can use this three-part framework—the ABCs—in drafting national law or policy designed to ensure the realization of rights. The framework can also be used for adapting specific programs, such as national welfare programs or nutrition programs, to conform to the human rights approach. The program's policies may be reformulated so that its clients have clear entitlements to its services, and so that the program makes explicit commitments to honor those entitlements. That commitment can be concretized by establishing a complaint procedure through which those who feel they have not obtained their entitlements can get a fair hearing and, if necessary, have the situation corrected. This rights-oriented approach can be taken not only by programs within nations but also by regional and global programs. For example, it could be adopted by international agencies that provide humanitarian assistance (Kent 1999).

The three core components are essential to any rights system. Governments and other agencies can establish rights systems on the basis of these components to ensure the realization of any sorts of rights, and not only those rights that are universal.

Studying Human Rights in National Governance

All human beings should enjoy the universal human rights. Whether these rights in fact can be enjoyed within a given state depends on the degree to which the rights are recognized and effectively realized.

Human rights can be recognized by states in various ways. Many countries have explicitly acknowledged the international human rights agreements in their constitutions. The South African Constitution of 1996 illustrates comprehensive recognition of the broad system of universal human rights. Older constitutions generally recognize only selected human rights, particularly those rights that seek to protect the person against abuse of power by state authorities.

The ratification of modern international human rights agreements signifies the nation's formal legal commitment to widely recognized human rights. Even if the nation's constitution recognizes human rights only in a fragmentary way, ratification establishes the nation's commitment to the broad human rights framework established in international law. The seriousness of that commitment is demonstrated by the array of institutional arrangements through which the national government carries out its human rights obligations.

As indicated in the preceding section, the major components of any rights system are the *rights*, the corresponding *obligations* and associated implementation mechanisms, and the *accountability* mechanisms. Anticipating the discussions of these three components in chapters 5, 6, and 7, here we pose a number of questions about the components that can help to focus and organize research on national human rights systems.

Questions about Rights

States signify their recognition of and commitment to specific human rights through their ratifications of international human rights agreements and through their national constitutions. However, it is important to know not only what commitments exist on paper but also which actually guide the government's activities. One can begin to gauge the sincerity of the government's commitments to human rights by asking the following sorts of questions:

- Which of the major international human rights agreements has the country ratified?
- What reservations, understandings, and declarations (RUD's) did the country assert upon ratifying these agreements? Why did it make these RUD's?
- What official explanation has the country offered for not ratifying some of the international agreements? What other explanations have been suggested?
- What commitments are expressed in the country's constitution with regard to human rights?
- Have the rights been concretized into specific, explicitly acknowledged entitlements?
- Do the people know their rights?
- Has the country acted to ensure that its national legislation conforms with its obligations under the international human rights agreements it has ratified?
- Apart from legislation, what other means has the government used to articulate its policy with regard to human rights, for example, in national development plans, policy papers, speeches, and the like?

One can ask such questions about human rights generally, and also about human rights relating to adequate food in particular. For example, one could ask questions such as these:

- What is the situation on these dimensions specifically with regard to the human right to adequate food?
- Does national law relating to food and nutrition set out specific entitlements for the people? For example, does the law on food safety say that people are *entitled* to safe food?

One particularly important question is, *Do the rights holders know their rights?* If not, it is not a properly functioning rights system.

Questions about Obligations

How clearly has the government acknowledged that it has specific obligations corresponding to the people's rights? This leads to further questions:

- Has the government acknowledged its obligations to ensure the realization of particular human rights? Is this understanding spelled out in the law or in particular policy documents?
- Does the government acknowledge that it has various forms of obligations: to respect, to protect, to facilitate, and to provide for the realization of human rights?
- Which agencies of the government have specific responsibility to carry out the government's obligations?
- Are the employees of these agencies fully aware of the relevant human rights and the corresponding obligations that their agencies are supposed to carry out?
- Do those employees grasp their role in their nation's human rights system?
- Are they aware that their agencies may be held accountable in their national human rights system?
- Has the government set out a plan of action for ensuring the realization of human rights generally?
- Has the government prepared a National Program of Action as called for at the World Summit for Children in 1990? What has been done with it? Does it acknowledge particular rights, and the corresponding obligations of government?

With regard to food in particular, one might ask:

- How clear are the commitments with regard to the human right to adequate food?
- Has the government taken steps to ensure that its people know their rights regarding adequate food?
- Has the government set out a plan of action for ensuring the realization of the human right to adequate food?
- Has the government prepared a National Plan of Action for Nutrition as called for at the International Conference on Nutrition of 1992? What has been done with it? Does it acknowledge particular rights, and the corresponding obligations of government?
- What sorts of food and nutrition programs does the government have in place? To what extent do people have entitlements to the services they provide?

One particularly important question is, *Do the obligation holders know their obligations?* If not, it is not a properly functioning rights system.

Questions about Accountability Mechanisms

What arrangements are there to ensure that the government carries out its obligations? This leads to such further questions as these:

- What mechanisms are there to ensure that the government carries out its obligations for the realization of human rights? Which individuals, and which agencies, have what roles?
- How responsive is the government to the UN agencies responsible for human rights? Does the government submit timely and thorough reports to the treaty bodies, as required?
- Are there any agencies in government, apart from those primarily responsible for carrying out the obligations, that monitor the government's human rights performance and call for corrective action when it is needed (e.g., the judiciary, ombudsmen)?
- Does the country have a national human rights commission? When was it created? What is its mandate? How powerful is it? How does it function? How effective is it?
- What role do nongovernmental organizations within the country play in monitoring the government's human rights performance?
- Do any outside nongovernmental organizations play a significant role in monitoring the government's human rights performance?
- Are there judicial or administrative remedies for people who feel their rights have been violated? For example, if people feel their food is not safe, are there specific legal remedies they can pursue?
- Do the people know their rights? Do they know what they can do about it if they feel their rights have been violated?
- How have the accountability mechanisms functioned specifically with regard to the human right to adequate food?

One particularly important question is, *Do the agents of accountability know what they are supposed to do, and why?* If not, it is not a properly functioning rights system.

Researching These Types of Questions

These questions are only suggestive. Many of them might be difficult to answer as a practical matter, but nevertheless, they are useful because they help to convey an understanding of the issues.

One could do analyses of national human rights systems taken as a whole, or one could focus on specific themes, such as the human right to adequate food: what entitlements, commitments, implementation mechanisms, and accountability mechanisms are in place relating to this particular issue? In all such specialized studies, it will be important to understand the particulars in the context of the nation's human rights system seen as a whole.

Many reports about human rights in particular countries focus on assessing performance; that is, gauging the extent to which particular human rights are realized. Though that is certainly important information, it does not say much about the structure and operations of the human rights system itself. One of the best sources for descriptive information on national human rights systems is the reports provided by national governments to the United Nations treaty bodies. Many of them can be accessed through the website of the Office of the United Nations High Commissioner for Human Rights (http://www.ohchr.org). Of course, these national reports should be viewed with skepticism because governments generally try to put their situations into the best possible light. Their reports should be cross-checked and compared with other sources, especially critics of the government's human rights performance.

Critics' accounts should be viewed with just as much skepticism. They, too, have particular positions that they are interested in advancing. Researchers should consult a broad variety of sources. The characterizations of countries' performance are always subject to contestation, and all assessments must be regarded as tentative and open to review. However, whereas assessments of performance may be sharply contested, descriptive accounts of a country's human rights system, in terms of its institutional structure, are less likely to be controversial.

The Role of National Law

Law should never be confused with justice. Law can be an instrument of justice, but it can also be used as an instrument of injustice. For example, the law may give priority to the rights of shopkeepers to protect their stocks while forcing others to starve. An extreme example of the law being used as an instrument of injustice is that of South African law during the apartheid period. Even in democratic states with voting rights for all, some sections of society are much more influential than others, and therefore are able to ensure that their concerns are given priority over the needs and interests of more vulnerable groups. The function of universal human rights is to provide a framework to achieve a more fully balanced, just system. The need for drawing the distinction between law and justice is highlighted by the Global Alliance for Justice Education (http://www .gaje.org). It works to make justice the principal goal of law school education worldwide.

One of the major tasks of human rights advocates is to lobby for law that conforms to human rights. Rights as they currently exist in any given nation's law may be quite different from what they ought to be from a human rights perspective. The task is to discuss, analyze, and argue about what they ought to be, with human rights as the frame of reference, and then to press for modification of the law so that it recognizes rights as they ought to be.

National governments, not international organizations, are the primary agents responsible for the realization of human rights. The international human rights instruments are concerned mainly with the obligations of states to their own people, not to people elsewhere. The United Nations and other global agencies may be called to take direct action when national governments fail to ensure the realization of human rights, but the situations in which this can be done are exceptional. The international community has an important role to play in setting out widely accepted guidelines, but once general principles are set out in international human rights agreements, the primary locus of human rights work is within nations. The front line of responsibility for the realization of human rights is in national governments.

A major issue with regard to international treaties is the question of whether, for states parties, they prevail over national law, and thus may be invoked directly in national courts. In a *monist* legal system, treaties are in principle also the law of the land. Upon ratification, a treaty is regarded as part of the national law, and it may be invoked in the national courts. This depends, however, on whether the treaty or particular provisions within it are self-executing. Sometimes the provisions are held to be too vague and general to be directly applicable. The approach to this varies greatly from country to country.

In contrast, in *dualist* systems, treaties are not directly applicable; national law and international law are viewed as two separate legal systems. National legislative action must be taken to incorporate the principles of the treaty into national law. Only national law, and not international law, is binding in national courts. In the Federal Republic of Nigeria, for example, article 12 of the 1999 Constitution says, "No treaty between the federation and any other country shall have the force of law except to the extent to which any such treaty has been enacted into law by the national assembly."

When they ratify international human rights agreements, states may choose to make reservations to some of their provisions. They are then not bound under international law to implement those provisions in national law. Sometimes they also state that the international human rights agreements they ratify shall be held to be non-self-executing in their national law. The United States has made a practice of doing this.

The distinction between monist and dualist systems was once regarded as simple and straightforward, but it has now become muddled. National courts frequently invoke international law even in dualist systems, if only to take note of that law's strong moral imperatives. They use the international standards as a tool for the interpretation of national law, basing themselves on the presumption that it was the intention of the lawmaker to give the law a content that was compatible with international human rights law.

Many nations with monist systems nevertheless modify their national law to conform to the international treaties they have ratified, and thus give them greater strength and visibility. In both cases, national lawmaking is used to set out local interpretations of international law.

A good example of a monist legal system is the one in Mexico. Referring to the International Covenant on Civil and Political Rights, article 133 of the Mexican Constitution says:

> international treaties concluded by the President of the Republic, with the approval of the Senate, shall together with the Constitution itself and the laws of the Federal Congress, constitute the supreme law of the entire nation; consequently, the covenant forms part of national legislation and may be the basis and foundation for any legal action.

Norway, which otherwise has a dualist system, has a provision in its Constitution committing the nation to the realization of internationally recognized human rights. To implement that provision, in 1999 the Norwegian parliament passed a law by which the European Convention for the Protection of Human Rights and Fundamental Freedoms and its associated protocols—the International Covenant on Economic, Social, and Cultural Rights; and the International Covenant on Civil and Political Rights—were made part of national law. The law also provides that in case of conflict between national law and the international agreements, the international agreements shall prevail.

Whether in monist or in dualist systems, it is important to ensure that human rights are clearly articulated in national law. Following ratification of international human rights instruments, concretization of human rights in national law reinforces, and is a major sign of, commitment to those rights.

The fact that a certain right forms part of universal human rights does not automatically mean that it is recognized and applied in a given national system. To illustrate, in one study (Cook and Brown 1996), the authors observe that adequate food is a basic human right, and on that basis view it as applying everywhere, including the United States. They did not address the fact that the United States has ratified neither the International Covenant on Economic, Social, and Cultural Rights nor the Convention on the Rights of the Child, and it has consistently refused to recognize subsistence rights in its courts (Good 1984). The people of the United States should be entitled to enjoy the human right to adequate food, like everyone else, but the U.S. government has not made a commitment to ensure its realization, as indicated by its failure to ratify the relevant international human rights agreements. Therefore the right cannot be claimed before courts in the United States. The U.S. position on the human right to adequate food is described more fully in chapter 10.

In the following chapter, the section titled "Having versus Realizing Rights" argues that one should determine whether people have particular rights in their nation's legal system before trying to assess the degree to which those rights are realized. There is not much use in arguing that a right exists and has not been realized when what is really needed is new legislation to firmly establish the legal right within the nation.

Many national constitutions contain references to the right to food, as demonstrated in the Food and Agriculture Organization of the United Nations' publication, *The Right to Food in Theory and Practice* (Food and Agriculture Organization 1998). However, most states have not given these provisions real effect in their national law and institutions. Nevertheless, these expressions of commitment in their constitutions are useful because the governments can be called to account with reference to them.

When states undertake obligations to honor particular human rights by becoming parties to international human rights agreements, they are expected to elaborate their understandings of those obligations by spelling them out in their own national law. Indeed, there is a positive obligation to do this. In the International Covenant on Civil and Political Rights, article 2, paragraph 2, says:

> Where not already provided for by existing legislative or other measures, each State Party to the present Covenant undertakes to take the necessary steps, in accordance with its constitutional processes and with the provisions of the present Covenant, to adopt such legislative or other measures as may be necessary to give effect to the rights recognized in the present Covenant.

In the International Covenant on Economic, Social, and Cultural Rights, article 2, paragraph 1, says that states parties will undertake to take steps to achieve the rights recognized in the covenant "by all appropriate means, including particularly the adoption of legislative measures." Article 4 of the Convention on the Rights of the Child begins by saying:

> States Parties shall undertake all appropriate legislative, administrative, and other measures for the implementation of the rights recognized in the present Convention.

While international bodies, both intergovernmental or nongovernmental, may help to elaborate the meaning of the human rights in international agreements, the most important interpretation is that made by the government that is to carry out the corresponding obligations. Except in extreme situations, interpretations cannot be imposed on it. As noted in the preceding chapter, the international human rights system is not based on having some sort of superior international authority tell countries what they must do. It is based on the principle of consent: Nations are bound by those rules to which they agree to be bound.

In principle, internationally recognized rights can be realized within nations even if those rights are not articulated in national law. However, they are much more likely to be realized when there is well-crafted law regarding these rights at the national level. National legislation provides highly authoritative articulation of the commitments accepted by the nation-state. It is a means of codifying and legitimizing institutionalized governmental action. Thus, lawmaking can be a major tool for advancing the realization of human rights.

National legislation relating to the human right to adequate food may be pulled together under the umbrella of a comprehensive *framework law*. In her keynote address "The Human Right to Food and Nutrition" at the meeting of the UN's Standing Committee on Nutrition in Geneva in April 1999, then–high commissioner for human rights Mary Robinson said, "Incorporating the right to food into a national framework legislation would be essential in establishing the ground work for a real accountability of the 'duty bearer'—the State—towards the 'claim holders'" (Robinson 1999, 3). In paragraph 29, *General Comment 12* says:

> States should consider the adoption of a framework law as a major instrument in the implementation of the national strategy concerning the right to food. The framework law should include provisions on its purpose; the targets or goals to be achieved and the time-frame to be set for the achievement of those targets; the means by which the purpose could be achieved described in broad terms, in particular the intended collaboration with civil society and the private sector and with international organizations; institutional responsibility for the process; and the national mechanisms for its monitoring, as well as possible recourse procedures. In developing the benchmarks and framework legislation, States Parties should actively involve civil society organizations.

The preparation of a framework law is an opportunity to formulate national strategy for dealing with malnutrition. It can be used to clarify national interpretations of the three core elements of rights systems that were discussed earlier in this chapter: rights, obligations, and accountability.

As the name suggests, the framework legislation may set out only broad outlines of the mechanisms and the strategy for ensuring the realization of the human right to adequate food. Once that foundation is established, it would be possible to take more concrete action within the framework. This should include improvements in previous legislation and the launching of appropriate new legislative initiatives.

Many nations already have different kinds of legislation relating to food and nutrition issues, including feeding programs, fortification, food quality control, trade practices, and so on. However, in most such legislation, the consumer has no specific entitlements. For example, where the law mandates salt iodization, usually the salt industry is answerable only to the government. Consumers have no powers under the law, so neither the industry nor the government is answerable directly to consumers themselves. In the perspective adopted here, food and nutrition legislation can become a form of human rights legislation only when consumers have specific, explicitly described entitlements under the law. The central function of legislation concerned with human rights is to create entitlements that are legally enforceable. One of the major distinctions between moral and legal rights is the fact that legal rights are enforceable through legal procedures.

A major motivating idea underlying the human right to adequate food is that establishing clear entitlements in the law, and ensuring the implementation of that law, can help to reduce malnutrition of different kinds. The establishment and effective implementation of such law will not be *the* solution to the malnutrition problem. Rather, it should be viewed as one among many tools for addressing the challenge, one that must be used together with other more conventional means such as feeding, health, education, and sanitation programs.

The human rights approach does not replace existing programs for alleviating malnutrition; rather, it augments and strengthens them. The human rights approach can make the usual kinds of programs more efficient and effective by making them more decisively goal-directed. Under such an approach, government no longer delivers services just to deliver services. Many nations already have substantial nutrition programs in place, but they are not organized in a unified, goal-directed effort. The human rights framework can provide a basis for aligning these assets so that they act together systematically to achieve the goal of eliminating malnutrition.

Human rights of every kind should be concretized locally through well-crafted national law. The law should specify individuals' entitlements and also the corresponding governmental commitments. It should specify the response mechanisms and the accountability mechanisms through which those obligations will be fulfilled. The effective implementation of comprehensive law of this sort can be a potent means for ensuring that human rights are realized.

In its early stages, international human rights law simply sets out standards and norms. However, as that law evolves, we see that it goes beyond clarifying standards and norms to also describe institutional mechanisms and procedures for ensuring that the rights are realized. At any level, well-crafted law spells out the means for its own implementation, with clear specification of agencies and their procedures. Of course the fine detail must be left to lower-level statutes and regulations, but the basic mandates for the implementation mechanisms can be set out in the law.

In contemplating possibilities for national action, the adoption of formal law may not be politically feasible in the short run. Nevertheless, proposals can be formulated as principles or guidelines, or perhaps as codes of conduct. These can be viewed as possible precursors to future law, and they could be used in the intervening period as lobbying instruments.

Legislation is only one of many possible means of action by government, and there are many possibilities for action by civil society. In addition to making new laws, national governments can use their executive and judicial powers in many different ways. Governments can help achieve human rights objectives by making adjustments in fiscal policy, export policy, welfare programs, agriculture support programs, and the like.

The preparation of appropriate national framework legislation is not the only means for ensuring realization of human rights, but it is an important one. Moreover, drafting legislation is a good means for working out the meaning of particular human rights in specific settings.

The lawmaking process can be understood as a form of referendum, a means for systematically assessing the views and positions of those in power. In a democracy, the views of the population at large have great influence in shaping the law, but lawmaking also takes places in nondemocracies, reflecting the views of the dominant power holders.

In general, the law, like other economic and social systems, tends to favor the interests of those who are more powerful, in both democracies and nondemocracies. Consider the extensive body of law many countries have to protect property rights. Nevertheless, the law can be used to serve the interests of those who are less powerful. Human rights law is one of those areas of law that is distinctly designed to serve the interests of those who are less powerful.

Several nations have articulated the right to adequate food in some form in their laws. Cuba's Constitution assures that "no child be left without schooling, food and clothing." The Italian, Spanish, and Greek Constitutions assure a right to health. In many countries there is language referring to other sorts of assurances, such as the right to social security (as in the Netherlands and Spain) that can be interpreted as implying the right to adequate food. In most cases, however, the assurances have not yet been concretized, and they have not been enforced through the courts or through other kinds of administrative measures. The meaning of the right to adequate food at the national level needs to be elaborated through national policy and national legislation.

The adoption and implementation of well-crafted national law requires not only legal language but also an advocacy process to ensure that it is acceptable to legislators and those behind them. Lobbying for new law is a focused process of political advocacy devoted to establishing new sustained patterns of governmental behavior. By helping to clarify individual positions and helping to build consensus on those positions, drafting legislation can become an instrument of political action for the realization of human rights. Thus, carefully crafted legislation designed to ensure the realization of the human right to adequate food can be an effective means for enhancing the power of the poor, and thus for reducing their malnutrition.

The law-based approach to human rights is important, but it may not always be essential. As Jack Goldsmith points out, outside the courtroom, human rights discourse

rarely depends on careful arguments about legality, and both the content and sources of international human rights law are much too diffuse for illegality to be the criterion of opprobrium it is in domestic legal systems. It is the moral quality of the acts in question, not their illegality, that actually triggers the international community's opprobrium. The successful characterization of an act as 'illegal' can of course change perceptions about the moral worth of the act, but it is moral worth, and not legality, that counts. (Goldsmith 1998, 365)

Human rights work always should be attentive to the law, either through implementing the law where it is sound, or creating new law where that is needed. Where something is decisively immoral and deserving of the international community's opprobrium, consideration should be given to affirming that in international human rights law. Similarly, in many countries, there is a need to strengthen existing national law or create new law to strengthen the national commitment to widely accepted international human rights law and principles. National framework legislation is needed as the basis for formulating new national law in support of the human right to adequate food.

Universal Human Rights and the Role of International Law

From the point of view of the international order, the major units of the international system are *states*, sometimes called *nation-states*. *State* is the formal name for a country or nation. The term *nation* can be confusing, because it is used in at least two different meanings. It can refer to the sum total of the population living in the country, held together in an organizational structure called government. This is its meaning when we use terms such as *international law*, or *United Nations*. But the word *nation* is also often used with a different meaning, referring to a group of people who feel they belong together because they have the same language, the same culture, and common historical experiences. These could be described as *ethno-nations*. Nations in this sense of the word can extend beyond the population of a particular country—such as the Russian nation or the Hungarian nation. In other cases, there can be groups living in the same country but belonging to different ethno-nations, as is often the case in federal states. Some ethno-nations—for example, Hawaiians, Kurds, and Palestinians—have no independent states.

As indicated in the section on the historical foundations of human rights in chapter 2, the basic normative principles underlying the operation of the international order are (1) *sovereignty*—there is no global government or other authoritative power over nation states, and (2) *noninterference*—states may not interfere in one another's internal affairs. Despite frequent deviations from these norms, these guiding principles have been in place since the Treaty of Westphalia of 1648 concluded the Thirty Years' War in Europe.

Usually, only states can become parties to international agreements under public international law. States are officially represented by their governments.

Governments act in behalf of their states. States become *states parties* to international agreements through a systematic, formal process. There are variations, but the common pattern is as follows. Most modern international human rights agreements emerge from negotiations mandated by the United Nations General Assembly. After the negotiations are completed, the proposed agreement is *adopted* by the General Assembly. It is then open to *signature* and *ratification* by the states of the world. The signing of an international agreement by an official representative of a state is an expression of its intention to ratify it. The ratification process entails taking the proposed agreement home to the national legislature, subjecting it to close scrutiny and obtaining the consent of the legislature, and then finally ratifying it. Ratification establishes the state's legal commitment to honor the agreement.

Draft agreements normally include provisions saying that they are to come into force upon ratification by a specific number of states. Thus, each international human rights treaty has two dates associated with it: its date of adoption by the United Nations General Assembly, and the date it came into force. To illustrate, the Convention on the Rights of the Child was adopted in 1989 and came into force in 1990 when it received its twentieth ratification. (See table 2.2 for the dates for several important human rights agreements.) Each state party to an agreement also has two distinct dates associated with it, the date on which it signed and the date on which it ratified the agreement (these dates can be found at http://www.unhchr.ch/tbs/doc.nsf).

Covenants and treaties are subject to the signature and ratification process, and thus they are legally binding on the states parties. In contrast, because declarations and resolutions are not subject to signature and ratification, they are not legally binding. However, there is something called *customary international law*. Under this doctrine, when a particular principle is very widely accepted, appears to have compelling moral force behind it, and appears to guide the behavior of most nations, then arguably the principle guiding that behavior becomes binding on all. When that happens is a matter of judgment, and thus it is frequently a matter of dispute.

Since the advent of the modern nation-state system with the Treaty of Westphalia in 1648, the world order has been based on the sovereign nation-state as the key actor. International law is based on the consent of these nation-states, just as government in a democracy is in principle based on the consent of the governed. States adhering to specific international declarations and agreements have considerable latitude in saying how they understand their obligations under those instruments. These interpretations may be expressed in a variety of ways—including reservations, understandings, and declarations enunciated at the time of accepting them; in the specifics of the national legislation through which they implement their obligations; and in national policy statements of various forms.

Much of the literature on human rights focuses on the role of international bodies, but one should not exaggerate the international character of the human rights system. Certainly, one should not suggest that governments adhere to human rights principles mainly because of pressures from the outside. As Richard Falk recognizes:

> The statist matrix of political life . . . means that the most substantial contributions to the realization of human rights arise from the internal dynamics of domestic politics. Far more significant than imposing human rights policies from outside is an effective commitment to their protection arising from within the body politic. (Falk 1992, 33)

As indicated in the preceding section, national legislation and policy are crucially important for the realization of internationally accepted human rights precisely because forces within countries play such a great role.

CHAPTER 5

Rights and Entitlements

Definition

We have rights to very few things. All of us have broad interests, such as having physical security, good friends, good jobs, good wine, and the like, but only a few of those things are—or should be—formally recognized as rights. Some good things, such as having friends, are things we do not feel ought to be claimed as rights.

We have different sorts of rights in different settings. Not all rights are human rights. The key distinguishing features are that human rights are about matters essential to human dignity, and they are universal. As stated in the preamble of the Universal Declaration of Human Rights, "recognition of the inherent dignity and of the equal and inalienable rights of all members of the human family is the foundation of freedom, justice and peace in the world." Thus, human rights can be understood as

> fundamental entitlements of persons, constituting means to the end of minimal human dignity or social justice. If persons have human rights they are entitled to a fundamental claim that others must do, or refrain from doing, something. Since governments speaking for states are primarily responsible for order and social justice in their jurisdictions, governments are the primary targets of these personal and fundamental claims. (Weiss, Forsythe, and Coate 1994, 105)

Or, more simply, if one has a human right, one can make a fundamental claim that a government authority or some other part of society must do—or refrain from doing—something that significantly affects one's human dignity (Forsythe 1991, 1). At its core, a human right is a claim against government, a claim that the government must do or desist from doing specific things to further human dignity.

The significance of rights must be recognized not only in philosophical and legal terms but also in psychological terms. Joel Feinberg's characterization is frequently quoted:

> Having rights enables us to "stand up like men," to look others in the eye, and to feel in some fundamental way the equal of anyone. To think of oneself as the holder of rights is not to be unduly but properly proud, to have

that minimal self-respect that is necessary to be worthy of the love and es-
teem of others. Indeed, respect for persons . . . may simply be respect for
their rights, so that there cannot be the one without the other. (Feinberg
1980, 151)

In the legal sense, human rights are held by all individuals simply by virtue of
their being human, by definition. They are universal. They are international. It is
redundant to speak of *international* human rights; they are international by
definition. They are different from what may be described as *local* rights, rights
that apply only in particular jurisdictions. For example, there is a right to
polygamy in some countries but not in others. The hospital near where I live has
a Patients' Bill of Rights. These are rights, but they are not human rights. The
term *human rights* is reserved for those rights that are universal.

The regional human rights bodies, which were described in chapter 2, are concerned with the realization of universal human rights, not with rights that are
particular to their regions. The rights are universal, but the means for ensuring
their realization are tailored to regional and cultural considerations. In much the
same way, the concretization of human rights within countries varies according
to local circumstances. As is explained later in this chapter, their application takes
different forms in different places.

The question of what should be recognized as a human right is closely linked
to the question of good governance, a point that is elaborated in the following
chapter. For what should all governments be responsible, and for what should
they not be responsible? Human rights refer to important things related to human dignity that should concern all governments.

Moral versus Legal Rights

Many of us have strong views on what ought to be recognized as human rights,
based on our sense of the essential requirements of justice and human dignity.
Often, these understandings are articulated in religious doctrines and in other
statements of fundamental or "natural" ethical principles.

At times, we find such statements in relation to food in particular. For example, in the seventeenth century, the Diggers squatted on the land of wealthy
landowners and tried to counter the property rights claims of the owners. Gerrard Winstanley, speaking for the Diggers, said:

Seeing and finding ourselves poor, wanting Food to feed upon, while we
labour the Earth, to cast in Seed and to wait till the first Crop comes up; and
wanting Ploughs, Carts, Corn and such materials to plant the Commons
withal, we are willing to declare our condition to you, and to all, that have
the Treasury of the Earth, locked up in your Bags, Chests, and Barns, and

will offer up nothing to this publike Treasury; but will rather see your
fellow-Creatures starve for want of Bread, that have an equal right to it with
yourselves, by the Law of Creation. (Winstanley 1941, 272)

In his famous "Four Freedoms" speech to the U.S. Congress in 1941, Franklin
Delano Roosevelt made comparable claims, but on a global scale:

The third is freedom from want, which, translated into world terms, means
economic understandings which will secure to every nation a healthy
peacetime life for its inhabitants—everywhere in the world. (Roosevelt
1941)

This speech inspired former U.S. Senator George McGovern to write a book titled *The Third Freedom: Ending Hunger in Our Time* (McGovern 2001). It also inspired the title of this book.

There are significant differences among us in our views of what is morally
right. We can move from saying that something *ought to be* recognized as a human right, out of deep personal conviction, to saying it *is* recognized as a human
right when we can somehow demonstrate that there is a strong and widespread
consensus on this conviction. One of the best ways to make this demonstration
is to be able to point to widely accepted resolutions, declarations, or treaties on
human rights. As suggested in the preceding chapter, the negotiation and ratification process leading up to the establishment of an international treaty can
be viewed as a kind of referendum for detecting and confirming widespread
agreement.

When human rights are articulated in widely ratified international law, human rights that had originally been advocated because of widespread and strong
moral conviction—*moral human rights*—become transformed into *legal human
rights*. Softer forms of law, such as resolutions and declarations, voice softer
forms of legal human rights, while harder forms of law, such as covenants and
treaties, articulate harder—and thus more legally binding—forms of legal human rights.

Local governments, agencies of government, and civil society organizations
may endorse any of the international human rights agreements. To illustrate, on
October 3, 1991, the Board of Education of the state of Hawai'i passed a resolution affirming its support of the Convention on the Rights of the Child. In 1998,
the cities of San Francisco, Berkeley, and Oakland in California all passed resolutions declaring that they supported and would honor the International Covenant on Economic, Social, and Cultural Rights. Three cities in Canada—Toronto;
Kamloops in British Colombia; and Prince Albert in Saskatchewan—have charters that affirm the right to food for their people. These resolutions and charters
were strong expressions of moral conviction, but they did not bind these cities
under international law. From the perspective of the international legal system,
only nation-states can officially become parties to the international human rights

agreements. However, any locality may choose to adopt the principles as a sign of its moral conviction. If they wish, governments of local jurisdictions may go further and incorporate them into local law and make them locally binding in that way.

Much of what we may agree ought to be recognized as human rights (rights in principle, matters of "natural law," or moral rights) are not rights in the written "black letter" law. It is always important to distinguish what *ought* to be rights in the law from what *is* actually found in the law. A *moral right* does not become a *legal right* simply by assertion; it becomes a legal right through legislative action. At the international level, the equivalent of legislative action is the well-established practice of negotiating draft agreements and then offering them up for signature and ratification by the states of the world.

In this book, when we speak of human rights, we generally have in mind legal human rights, that is, human rights explicitly stated in international law. We are concerned with the ways in which these rights affirmed in international law lead to legal rights locally, manifested in national and subnational law. In our view, all human rights work is about the law, either to ensure the realization of rights already established in the law, or to establish and strengthen that law. This point is elaborated further in chapter 7.

Soft versus Hard Rights

Soft rights are defined here as rights that are not spelled out in the law, or if they are in the law there is no strong and effective institutional mechanism to ensure their realization. For example, several national constitutions have comprehensive provisions regarding human rights that are thoroughly ignored. Without good implementation mechanisms, rights in law are little more than empty promises.

Of course, soft rights can be useful in a transitional stage. The articulation of rights in the law is important even where there are no special means to ensure their realization. The Universal Declaration of Human Rights, for example, has been one of the most important statements of international law even though it is not binding and does not include any implementation mechanism. Its power arises from its cogent articulation of the near universal imperative: *Do the right thing. This is the right thing.*

Hard or *strong* rights are clearly articulated in the law, and there are effective mechanisms for implementing that law. There are designated agencies responsible for carrying out the law, and there is adequate funding to do the job. Hard rights have a history of cases through which the meaning of the right is tested and refined. There is clear recourse in law for individuals whose rights are not realized, and clear public accountability. This is illustrated by, say, the right to freedom of religion in the United States. The right is stated in just a few words in the First Amendment to the U.S. Constitution ("Congress shall make no law respecting an establishment of religion"), but the meaning of that right is then elaborated in more detailed federal law and in judicial interpretations. There will always be some ambiguity around the edges, but the meaning of that right has now been extensively elaborated and tested in practice in the United States.

Without clear, hard rights, those who are more powerful, more highly educated, or better connected have an advantage in obtaining protection and other kinds of services. Firmly established rights can empower the weak, leveling the playing field a bit so that the weak are not so disadvantaged.

Rights can be truly hard—that is, clearly articulated and systematically realized—only where there is a strong and effective legal system in place. In many countries, there is no such system. However, even where the legal system is weak, it is worthwhile to advocate the hardening of rights. Even if government does not effectively implement them, rights enshrined in the law can provide a strong basis for political action by civil society organizations and others. Establishing hard rights is not always immediately practicable, but the vision should be kept in view as an ideal, helping to set the course in long-term efforts to strengthen human rights.

With some exceptions, all people have all human rights, as a matter of definition. The fundamental human rights have been articulated in the Universal Declaration of Human Rights of 1948. If all people have all these rights, what then is the function of the subsequent human rights agreements? The answer is that these agreements continue the steady progress of hardening these rights. The main function of the Convention on the Rights of the Child, for example, is not to create new rights for children but to clarify and strengthen rights that had already been articulated, for all people, in the Universal Declaration of Human Rights and the two covenants.

When states ratify international human rights agreements, they agree to be legally bound to work for the realization of those rights. People in countries that have not ratified, say, the International Covenant on Economic, Social, and Cultural Rights nevertheless have those economic, social, and cultural rights. They are, after all, rights held by all human beings. The difference is that where countries have not ratified particular human rights agreements, their governments have not made commitments to act on them. The people have these rights, but they remain soft.

The hardening of human rights takes place through legislation, through practice, through scholarly analysis, and through the authoritative interpretations offered by human rights agencies at the global, regional, and national levels. As explained in chapter 3, *General Comments* issued by the United Nations treaty bodies help to clarify and harden the meaning of the human rights treaties.

The international human rights treaties are binding in principle, but the rights and obligations are not set out in detail, and implementation mechanisms are not fully specified in those treaties. The rights can be transformed into hard rights by national governments creating suitably strong and specific laws and policies, along with effective agencies with adequate resources to implement them. The relatively soft international human rights law can be understood as a guide to the formulation of national human rights law. It is at the national level that rights are likely to be hardened first. In the long term, as we move toward more effective global governance, it may be possible to have human rights hardened at the global level as well.

Critics sometimes complain that human rights law is not clear enough. They ask, for example, what exactly are the "best interests of the child." They want the international documents to lay out the specifics in great detail, with unambiguous rules to be applied in concrete situations.

That is not how the human rights system works. Rather than having the specifics formulated at the global level and imposed downward, they must—within broad limits—be worked out locally, in each society, through democratic processes of governance. After a time, norms at the global level may evolve out of careful scholarly analysis and practice rooted at the local level (cf. Alston 1994). To draw an analogy, in a country with a federal form of government, the central government may determine that it is important for all the member states to have speed limits on their roads, but leave it to the separate states to determine those limits, not arbitrarily, but in accordance with established guidelines. Many aspects of human rights law provide a broad, but not unlimited, latitude for interpretation. There are some areas where there is no latitude for varying local interpretations. In most cases, however, the international law is deliberately soft, with the intention that it will be interpreted and hardened locally.

The human rights system is based on having clear global norms, and some latitude in application depending on local circumstances. On some issues, such as torture, there is no room for interpretation. Where the state has latitude in interpreting its human rights obligations, this is controlled latitude. It is controlled through the accountability of the state to the rights holders themselves, to the United Nations treaty bodies, and to other agencies as appropriate. As the European Court of Human Rights has put it, there is a "margin of appreciation" for local circumstances that permits variation in the application of human rights (Advisory Council on International Affairs 1998; Yourow 1996). The norms must be interpreted and applied at the local level through democratic processes. Then, through legislation or through other means of policy articulation, governments should specify how they will interpret and apply their human rights obligations.

Rights as Goals

It can be useful to think about human rights in terms of the goals they imply. It then becomes clear that there is always a need to work out strategies and to commit resources for the achievement of those goals. When a government works toward the realization of a right, it should clarify the corresponding goal and the strategy that is to be pursued to reach it.

Goals and Targets

The term *goal* is here taken to refer to an ideal desired state, such as "no food insecurity in the world," while "target" is understood to refer to an achievement to be reached along the path to the goal by a specific time, such as "reduction of food insecurity by half by 2015." Goals may be described comprehensively (e.g., no food insecurity in the world), or they may be divided into their component elements (e.g., no protein-energy malnutrition, no iodine deficiency disease, no vitamin A deficiency).

Often, the global community proposes specific targets to be met in the process of achieving goals. For example, the World Summit for Children of 1990 called for the reduction of severe and moderate malnutrition to half their 1990 level by 2000. Such targets are based on measurable indicators that allow for judgments as to whether the "trajectory" is directed toward the goal, and whether the motion is rapid enough to achieve the target by the intended time. With well-formulated targets, when the time comes, it is possible to say whether the target has in fact been successfully reached.

At times, the international community formulates goals in great detail. High-level international meetings have formulated specific goals in relation to health, education, the environment, and the like. As was indicated in chapter 3, concrete goals in relation to nutrition were set out at the World Summit for Children in 1990, and subsequently endorsed by many other bodies. On September 5, 2000, the United Nations Millennium Assembly agreed on an ambitious group of Millennium Development Goals. The nations participating in these international goal-setting exercises may make binding commitments to the goals. In most cases, however, these issue-oriented meetings (food, education, children, environment, etc.) conclude with "final declarations" and "plans of action" that are not legally binding on the participants. The goals with regard to nutrition, reaffirmed at several other global conferences, may be understood as strong recommendations, suggesting how national governments might sensibly formulate their own commitments.

Most of the goals set by the international community at these meetings are not met. Nevertheless, the exercise of setting goals and targets is useful for guiding the formulation of commitments, whether at the global or national level. For example, any nation could reasonably take as a major nutrition target the reduction of severe and moderate malnutrition among children younger than five years of age by half during the next ten years. The effective use of national resources in terms of law, governance, and commitment can make goal seeking more realistic at the national level than at the global level.

Rights Imply Goals

Goals indicate a desired direction of action. However, the fact that a government, agency, or program declares that it has particular goals does not necessarily mean that any individual has any rights in relation to that government, agency, or program. The goal may say that everyone ought to get a particular outcome or service (e.g., adequate food, free primary education, a clean environment), but the statement of a goal does not in itself mean that people are entitled to these things. The core implication of a right is that if I am entitled to something, I have a strong basis in law and policy for claiming it, and there are specific actions I can take to remedy the situation if I do not get that to which I am entitled.

Although goals do not necessarily imply human rights, human rights do imply goals. The rights described in the major international human rights agreements can be understood as expressions of global goals: There should be no slavery, no discrimination, no genocide, no malnutrition, and so on. All people should have various freedoms, and all should enjoy an adequate standard of living. When countries ratify international agreements, they make commitments to pursue these goals for their own countries. However, nations have considerable latitude (or "margin of appreciation") in determining how they will interpret and apply these goals in their own settings.

But Rights Involve More Than Goals

Setting out goals and targets can be very helpful to governments as they design their social-sector programs. However, it must be recognized that having a right to the achievement of a particular goal requires more than just having the government set the goal. To illustrate, imagine that a country's commitment to the target of reducing food insecurity among its people by half over the next ten years is so serious that it is willing to assure its people that they had a right to its achievement. Imagine that the government was willing to take on its achievement as a real obligation, one on which it could be called to account for its performance. This implies that a substantial planning effort and commitment of resources would have to be made to achieve the specified reduction of food insecurity within the stated time frame. These commitments could be made through appropriate national law. Commitments could be made to achieving such objectives in much the same way a commitment could be made to building a bridge across a river.

Of course, it may be that the goal just outlined is too demanding, and the government is not able to make such a broad commitment because of its resource constraints. Other formulations could be substituted. For example, the government might be willing to make a strong commitment only if it was limited to children under three years of age, only if it was limited to severe cases, or only if it had twelve years to achieve the goal. The specifics are open to discussion. The point is that, whatever the detail of its formulation, one way to interpret human rights is in terms of a firm legal commitment to a specific goal, such as the goal that all people will have adequate food. Rights can be defined in terms of the direction in which individuals and the society as a whole ought to be heading.

If people have a human right to adequate food, countries must have the goal of ensuring that all people have adequate food. That goal should be used as the basis for designing a specific goal-directed strategic program of action. The goal and the strategy should be outlined in the law. One major element of the strategy should be the establishment of specific intermediate targets, in terms of particular levels to be reached on specified indicators by definite dates. For example, the government might say that it will reduce the proportion of food-insecure people in its population by 10 percent within one year, and 25 percent within two years. In this approach, *the process of realizing rights is the process of pursuing a strategy to reach a goal.*

At all levels—global, regional, national, and subnational—the strategy for moving toward achievement of these goals can be based on the explicit formulation of intermediate targets, for example, reducing certain types of food insecurity by a certain degree on a specified measure by a certain date. Strategic planning and resource allocation need to be guided by plausible, concrete objectives. There must a possibility of midcourse corrections, possibly based on the reallocation of resources. In other words, there must be continuous steering of the effort if the target is to be achieved.

Many social programs define their tasks in terms of the services they provide, that is, in terms of the "inputs" they deliver to their clients, such as inoculations, subsidies, school meals, and drinking water. They often leave the ultimate goal unspecified and thus function as if they expect to continue the same activity eternally, with no real abatement of the problems they claim to address. By endlessly ameliorating the stress caused by the problems, these programs may actually help to perpetuate them.

The entitlements corresponding to specific human rights can be described in terms either of inputs delivered to clients or of desired outcomes, results, and targets that constitute steps toward achieving particular goals. Rights to specific inputs and outcomes are the counterparts to what are described in human rights discourse as "obligations of conduct" and "obligations of result."

Social programs can be made more effective if there are clear goals guiding their actions. The purpose of providing school lunches, for example, should not be simply to provide school lunches. Presumably, the objective is to obtain better outcomes in terms of, say, health status, school attendance, and school performance. In dealing with vitamin A deficiency, the goal is not to deliver vitamin A capsules to everyone but to eliminate the deficiency. Goals should be plainly articulated.

The Importance of Local Participation

In both service-oriented and goal-oriented programs, careful attention should be given to the process through which rights are realized. The rights holders should not be treated as passive beneficiaries of a government-directed program but should be fully engaged, with high levels of participation, community ownership, sustainability, and empowerment (Jonsson 1997).

This means that the clients, the purported beneficiaries, should be active participants not only in the implementation of social programs but also in the formulation of their goals and targets. Goals and targets should emerge from a broadly participatory consensus-building effort. The goals and targets set out at the major global conferences or at national meetings of policymakers should not be treated as objectives to be imposed on local communities by outsiders.

International human rights law articulates goals that have emerged from a broadly participatory global consensus-building effort. It acknowledges the reality and the value of local differences by encouraging localized interpretation and the application of the agreed-upon principles. Rights need to be concretized locally as specific entitlements and specific targets. The most important means of adapting global goals to local realities is to ensure that local people participate in shaping the policies for achieving them. If outsiders were to come in with their own analyses of local problems, and also their own remedies, that would violate the rights of local people to participate. Local people must be actively engaged not only in the implementation of the programs but also in their design and management. They must share in the formulation of the goals as well as in shaping the means for reaching them.

Strategizing

Goals and targets do not fulfill themselves. They mean little in isolation but they become important when embedded into coherent strategies for action. Consider, for example, the goal of ending stunting among children. If we are serious about this, we need to think through what might be a plausible path to the goal and what resources would be needed. We need to think about who would have to take what actions to make sure the goal is reached. We need to ensure that the required incentives are available at the right places and at the right times to induce the people who need to act to do whatever needs to be done. That is how bridges and buildings get built. Similar procedures are needed for building social structures.

Human rights can be an important instrument contributing to the achievement of social goals. We can go beyond saying that children ought to get the food, health, and care that they need to say that they are entitled to these things. The specifics of these entitlements will vary in different places according to both local circumstances and the conditions of the child. However, we begin with the premise that every child is entitled to whatever it takes to ensure that she or he is not stunted.

The goal of abolishing stunting cannot be achieved instantaneously. However, a national government could make a commitment to reducing the proportion of stunted children by, say, 5 percent a year. That commitment could be enshrined in national law by saying that children collectively are entitled to expect that in their nation stunting will be reduced by 5 percent a year, and if it is not, the resources allocated to the achievement of that target would be increased according to a specific formula.

This sort of commitment would establish a clear incentive for using resources efficiently and effectively, and to ensure that the effort stays on track. A willingness to make this sort of commitment to the allocation of resources in national law would be the clearest indication of genuine commitment by a national government to achieve the goal.

Such commitments need to be made by national governments, taking into account their resource limitations. Because all children everywhere have a right to not be stunted, there also should be a commitment by the international community to the realization of this right and goal. There needs to be a commitment of significant resources to help the poorest countries in their efforts to eliminate stunting. Emphasis could be placed on in-kind assistance, such as advisory services and capacity building. There must also be institutional mechanisms in place to call nations to account when they do not do what they can to eliminate stunting.

General Comment 12, the UN's authoritative explanation of the meaning of the human right to adequate food, is explicit about the requirements of strategy to ensure the implementation of the right at the national level. For example, in paragraphs 21 through 28, it says:

> the Covenant clearly requires that each State party take whatever steps are necessary to ensure that everyone is free from hunger and as soon as possible can enjoy the right to adequate food. This will require the adoption of a national strategy to ensure food and nutrition security for all, based on human rights principles that define the objectives, and the formulation of policies and corresponding benchmarks. . . . The strategy should be based on a systematic identification of policy measures and activities relevant to the situation and context. . . . Appropriate institutional mechanisms should be devised to secure a representative process towards the formulation of a strategy, drawing on all available domestic expertise relevant to food and nutrition. The strategy should set out the responsibilities and time-frame for the implementation of the necessary measures. (United Nations, Economic and Social Council 1999d)

Systematic strategies need to be formulated and implemented at every level if the goal of fulfilling every person's human right to adequate food is to be achieved. In these strategies, there must be clear incentives for the actors to do what needs to be done, and there must be institutional mechanisms to ensure that all actors are held accountable for doing their jobs. Just as the construction of a building or a bridge is only possible with detailed planning and periodic course corrections during the process of working toward the goal, the human right to adequate food can only be fully realized through carefully designed and implemented programs of action. The formulation of clear goals and targets is only one step in the formulation of strategies.

The Commission on Nutrition Challenges of the 21st Century made a major contribution to this effort in its report to the Sub-Committee on Nutrition of February 2000, *Ending Malnutrition by 2020: An Agenda for Change in the Millennium* (United Nations System Standing Committee on Nutrition 2000). However, much more strategic thinking is needed if the goal of ending malnutrition by 2020 is to be taken seriously. The requirements of strategy formulation at the global level are discussed further in chapter 17.

Rights Imply Entitlements

The application of the human rights enumerated in the Universal Declaration of Human Rights and other international instruments must be worked out at the national level. National governments, representing their respective states, are expected to elaborate and concretize these rights through their national law, policy, and practice. Thus, human rights are concretized locally in the form of specific entitlements. In doing this, national governments make commitments to ensure the realization of these rights, through means appropriate to the particular local circumstances.

Table 5.1 outlines the terminology used here. Entitlements and commitments are the nationalized versions (the adaptations to local circumstances) of global human rights and their corresponding national obligations.

Local (nonuniversal) commitments usually will be made at the national level, but they may also be made at regional or subnational levels. If one has a right to an adequate standard of living, including adequate food, one must have specific entitlements. Entitlements are

enforceable claims on the delivery of goods, services, or protection by specific others. Entitlements exist when one party effectively controls produc-

TABLE 5.1. RIGHTS/OBLIGATIONS
AND ENTITLEMENTS/COMMITMENTS

Global	National
Human rights	Entitlements (national rights)
National obligations	National commitments

tive resources or can insist that another delivers goods, services, or protections, and third parties will act to reinforce (or at least not hinder) their delivery. (Eide 2001, 139)

Saying that entitlements are *enforceable* claims means that there must be some sort of institutional arrangement to which claims holders whose claims are not satisfied can appeal to have the situation corrected. Enforceability means that those who are to fulfill rights or entitlements must be obligated to do so, and they must be held accountable for their performance. As argued above, there are three key parties: the holder of the right or entitlement (discussed in this chapter), the party obligated or committed to ensuring the realization of that right or entitlement (discussed in chapter 6), and the party who oversees the relationship and ensures that the obligations or commitments are in fact fulfilled (discussed in chapter 7).

Where there is an entitlement to something, there must be some sort of remedy that can be pursued if the rights holder does not get that to which he or she is entitled. If there is no institutional mechanism through which one can press one's claims, there is no genuine entitlement. It is these institutional arrangements that make the claim enforceable.

In some cases, there is an explicit legal arrangement spelling out the rights or entitlement, the obligations or commitments, and the accountability system. However, the arrangement also can take nonlegal forms, such as widely understood and accepted moral codes, overseen by recognized authority figures in the society.

If you rent an apartment, the owner is entitled to a rent payment from you each month. That has nothing to do with human rights. However, this relationship illustrates the meaning of entitlement. The apartment owner is entitled to your monthly payment. You do not pay just if and when you feel like it. You do not give your rent money as a kind of charity. You owe it. And most important, if the owner does not get the rent money when it is due, there are some specific actions she can take to correct the situation, such as evicting you or taking you to court.

All contracts imply entitlements. If I have a contract with you to paint my garage, and I give you the amount of money specified in the contract, I am then entitled to have the job done. If you do not fulfill your obligation, there are agencies to which I can take my complaint. The special thing that distinguishes contracts from other sorts of agreements is that they are enforceable. A fundamental aspect of legal systems is the mechanism for enforcing contracts, to ensure that important agreements are in fact honored. In sophisticated contracts, the procedures and penalties for dealing with noncompliance may be spelled out in detail.

Not all entitlements are derived from human rights. A city may allow all senior citizens to use the public transport system without charge, but there is no human rights basis for such an entitlement. Free transport may be a local entitlement; it is not a human right.

Entitlements can be specified in terms of services, concretized in statements of the form, "If you meet criteria *x*, you are entitled to services *y*." For example, it might be specified that "All persons over sixty-five years of age will get free health services" or "All children attending public schools up to grade six will be given a free lunch on school days." Such entitlements are not universal, but they may be derived from or implied by universal human rights.

Although not all entitlements are derived from human rights, all human rights imply entitlements. More specifically, they imply entitlements to action by government. In the formulation, "If you meet criteria *x*, you are entitled to services *y*," the word *services* can be interpreted broadly, and understood to include material goods, protection, respect, and other things of value. Thus, under the freedom of religion, we can say, "If your neighbor threatens your freedom to practice your religion, you are entitled to protection from your government." It is not only economic rights that imply entitlements; all human rights imply entitlements to government action.

With regard to food and other necessities, governments have an obligation to establish institutional arrangements under which people can provide for themselves. However, no matter how good these are, even in well-functioning social systems, there are likely to be people who, for various reasons, "fall through the cracks" and require special care. There should be special programs for these people, to deal with poverty, hunger, physical and mental disability, and others kinds of stresses. These people should be entitled to special services because of their special needs.

Many governments have programs designed to deliver specific social services. Sometimes, the clients of these programs are formally entitled to these services, but often they are not. Many social programs can be adapted to fit into the human rights approach by specifying that their clients are entitled to particular services and by providing the clients with effective remedies they can pursue if they feel they have not gotten that to which they are entitled.

The right to adequate food can be concretized locally either in terms of specific services (e.g., every child is ensured an intake of at least so many calories per day) or in terms of specific outcomes (e.g., good nutrition status, measured anthropometrically). It is generally preferable to frame entitlements in terms of desired outcomes (results) and to then call for the appropriate services (inputs) needed to achieve that outcome. Those services need not be spelled out in detail in the law. The law could say that the government is obligated to provide nutritional services, in accordance with the best professional advice of nutritionists, until the child no longer meets the entitlement criteria. Details regarding the exact nature of the services would not have to be spelled out in the main body of the law, but statutes and regulations could be formulated to provide guidance. The services might vary according to particular local circumstances.

States are obligated to ensure that their people get adequate food as part of an overall adequate standard of living. Various means to that end may be pursued, as long as they do not violate other human rights. "The duties of states to ensure an adequate standard of life for everyone within their jurisdiction are partly obligations of conduct, partly obligations of result" (Eide 2001, 139). Obligations of conduct can be understood as equivalent to obligations to deliver specific services.

Some writers say human rights *are* entitlements (e.g., Wiseberg 1996, xix). It is better to say that human rights *imply* entitlements. Entitlements are the local concretizations of human rights. They should be identified through an informed, open, democratic debate based on a good understanding of both international human rights law and local circumstances.

Determining Local Entitlements

Critics of government frequently complain that this or that government action was a violation of human rights. How do they know? Surely, human rights must be interpreted. But how? And who gets to make authoritative interpretations? One of the most difficult aspects of human rights work is translating broadly stated human rights as described in the international human rights instruments into concrete forms in the local setting.

In the preceding section, we said that human rights are concretized locally in the form of specific entitlements. What should be the content of these entitlements? The analysis must begin with the premise that people *are entitled to the realization of their human rights*. This means that they must have the means needed to achieve the end, the required outcome, the realization of their rights. Thus, for any particular right, we have to make a means–ends analysis. This is a question of empirical and scientific knowledge. If people in a particular setting are to have adequate food, what would bring about that outcome on a sustainable basis?

It may be that in some places there is only one feasible means to that end, perhaps land ownership. Then in such a situation we can say that people must have a right to land. This would be a local right, an entitlement. The people in that locality could be described as having a *compelling claim* to land.

To take another example, suppose someone says that "people have a human right to iodized salt to protect them from iodine deficiency disease." That is incorrect. There is no assertion to this effect in international human rights law. However, one might make an argument saying that because of the assertions in international human rights law regarding food and health, and the conditions currently prevailing in this particular country, people there (not people everywhere) should have an entitlement (a localized right) to iodized salt.

A compelling claim is a strong argument that people are entitled to something in the concrete local circumstances because of the existence of specific human rights. Compelling claims that apply everywhere could become human rights in themselves, because they are not merely local. Claims are weaker than rights precisely because their strength depends on the argument linking the universal human right and the local conditions. For most city dwellers, there is no good argument for land rights, and in many countries there is no good reason to insist on iodized salt.

In many situations, there are several possible means to any particular end. People might be helped to obtain adequate food by having good jobs or by having good markets in which to sell their produce. In such a situation, there is no compelling claim to any one means, and thus no specific entitlement in terms of services (or "inputs," in the language used in the discussion on rights as goals). If there are many possible paths to the goal, one's claims to any particular one of them are diminished.

However, there is always a compelling claim that *something* must be done to allow people to obtain adequate food. Government must do something to ensure that you can get enough food. However, your choices regarding how that food is to be obtained may be limited. You may have opportunities to get land, a job, money, or some kind of education. The options you are presented with must be reasonable and culturally sensitive, respecting all your human rights. Any of these could fulfill the government's obligation *if* in the local circumstances it can reasonably be expected to allow you to obtain adequate food on a sustained basis. In most cases, you should not expect to have food provided to you directly, but you do have a right to expect reasonable opportunities to provide for yourself.

If the government, say, arranges for you to get a job, and you refuse, the government might say that in offering the job it has fulfilled its obligations. Obviously, this would not be an acceptable option if it was a degrading job or if it paid very poorly, or if it was offered to a child or to someone who was severely disabled and incapable of carrying out the job. What is reasonable is a matter for judgment by the government and by those agencies that hold the government accountable for its human rights performance.

The entitlement is to whatever it takes to achieve the required outcome in a way that respects all other human rights. Government does not have to take every possible action, but it must take some action that can be expected to achieve the required outcome. The entitlement could be specified not in terms of a service (an input) but in terms of the particular result or target or outcome to which the individual is entitled. You are then entitled to whatever it takes to reach the goal and stay there on a sustained basis.

If what the government is currently doing is not moving the population toward the goal of ensuring adequate food for all, this is prima facie evidence of that action's inadequacy. Something else must be done, something that is likely to be effective in reaching the goal.

Of course, we cannot expect instantaneous achievement of the goal. One can only expect progressive realization—steady and decisive movement—toward the goal, at a pace depending on local resources and local circumstances. However, zero movement is always an unacceptable pace.

Within broad limits, the primary source of authoritative interpretation of human rights is the national government. It is obligated to translate human rights into local entitlements and commitments through its executive, legislative, and judicial arms. The entitlements and the corresponding commitments should be articulated through explicit policy statements and national legislation. Of course, the legislative process should be democratic, and it should be informed by the requirements of international human rights law and by relevant scientific information. The UN treaty bodies and other international human rights agencies, the civil society within the country, and specialists with expert knowledge in the technical field in question (e.g., nutritionists) should help to guide that legislative process to make sure that the local interpretation is faithful to the meaning of the human rights at issue.

Having versus Realizing Rights

One way to find out how individuals think about human rights is to ask how they would assess the status of particular human rights in a particular country. For many (e.g., Jabine and Claude 1992; Spirer and Spirer 1993), the answer is that you look at the situation and see if people speak freely, practice their religions, are adequately nourished, and so on.

This approach misses something important. One can sometimes speak freely even if there is no specific freedom of speech; one can be employed even if there is no right to employment; one can obtain adequate food even if there is no right to adequate food. It is important to know whether the human rights that we all have are translated into hard local rights in the form of specific entitlements and commitments.

All people have all human rights described in the Universal Declaration of Human Rights and the two covenants. That is, they have all human rights in principle. But one must also ask about practice. Are those rights recognized in local law and given practical effect? Where governments take human rights seriously, there are laws and institutional arrangements to ensure their realization.

If you want to know whether people *have* a particular legal right locally, you look at the law. The first place to look is national law, but it could also show up in the law at lower levels—for example, provincial law or state law in federal systems, such as those of India and the United States.

If you want to know whether the right is *realized*—which is a different question—you look at how people are living, and compare that with the law. To illustrate, Humana asked whether "everyone has the right to freedom of movement and residence within the borders of each state" in each country of the world (Humana 1992). He should have distinguished two different questions: Does the country have that right clearly enshrined in national law? And if it does, is the right fully realized by all of its people? Assessing the extent to which a goal is realized means assessing not simply a status (e.g., numbers of children who are malnourished), but the degree of shortfall from achievement of an explicitly identified goal.

It is important to distinguish between, say, speaking freely and having a right to free speech, or between having adequate food and having a right to adequate food. To draw an analogy, you cannot tell how much protection people have against fire by asking people if their houses are on fire at the moment. To assess the quality of the protection, one has to look into the institutional arrangements that are in place, ready to act if and when disaster threatens. The human right to adequate food requires action by government to protect against the occurrence of inadequacy and to remedy it if it does occur. Drawing on the distinction made in chapter 1, the right is about food security, not just current food status. The realization of the human right to adequate food requires appropriate institutional arrangements to ensure that people have adequate food now and can expect to have it in the foreseeable future.

The fact that most people in any given country are well fed tells us nothing about the situation of marginalized people, and it says nothing about what might happen in the future if wealth declines or government priorities change. In the United States, for example, most people have adequate food, and there are major programs to help needy people obtain food, but there is nothing in national law that establishes a national right to adequate food.

National legislation is not required to ensure that people have particular rights. Human rights are universal—by definition. Thus, children in Somalia and the United States have all the rights enumerated in the Convention on the Rights of the Child. The fact that their governments have not ratified the convention only means that their governments have not made a commitment to ensure the realization of those rights. Ratifying human rights agreements, and following up with appropriate national legislation, are strong signs of a nation's commitment to their realization. Appropriate national legislation increases the likelihood of the realization of particular human rights.

CHAPTER 6

Obligations and Commitments

Moral Responsibilities

Before examining the character of obligations with regard to human rights, it is useful to establish a framework for understanding moral responsibilities. In some ways, all of us are vulnerable. We face threats to our families, our freedoms, and our resources. We aspire to take care of ourselves, but at times we need support from others. Thus we do not live as hermits but as social beings who provide support to and draw support from the people around us. We aspire to a measure of self-sufficiency, but we are vulnerable, especially at the beginning of the life cycle and at the end.

Consider the example of children, those who are in training for independence. As highly dependent beings, small children need to have others take care of them. Who should be responsible for children? The first line of responsibility is with the parents, of course, but others have a role as well. In asking who is responsible, the question is not whose fault it is that children suffer so much (Who caused the problems?) but who should take action to remedy the problems. Many different social agencies may have some role in looking after children. What should be the interrelationships among them? What should be the roles of churches, nongovernmental organizations, businesses, and local and national governments?

Many children have two vigorous advocates from the moment they are born, and even before they are born: their parents, who devote enormous resources to serving their children's interests. These are not sacrifices. The best parents do not support their children out of a sense of obligation or as investments. Rather, they support their children as extensions of themselves, as part of their wholeness.

In many cases, however, that bond is broken or is never created. Fathers disappear. Many mothers disappear as well. In some cities, hundreds of children are abandoned each month in the hospitals in which they are born. Bands of children live in the streets by their wits, preyed upon by others. Frequently, children end up alone as a result of poverty, disease, warfare, or other crises. Many children are abandoned because they are physically or mentally handicapped. Some parents become so disabled by drugs, alcohol, or disease that they cannot care for their children.

Often, the failures are not the parents' own fault but a result of the fact that others have failed to meet their responsibility toward the parents. For example, parents may be willing to work hard and do whatever needs to be done to care for their children, but they may not be able to find the kind of employment opportunities they need to raise their children adequately.

Sometimes, others look after children who cannot be cared for by their biological parents. In many cultures, children belong not only to their biological parents but also to the community as a whole. The responsibility and the joy of raising children are widely shared.

In many places, especially in "developed" nations, that option is no longer available because of the collapse of the idea and the practice of community. Many of us live in nice neighborhoods in well-ordered societies, but the sense of community—of love and responsibility and commitment to one another—has vanished. In such cases, the remaining hope of the abandoned child is the government, the modern substitute for community. People look to the government to provide the human services that the local community no longer provides.

As children mature, the first priority is to help them become responsible for themselves. As long as they are not mature, however, children ought to get their nurturing from their parents. Failing that, they ought to get it from their relatives. Failing that, they ought to get it from their local communities. Failing that, they ought to get it from the local government. Failing that, it should come from their national government. Failing that, they ought to get it from the international community. The responsibility hierarchy looks something like this:

Child
Family
Community
Local government
State government
National government
International nongovernmental organizations
International governmental organizations

As is suggested in figure 6.1, this hierarchy can be pictured as a set of nested circles, with the child in the center of the nest, surrounded, supported, and nurtured by family, community, government, and ultimately international organizations. Of course, there are exceptions. For example, central governments often may provide services to the needy directly, bypassing local government, on the basis of an agreed-on division of labor and an understanding that services are likely to be distributed more equitably if they are funded by the central treasury. Similarly, some programs, such as immunization, cannot be completely managed locally. Nevertheless, the general pattern is that we expect problems to be handled locally, and we reach out to more distant agents only when local remedies are inadequate.

This is straightforward. The idea that needs to be added is that in cases of failure, agents more distant from the child should not simply substitute for those

INTERNATIONAL GOVERNMENTAL ORGANIZATIONS
INTERNATIONAL NONGOVERNMENTAL ORGANIZATIONS
NATIONAL GOVERNMENT
STATE GOVERNMENT
LOCAL GOVERNMENT
COMMUNITY
FAMILY
CHILD

Figure 6.1. Rings of Responsibility

closer to the child. Instead, those who are more distant should try to work with and strengthen those who are closer, to help them become more capable of fulfilling their responsibilities toward children. Agencies in the outer rings shown in figure 6.1 should help to overcome, not punish, failures in the inner rings. They should try to respond to failures in empowering, positive ways. To the extent possible, local communities should not take children away from inadequate parents but rather should help them in their parenting role. State governments should not replace local governments, but instead they should support local governments in their work with children. The international community should help national governments in their work with children.

Government's responsibilities with regard to ordinary children in ordinary circumstances should be limited. The family should provide daily care and feeding. However, for children in extreme situations who are abused or who suffer from extremely poor health or serious malnutrition, governments have a role to play. If there has been a failure in the inner rings of responsibility and no one else takes care of the problem, government must step in.

Empowerment—or development—means increasing one's capacity to analyze and act on one's own problems. Thus, empowerment is about gaining increasing autonomy, and decreasing one's dependence on others. The concept applies to societies as well as to individuals.

There are similar rings of responsibility for others who cannot care for themselves, such as victims of disasters, the physically disabled, and the mentally ill. These responsibilities need to be clarified so that the care of those who are unable to care for themselves is not left to chance. Thus, this framework may be used in relation to all individuals who need protection and support, and not only children.

When Do Governments Do Human Rights Work?

When and how do states—or more precisely, the national governments that represent them—do human rights work? Can a ministry of health say that all its effort is on the human right to health simply by virtue of the fact that it does health work?

I suggest that there are two major criteria that must be fulfilled to warrant describing specific government activity as related to human rights. (The issue of how we identify human rights work by nonstate actors will be addressed later in this chapter.) First, it must be possible to link it to specific human rights law; and second, those carrying out or directing the action must be aware that the action is taken in response to a specific legal commitment under human rights law.

Some people describe almost any sort of activity in support of human dignity or social justice as human rights work. However, I find it useful to be something of a legal positivist, and take the position that human rights work is about human rights law, either in terms of deliberately implementing that law or deliberately strengthening it. Thus, moral responsibilities are one thing, and legal duties are another. Though all duties under human rights law ultimately derive from moral concerns, not all moral concerns are enshrined in the law. Not all moral responsibilities are legal duties.

The existence of relevant human rights law is not enough. As was argued in chapters 4 and 7, in a properly functioning human rights system, those who have particular rights must know it. Just as rights holders must know their rights, the agents of government responsible for the realization of those rights must be aware of those obligations as ones based on human rights. Often they are not aware. Consider, for example, this account in a report on extrajudicial, summary, or arbitrary executions for the UN's Commission on Human Rights in relation to the United States:

> Government officials and members of the judiciary at the federal and state levels with whom the Special Rapporteur held meetings (with the exception of officials in the Department of State) had little awareness of the International Covenant on Civil and Political Rights and international legal obligations of the United States regarding the death penalty. Few knew that

the United States had ratified this treaty and that, therefore, the country was bound by its provisions. It was brought to the attention of the Special Rapporteur that state authorities had not been informed by the Federal Government about the existence and/or ratification of this treaty, and were consequently not aware of it. No efforts appeared to have been undertaken by the Federal Government to disseminate the ICCPR. (United Nations, Economic and Social Council 1998, para. 105)

The South African Human Rights Commission found similar unawareness of the government's obligations with regard to human rights in the agencies having primary responsibility for assuring their implementation. It found that no department in the government was charged directly with monitoring or ensuring the realization of the right to food, and no agency collected information on the implementation of this right. The right to food is assured in section 27 of South Africa's Constitution, which means that, in principle, the people of South Africa would have this right even if the government had not ratified any of the relevant international human rights agreements. This sort of unawareness probably would be found in many other countries as well.

When government employees are asked about their agency's human rights performance, some might answer with zealous confidence that everything they do is in the name of human rights, and others might react with puzzlement. Some staff members might have little knowledge or understanding of their agency's roles in relation to human rights, either with regard to international law or even with regard to the relevant national law. They might have some sort of understanding of their agency's objectives, but often it will be assumed that the agency is there to deliver a specific service, and not to reach any particular goal. If they do recognize that the agency has goals, few agency employees are likely to understand those goals in terms of the human rights framework. Few will view their agency's clients or beneficiaries as having any particular entitlement to their services. As has been argued, in a properly functioning human rights system, the agencies responsible for carrying out these obligations need to know and understand them.

In chapter 5, we discussed the view that rights can be formulated as goals. Just because one happens to be moving toward a goal is not a sufficient basis for saying that one is pursuing that goal. One needs to know the goal and pursue it deliberately. The view taken here is that, while government agents may do many things that happen to conform to their obligations under human rights law, that in itself is not an indication of a properly functioning human rights system. It is difficult to see how a government can claim a commitment to the realization of human rights if its agents are not aware of that commitment. If people at the front lines have no conception of the goal and no understanding of the commitment to pursue that goal, they are not doing human rights work. Government agents must act *deliberately* to conform their actions to their obligations under human rights law.

The distinction here is comparable to that drawn by the philosopher Immanuel Kant between the moral worth of an action that is done *in accordance* with an obligation and one done *for the sake of* the obligation. One's actions may sometimes just accidentally align with a particular obligation or goal. Morally, that must be assessed quite differently from an action that is motivated by consideration of the obligation or goal.

Levels of Government Obligation

All parties—all governments, all organizations, and all individuals—are obligated in some ways by human rights, at least morally, if not explicitly in the law. The challenge is to determine what these obligations are: What are different parties obligated to do or not do in concrete situations? As long as we are dealing with moral human rights, it is frequently difficult to make that determination. Transforming moral human rights into legal human rights can make that determination easier.

Well-crafted human rights law should be clear not only about the nature of the rights but also about the nature of the corresponding obligations. The law should clarify obligations not only for the state itself but also for other parties in its jurisdiction. As was indicated in the section titled "Right Imply Entitlements" in chapter 5, at the local level we need to be clear about the local entitlements and commitments through which internationally recognized human rights are to be implemented. These should be spelled out in national and subnational law. (The term *law* here is taken to include implementing statutes, administrative rules, etc.) Thus, well-crafted national law should refer to the international human rights instruments and, with respect to each group of rights, specify the entitlements derived from these universal human rights. The corresponding commitments made for realization of these entitlements should be spelled out as well.

Entitlements sometimes emerge out of a history of practice. If, for example, the government has subsidized bread for a very long time, people may come to feel they are entitled to that subsidy. However, we know that long-established practices can suddenly be discontinued. Entitlements are much "harder" (in the sense discussed in chapter 5) when they are spelled out in clear law with well-designed means of implementation and accountability. Of course, the law itself can be changed or violated. In the real world, commitments may be more or less hard, but they are never completely immutable. In the United States, Social Security is one of the people's strongest entitlements, but many still fear that it may one day be severely diminished or even dismantled.

On first hearing about the human right to adequate food, some people assume this means that governments will be obligated to feed everyone directly. This is a mistake. There may be some obligations for the government to provide for people directly, but that is required only in exceptional circumstances, when other means fail. The premise is that under normal circumstances people will provide for themselves.

In chapter 1, we discussed different types of action that governments can take to promote food and nutrition security. Now, in the context of our discussion of human rights, we can draw on those categories to describe the varieties of government obligation. As was indicated in chapter 3, the four categories are described in *General Comment 12* as obligations to (1) respect; (2) protect; (3) fulfill, in the sense of facilitate; and (4) fulfill, in the sense of provide.

Historically, these distinctions among different levels of obligation can be traced back at least to Henry Shue's discussion of levels of obligation in his essay "The Interdependence of Duties" in Alston and Tomaševski's 1984 book *The Right to Food*. G. Van Hoof drew similar distinctions in his essay in that volume, "The Legal Nature of the Rights Contained in the International Covenant on Economic, Social, and Cultural Rights: A Rebuttal of Some Traditional Views." Shue revisited the issue in the first edition of his book *Basic Rights: Subsistence, Affluence, and U.S. Foreign Policy,* published in 1986, and he discussed them again in the second edition, published in 1996. Thus there has been a long struggle to work out clear and agreed-on conceptual terminology for these levels of obligation.

This discussion has focused on the right to food, but these distinctions are useful in examining all other rights as well. Their relative importance is different for different rights. For example, with respect to, say, the freedom of speech or of religion, the primary obligations are at the level of *respect* and *protect.* The right to housing is understood to mean that government must respect and protect one's existing housing arrangements, but it does not mean that government must provide housing. Similarly, the common interpretation of the right to employment is that government must respect and protect, but it is not normally obligated to fulfill the need by providing employment opportunities to every individual. In contrast, the right to education is commonly understood to mean that government itself must fulfill the need by providing educational services directly.

The following paragraphs elaborate the four categories specifically as they relate to the human right to adequate food. Each section begins with the explanation provided by Asbjørn Eide in his 1999 update of his 1989 study on the right to food.

Respect

According to Eide (United Nations, Economic and Social Council 1999c, para. 52a):

Since State obligations must be seen in the light of the assumption that human beings, families or wider groups seek to find their own solutions to their needs, States should, at the primary level, respect the resources owned by the individual, her or his freedom to find a job of preference, to make optimal use of her/his own knowledge and the freedom to take the necessary actions and use the necessary resources—alone or in association with others—to satisfy his or her own needs. The State cannot, however, passively leave it at that. Third parties are likely to interfere negatively with the possibilities that individuals or groups otherwise might have had to solve their own needs.

The *Limburg Principles on the Implementation of the International Covenant on Economic, Social and Cultural Rights* (United Nations 1986) and the subsequent Maastricht Declaration (*Human Rights Quarterly* 1998; also see Dankwa, Flinterman, and Leckie 1998), introduced in chapter 3, reaffirm that states that are parties to the covenant, no matter how poor they may be, are obligated to ensure respect for minimum subsistence rights for all. States must not do anything that interferes with people's ability to provide for themselves and their families. They must not be taken off their land, they must be free to work and earn money, they must not have their goods confiscated by the government, they must not be taxed excessively, and the like.

Protect

According to Eide (United Nations, Economic and Social Council 1999c, para. 52d):

At a secondary level, therefore, State obligations require active protection against other, more assertive or aggressive subjects—more powerful economic interests, such as protection against fraud, against unethical behaviour in trade and contractual relations, against the marketing and dumping of hazardous or dangerous products. This protective function of the State is widely used and is the most important aspect of State obligations with regard to economic, social and cultural rights, similar to the role of the State as protector of civil and political rights.

Just as one's capacity to provide for oneself and one's family should not be threatened by government action, it should not be threatened by others who may be motivated to interfere. One of the major duties of governments everywhere is to provide their people with a measure of security against threats originating from within or from outside country. Thus, if your neighbor is stealing your crops, your government should do something to stop that. Those who are poor and vulnerable need protection not only from illegitimate acts, such as theft, but also from legal measures that may threaten their livelihoods. For example, if a poor family is forced to sell off its land because of excessive debt, the government should take measures to assure that it is left with means to provide for itself. There should always be some sort of social safety net to assure an adequate standard of living despite periodic crises.

Fulfill (Facilitate)

According to Eide (United Nations, Economic and Social Council 1999c, para. 52c):

> At the tertiary level, the State has the obligation to facilitate opportunities by which the rights listed can be enjoyed. It takes many forms, some of which are spelled out in the relevant instruments. For example, with regard to the right to food, the State shall, under the International Covenant (art. II [2]), take steps to "improve measures of production, conservation and distribution of food by making full use of technical and scientific knowledge and by developing or reforming agrarian systems."

In dealing with the human right to adequate food, particular attention should be given to facilitation. States must create institutional arrangements—such as systems of currency, transport, marketing outlets, extension services, and standards regarding food safety—that will allow and help people to provide for themselves. Government thus must provide an "enabling environment" that allows people to provide for themselves.

As Cheryl Christensen observed, in any type of economy, it is the duty of governments to assure that all their people can at least subsist:

> In this concept of subsistence rights and duties, the emphasis lies, not on "feeding" or "maintaining" people but on creating a social and economic environment which fosters development and hence need not depend upon charity. To take seriously the notion of subsistence rights and to value them as universally applicable "minimal reasonable demands" on the rest of society means that the satisfaction of basic human needs must be a primary and explicit focus of development. (Christensen 1978, 33)

Or, more simply, "A government's basic job is to provide a system in which people can meet their own and their children's basic needs" (Timberlake and Thomas 1990, 248).

It is the duty of governments to structure their societies in a way that assures adequate food for all. Under ideal governance, there would be no need to even raise the question of a right to adequate food. The idea of the human right to adequate food, or any other right, comes up only because communities and governments are imperfect.

The best way to end food insecurity is to achieve sound development in all countries. What then can we say about so-called developed countries such as the United States in which (as we will see in chapter 10) there is still widespread food insecurity? The only possible conclusion is that they really are not yet fully developed in any proper understanding of that term.

When faced with hungry people, many agencies respond by asking, How can we feed them? Instead, it is better to ask, How can we help them feed themselves? How can we help them increase their capacity to provide for themselves? When this way of responding is applied not only to food but also to housing, health care, and other basic human needs, we have what is called the *livelihood approach* to development (Frankenberger and McCaston 1999). This approach recognizes the need to facilitate people in their own pursuit of an adequate livelihood. The right to an adequate livelihood means that those who are capable should have a decent opportunity to work for it. It does not mean that they should expect it to come effortlessly, as a gift.

Fulfill (Provide)

According to Eide (United Nations, Economic and Social Council 1999c, para. 52d):

> At the fourth and final level, the State has the obligation to fulfil the rights of those who otherwise cannot enjoy their economic, social and cultural rights. This fourth level obligation increases in importance with increasing rates of urbanization and the decline of group or family responsibilities. Obligations towards the elderly and disabled, which in traditional agricultural society were taken care of by the family, must increasingly be borne by the State and thus by the national society as a whole.

The respect, protect, and fulfill (facilitate) functions may fail to assure that every individual is adequately nourished. For those who "fall through the cracks" of the system, or in disaster situations where normal means of self-provisioning become unavailable, there is some obligation for the government to provide for people's food needs directly. In an earlier work, Eide and his colleagues explained:

> The obligation of the state as provider can range anywhere from a minimum safety net, providing that it keeps everyone above the poverty line appropriate to the level of development of that country, to a full comprehensive welfare model along the lines of the Nordic countries. That the state has obligations in this direction was already recognized in 1948 by Article 25 of the [Universal Declaration of Human Rights], which provides for "the right to security in the event of unemployment, sickness, disability, widowhood, old age or other lack of livelihood in circumstances beyond his control."
>
> Special measures must be taken by the state to ensure the adequate standard of living for children (Article 27 of the CRC). Children can never be blamed for not doing their utmost to take care of their own needs, and

they cannot be blamed for their choice of parents when they are insufficiently responsible. Consequently, there is an obvious need for the society to assist.

Individuals deprived of their freedom (detained person in prisons and institutions) can obviously not by their own means ensure their enjoyment of basic needs. Provisions must therefore be made by those who have detained or institutionalized the persons concerned. (Eide 2001, 145)

Some have taken the position that government's obligations do not go beyond *facilitating* (providing an enabling environment so that people can provide for themselves), but most analysts concur that when other means fail, there are some obligations to *provide*.

The obligation to fulfill by the government's directly *providing* what is needed is a kind of residual category, becoming operational when *respect, protect*, and *facilitate* prove inadequate. The government is the provider of last resort, but only for certain categories of people in certain kinds of extreme conditions. The government does not have the obligation to fulfill the needs of those who are healthy and have reasonable access to employment or to productive resources (e.g., land, fishing opportunities) and thus should be expected to provide for themselves. Governments must do some things to prevent food inadequacies; they do not have to do everything.

We have all heard the saying, "Give a person a fish and feed them for a day. Teach them to fish and feed them for a lifetime." The first is about providing directly, whereas the second is about helping people to provide for themselves. (See the section titled "Questionable Charity" later in this chapter for some cautionary notes about this old fish tale.)

Facilitating is generally cheaper and easier for governments than *providing* directly. Therefore, a clear and strong obligation to provide if other means fail can help to motivate governments to work harder at facilitating, and thus enabling people to provide for themselves.

In chapter 4, we discussed the role of national law in assuring the realization of the human right to adequate food for all. This outline of different levels of obligation can help to guide the drafting of such legislation and, more generally, it can help in the formulation of national policy. Details regarding concrete obligations in all four categories should be spelled out in national legislation and policy.

Where people have a right to something, simply having *some* programs that provide *some* of that thing does not discharge the obligations of governments. Every individual who meets the relevant criteria has specific entitlements, so there must be institutional arrangements in place to make sure that every individual gets what he or she is due. Much too often, programs reach only a fraction of the people who ought to get them. In the United States, for example, in September 1997 only about 62 percent of the households eligible for food stamps actually got them (U.S. Department of Agriculture 2000b).

Having laws and programs pertaining to an issue does not necessarily mean that people have rights. Consider, for example, that many countries with widespread iodine deficiency disorder have laws that require the iodization of salt, an effective means for combating the disease. In Brazil, most salt mills have simply ignored a law enacted in 1956 requiring the iodization of salt (Medeiros-Neto 2000). The law does not provide for any remedies to salt consumers who might discover that their salt is not iodized. As a result, the iodization program in Brazil continues to be plagued with problems, and iodine deficiency disease levels remain high.

In the iodization laws of Brazil and many other countries, the people are treated as passive objects, and the only real players are government agencies and the companies that produce and market salt. The laws are not based on the premise that the people are *entitled* to iodized salt. It would not be difficult to formulate legislation that is based on the idea that people are entitled to iodized salt. The people could be given access to simple test kits, or they could be invited to bring samples to laboratories, and they could be given specific means for filing complaints if they find that their salt is not iodized. They might even be given small rewards or recognition for filing complaints. This change in perspective would likely have important positive effects not only on the iodization program itself but also on the people's own understandings of their proper role in society.

The same observation can be made with regard to food safety. Though many countries have detailed laws pertaining to food safety, this legislation is not based on the premise that people are entitled to safe food. Consumers are treated as bystanders to a relationship that is mainly between the food industry and the government. It would not be difficult to have at least some safety laws that are based on the active engagement of consumers.

School meal programs provide another example. These programs generally are overseen by government agencies and are subject to a broad array of rules regarding the nutritional value of the meals, the costs, and so on. In a human rights approach to school meal programs, school children would have specific entitlements with regard to their school meals. Thus, instead of simply having a rule saying that the meals must meet certain nutritional criteria, it might be established that students are *entitled* to meals that meet those criteria. Such a commitment could be made at the national level, the state level, the county level, the community level, or possibly even the school level. With entitlements, there are not only standards but also mechanisms of accountability to assure that the standards are met.

If the requirements were formulated as entitlements enjoyed by the students, they would then have reasons to learn and understand the requirements. If officials said that students in our jurisdiction are entitled to particular nutrient levels in their school meals, that could be used as the basis for an educational program for the students and their parents, explaining why they should be interested in having those nutrient levels available to them.

In considering mechanisms of accountability, students could be provided with appropriate means for determining whether they were in fact getting that to which they were entitled. Some nutrients are invisible and thus are difficult to identify, but some qualities of meals are—or can be made—visible. Part of the educational program could involve showing students how to make simple assessments of the nutritional qualities of their meals.

Students should have some institutional mechanism available to them for complaining if they do not get what they are entitled to, and this should lead to corrective action. For example, a home economics teacher might become a kind of "school meals ombudsman," responsible for receiving complaints and for passing them on to appropriate authorities.

With these kinds of rights-oriented procedures, students, parents, teachers, and administrators all would become more active participants than they would be if there were no explicitly stated entitlements. Thus, there would be considerable benefits not only in nutritional terms but also in terms of the students' social studies education.

In dealing with issues of food adequacy with the human rights approach, government's obligation is not simply to offer more of the same old policies and programs. If they are to be rights centered, policies and programs must be explicitly based on the idea that the beneficiaries are entitled to something. The beneficiaries should be able to be active participants in making sure they get that to which they are entitled.

Economic Rights

Government officials and others tend to be very concerned that the realization of economic rights might be very costly and might not be affordable. This is a serious concern, one that must be addressed very carefully. Seven distinct points need to be made.

First, all human rights entail costs. Some observers suggest that civil and political rights are negative rights requiring no substantial action, and thus are virtually cost free. They say that only economic, social, and cultural rights require substantial action and thus are costly to realize (Shue 1996). The idea that some broad categories of rights are "negative" and do not require significant government action, and thus cost nothing to realize, is untenable. Surely, a strong national government might be able to instruct its agents to do some things, such as end torture, almost instantaneously and with little cost. But a large country with limited control over its agents might have to undertake an extended effort to reach the objective of ending torture.

Similarly, the right to not suffer from discrimination means that the government must not discriminate, and it also means that the government must protect its people from discrimination. It must do so actively. Generally, significant costs must be incurred for the realization of all kinds of human rights (Holmes and Sunstein 1999). These costs are in terms not only of money but also of time, effort, and attention. Civil and political rights, as a category, are not exempt from such costs. It is now widely acknowledged that implementing civil and political rights can require substantial positive action by governments.

Poor countries are not to be excused from working for the realization of the human right to adequate food and other economic, social, and cultural rights on the grounds that they cannot afford it. There is a positive requirement for the *progressive realization* of the goals based on clear plans and the commitment of resources commensurate with the nation's capacity. In the language of the *Limburg Principles on the Implementation of the International Covenant on Economic, Social, and Cultural Rights*:

> The obligation "to achieve progressively the full realization of the rights" requires States Parties to move as expeditiously as possible towards the realization of the rights. Under no circumstances shall this be interpreted as implying for States the right to defer indefinitely efforts to ensure full realization. On the contrary, all States Parties have the obligation to begin immediately to take steps to fulfill their obligations under the Covenant. (United Nations 1986, para. 21)

Very poor nations might limit their initial commitment to providing service only to malnourished children less than five years of age, whereas others might immediately guarantee services for all who lack adequate food. These details would have to be worked out. The important thing is to establish the principle that people are entitled to adequate food as a matter of right and to design and launch a program that will assure the realization of that right.

It should not be assumed that the concept of progressive realization applies only to economic rights and not to other kinds of rights. Some economic rights can be realized quickly, and with few resources. For example, a farmer's right to protect his crops from theft by soldiers should not be difficult to implement. Similarly, providing support for breast-feeding mothers need not be costly.

In the International Covenant on Economic, Social, and Cultural Rights, progressive realization applies generally, in article 2(1), and to education in particular, in articles 13 and 14. In the Convention on the Rights of the Child, there are references to progressive realization only in relation to education, in articles 24(4) and 28(1). The concept does not appear in the International Covenant on Civil and Political Rights. Nevertheless, it should be understood to apply to all human rights. The Universal Declaration of Human Rights speaks of the need for *progressive measures* to secure the realization of human rights. There are few circumstances in which any human right can be fully realized instantaneously. It takes work and resources. All human rights must be fully realized as rapidly as possible, taking into account local resources and circumstances. The idea of progressive realization acknowledges that the pace of realization of some rights may be constrained by the availability of resources. This is relevant for all categories of rights, and not just economic rights.

Second, all human rights are aspirational. All rights—not just economic, social, and cultural rights—are aspirational in the sense that it takes resources (money, time, effort, attention) to ensure their full realization. Human rights reflect a common desire to achieve a particular status in the human condition. If a right had already been fully realized everywhere, there would be no purpose in setting it out as a goal.

Third, the categories regarding levels of obligation can apply to all rights. Obligations to respect, protect, fulfill (facilitate), and fulfill (provide) may apply to all kinds of human rights, though perhaps to different degrees. The human right to adequate food must be protected and respected as much as any civil or political right. Similarly, there are many things governments can do to facilitate—as well as respect and protect—civil and political rights.

Fourth, fulfill (provide) as a last resort. People normally should try to meet their own needs directly, out of their own resources. Thus it should be sufficient for the government to respect, protect, and facilitate. Usually, only if these things are not done well will there be a need for the government to directly fulfill needs. Setting up enabling conditions so that people can provide for themselves will be less costly to governments than having to feed people directly.

To illustrate, governments may find that the most cost-effective means for *preventing* children from becoming underweight is through establishing a good immunization program, maintaining effective sewage systems, and educating mothers about family budgeting and food handling. Governments could achieve the required results in different ways, depending on local circumstances. Usually, the objective of realizing the human right to adequate food can be achieved—and always preferably should be achieved—through effective programs of respecting, protecting, and facilitating that right. The cost of direct provision of food can be avoided by helping people meet their own needs. In a normal, healthy society, people provide for themselves, and government sees to it that they have decent opportunities to do so.

Fifth, assistance need not be costly. Many forms of assistance cost little in terms of material resources. To illustrate, in some contexts, the government's helping to identify malnourished individuals may be sufficient to induce the family and the local community to help provide the care, health services, and food needed to bring those individuals to a good nutrition status. Similarly, agricultural extension and nutrition education do not require the delivery of costly products. As Amartya Sen observes, "A poor economy may *have* less money to spend on health care and education, but it also *needs* less money to spend to provide the same services, which would cost much more in the richer countries" (Sen 1999, 48; emphasis in original).

Sixth, children do not eat much. Small children, who are most vulnerable to malnutrition, do not need large and costly amounts of food. Individually, they do not eat very much, and even in significant numbers, small children can be fed quite economically. Strong support for breast-feeding can make a big difference. Often, correcting improper diets and providing basic services can meet their needs. Older children can help to produce the food they need, whether at home or at school. Solving the problem of children's chronic malnutrition usually can be accomplished through the better use of local resources, and it is not likely to require massive shipments of food from the outside.

Seventh, entitlements need to be capped. The cost factor for implementing economic rights should not be exaggerated. It should not be ignored either. Government officials sensibly fear open-ended or uncontrolled commitments. Proposed laws that open the government to potentially unlimited obligations will not be accepted, or if accepted will not be taken seriously. When establishing clear entitlements in law and policy, it may also be necessary to cap the entitlements. Upper limits might be set by, say, limiting the total number of beneficiaries or by limiting the total budget for specific programs or services. Of course, the limit must be reasonable and not undermine the prospects for realizing the rights.

The Obligation of Good Governance

We have been especially concerned with governments' obligations with regard to the human right to adequate food. These or any other specific obligations should be seen in the context of a prior obligation for general good governance.

The fundamental question of governance is: What is the proper role of the state, and thus of the government that represents it? The extended version is: What is the proper role of governing bodies at every level—subnational (e.g., provincial, county), national, regional, and global? Governing bodies may be parts of integrated governments, as they are in national and subnational governments, or they may be separate bodies with specific functions operating more or less independently, as they are at the regional and global levels.

There is no global government, but there is global governance, which is exercised through organizations such as the World Health Organization, the Food and Agriculture Organization of the United Nations, and the United Nations Environmental Program. The authority of these bodies is limited, but they do have some specific powers delegated to them by their member nations. Governance at the global level is discussed further in chapter 17.

For much of human history, there was very little governance. The family and the local community met most human needs. With the advent of the modern nation-state system in the seventeenth century, the state's primary function was to provide security from attack from the outside. What went on within the boundaries of the state was not the business of government.

Then the state began to become more involved, first as a minor participant, but later as the dominant provider of various services. In the eighteenth century, there was a backlash in the economic sphere, expressed in Adam Smith's call for laissez-faire policies toward commerce. Even so, the role of government continued to grow. By the middle of the twentieth century, government had become the primary provider not only of defense but also of health, education, and numerous other services. The process was fueled by rapidly increasing taxation, especially by the taxing of personal incomes. France had an income tax in 1793, and Great Britain had one in 1799. In the United States, an income tax was levied during the Civil War from 1860 to 1865 but dropped after a few years. The 2 percent income tax approved by Congress in 1894 was ruled unconstitutional. It was not until 1913 that the Sixteenth Amendment to the Constitution authorized Congress to collect income taxes.

The taxation of personal incomes in periods of vigorous economic growth helped to fuel the growth of central governments. It all worked reasonably well in the developed countries. Governments were able to take on more and bigger functions by demanding more taxes from individuals and corporations under their jurisdiction.

But what happened when these large-scale services were expected from governments that did not have the resources—the tax base—to provide them? Previously self-sufficient countries that had functioned on the basis of strong communities became incapable of providing these services, not because their resource levels had declined but because the demands on their governments had increased. Because of new expectations, imported from the outside, they were now labeled as poor and in need of assistance and advice—from the outside.

Perhaps poor countries never should have taken on extensive duties regarding social services, but such detachment by national governments is feasible only if families and communities can adequately fulfill people's needs. Local capacities to provide basic health and education services often have been undermined by the intrusion of outside influences, particularly the influence of the market system. The market is seductive because it provides enormous benefit to some, but in the competitive race many others are left behind, and some become even worse off than they had been earlier. The current globalization of the world economy shows that rather than raising all ships, the rising economic tide can engulf the less seaworthy ships.

It is fascinating to reflect on what life and governance in poor countries might have been like today if there had been no intrusion by outsiders. But we cannot rewind the tape of history. It is now more important to think out the proper role of the state and of governance at every level in our own times, in the face of social and economic situations as they are.

Human rights law and principles are mainly about the obligations of government. Thus, they imply clear norms for governance, especially as it relates to human dignity. It follows that good governance is that governance which assures the realization of all human rights for all.

Following John Locke, Jack Donnelly sees governments as bound by the rights of those over whom they have jurisdiction:

> Government thus can be considered legitimate insofar as it furthers the effective enjoyment of the human rights of its citizens. And citizens are entitled to such a government. (Donnelly 1989, 63)

With good governance, there is general accountability of the government to all the people, through the media and other more formal arrangements. With good governance, broad government accountability arises out of the fact that the people can remove government officials who do not perform satisfactorily. If this works well, there may be no need for special mechanisms of accountability to ensure the realization of the human right to adequate food or any other right.

Until broad and general accountability of governments to all their people is perfected, it is important to establish distinct institutional arrangements, such as effective national human rights commissions and effective international treaty bodies, to ensure that all people make steady progress toward the goal of realizing all human rights.

Food security is a good, concrete test of the quality of governance generally. It is easy to present data on food security in a given area. Numbers can be assembled to show, reasonably accurately, the average calorie intake, specific micronutrient deficiencies, the numbers of children underweight, and so on. Many of these things may be seriously problematic from the nutritionist's point of view. However, it does not automatically follow that the government should take on each of these issues. It does not follow that if I am hungry the government should provide me with lunch. The question is: Which of the many issues of concern should be regarded as matters for government? And how far should governments, with their limited resources, be expected to go in addressing these concerns? The raw descriptive data do not answer those questions.

In the four categories of obligation, the third category, *facilitation*, encompasses the broad obligation of national governments to assure that there are sound institutional arrangements for the functioning of society as a whole. With good governance, *enabling conditions* allow people to work effectively and productively, and thus provide for themselves. Under good governance, governments do not need to pay much attention to food and nutrition (except for safety measures) because most people take care of themselves, and there are no serious and widespread food and nutrition problems. With good governance, most people are not much concerned about their human right to adequate food because that right is not violated.

Obligations of Nonstate Actors

When a couple takes in a foster child, are they doing human rights work? When a church runs a soup kitchen for the poor, is it acting as an agent of human rights? Does every physician advance the realization of the human right to health? Some providers of human services insist that their work is about the realization of human rights, even when they know little about the global human rights apparatus.

The primary responsibility to ensure the realization of human rights rests with states, and thus with the governments that represent them. This arises in part from the fact that it is national governments that sign and ratify international human rights agreements. However, nonstate parties have responsibilities as well. The preamble of the Universal Declaration of Human Rights says:

THE GENERAL ASSEMBLY,

Proclaims this Universal Declaration of Human Rights as a common standard of achievement for all peoples and all nations, to the end that every individual and every organ of society, keeping this Declaration constantly in mind, shall strive by teaching and education to promote respect for these rights and freedoms and by progressive measures, national and international, to secure their universal and effective recognition and observance.

In a similar vein, the preambles to both the International Covenant on Civil and Political Rights and the International Covenant on Economic, Social, and Cultural Rights say that

the individual, having duties to other individuals and to the community to which he belongs, is under a responsibility to strive for the promotion and observance of the rights recognized by the present Covenant.

The nature of these responsibilities remains a point of debate among human rights specialists.

As was argued earlier in this chapter, the moral rights of individuals lead to corresponding moral responsibilities on the part of government and other parties, and legal rights lead to corresponding legal obligations on the part of government and other parties. Legal rights are less ambiguous than moral rights because they are spelled out in the law. Nonstate actors have those legal duties with regard to human rights that are specified in the relevant human rights law, whether international or national.

The legal duties of nonstate actors with regard to human rights law can be examined within the framework of the four levels of obligation described earlier in this chapter. There is a broad consensus that nonstate actors must respect the human rights of others and not do anything to violate them. However, there is no general agreement that they must actively protect others whose rights are being violated. Very few writers seem to think that nonstate actors have a positive obligation to act to fulfill others' human rights, whether through facilitation or direct provision of goods or services. Some say there *ought to be* an obligation to take positive steps to ensure that others' human rights are realized, but hardly any claim that such an obligation already exists under present international law.

Several of the international human rights treaties specify particular responsibilities of nonstate actors. For example, the Convention on the Rights of the Child specifies a number of family responsibilities. The national law in which human rights are elaborated may elevate these responsibilities to the level of legal duties. These specifications of legal duties generally vary among nations. For example, there is a duty of individuals to assist those who are needy in some nations, but not in others (Glendon 1991).

Nonstate actors include not only individuals and organizations within nations but also international organizations, both governmental and nongovernmental. International governmental agencies—such as the United Nations, its specialized agencies and funds, and international financial institutions like the World Bank—have legal duties under international human rights law. This follows from the fact that these agencies are constituted by states and serve as their agents. As states' agents, they are under the same obligations with regard to human rights as are states (Kent 1994). Similarly, international nongovernmental organizations (including transnational corporations) are in principle under the jurisdiction of states, and thus they too have duties under international human rights law.

International organizations, whether governmental or nongovernmental, are not above or outside international human rights law but rather are subject to it. They are not the primary parties to that law, as are the states that sign and ratify the treaties, but they do have derivative obligations. Much work remains to be done to interpret the application of that law to nonstate actors at every level. The basic premise, however, is that they are in fact subject to human rights law.

On December 9, 1998, the United Nations General Assembly adopted the *Declaration on the Right and Responsibility of Individuals, Groups and Organs of Society to Promote and Protect Universally Recognized Human Rights and Fundamental Freedoms* (United Nations, General Assembly 1999). It is sometimes described as the Human Rights Defenders Declaration because it emphasizes the right of nonstate actors to promote the realization of human rights.

Article 3 of the declaration asserts that domestic law constitutes the juridical framework within which human rights should be implemented. Apart from that, the declaration offers no concrete guidance with regard to the duties of individuals or any other nonstate actors. During the many years devoted to drafting this declaration, there were several attempts to articulate the obligations of individuals. However, there was a great deal of resistance to this, partly because some felt that international law should deal with the obligations of states, not of individuals.

The question of who has what rights or obligations to act in support of the human rights of others is not a trivial one. To illustrate, in the United States, the state of Massachusetts had a "Burma law" that restricted the state government from purchasing from companies doing business in Burma (Myanmar) because of its alleged human rights abuses. This was held unconstitutional by a federal appeals court because under the U.S. Constitution foreign affairs are supposed to be the exclusive domain of the federal government. In June 2000, the U.S. Supreme Court unanimously struck down the Massachusetts law as unconstitutional, saying that it would "compromise the very capacity of the president to speak for the nation with one voice in dealing with other governments" (Greenhouse 2000, 23).

Many civil society organizations such as CARE and Médecins Sans Frontières provide humanitarian assistance and are therefore sometimes described as human rights agencies. It is important to recognize that humanitarian assistance and advocacy for human rights are quite different. A number of civil society organizations do useful work in providing humanitarian assistance directly to the needy, but that is different from insisting that governments should provide this assistance because it is their legal right. Not every effort to protect human dignity or improve human well-being should be described as human rights work.

Similarly, it is sometimes suggested that specialized agencies of the United Nations, such as the Food and Agriculture Organization (FAO) and the World Health Organization (WHO), are human rights bodies because they help to fulfill important human needs. However, until recently their efforts have not been *explicitly* tied to codified human rights. Historically, international governmental agencies such as FAO and WHO have rarely explained their actions as being intended to fulfill specific, codified obligations under the law—although that is now changing under the new United Nations Development Assistance Framework.

If we were to accept that battling injustice or providing human services of any kind means doing human rights work, we would miss some important distinctions. Perhaps the claim that nonstate actors are doing human rights work should be based on an awareness and conscious use of the relevant human rights framework, matching the requirements for state actors, as outlined earlier in this chapter. Human rights work can then be identified by the fact that it makes explicit reference to human rights law. Thus, in this perspective, we would say that the United Nations Children's Fund (UNICEF) began to function as a human rights agency when its Executive Board decided in 1991 that thereafter UNICEF's work would be based on the Convention on the Rights of the Child. Many other United Nations agencies are reorienting their efforts to a more explicit human rights approach. Thus, they also are beginning to become human rights agencies.

The question of what constitutes human rights work is relevant not only for large international organizations but also for small local ones. Consider what happens when churches set up soup kitchens for the poor. Such programs certainly help poor people, but they do nothing to ensure that the government fulfills its obligations to them. When the private sector provides services directly because the government fails to do so, it may in fact be relieving the government of its obligations. In allowing governments to escape their obligations, such organizations may be undermining people's human rights at the same time they provide them with good food.

In some cases, civil society organizations may work cooperatively with government and serve as its agent, helping it to meet its obligations. As is argued in the following section, this is very different from what happens when such organizations step in and, on their own initiative, provide services to fill voids left by government's omissions and failures. Such work certainly may be necessary. However, from a human rights perspective, it is always important to press for clarification and fulfillment of the government's obligations to help meet basic needs.

It is useful to contrast the typical soup kitchen with the operation of the civil society organization named Food Not Bombs, which set up feeding programs for the poor in San Francisco in a way that highlighted the point that the government was not doing enough to make sure that people would be able to feed themselves. The Food Not Bombs staff may or may not have been aware of the relevant international law, but they certainly were clear about the need to press government to fulfill its responsibilities to its people.

In chapter 1, it was shown that government actions with regard to food or other sorts of problems can usefully be distinguished into four categories: respect, protect, facilitate, and provide. Earlier in this chapter, we showed how these terms have been used to categorize the obligations of government under international human rights law: Governments have certain obligations to respect, protect, facilitate, and provide for people in relation to their food needs. Not everything that *can* be done in these four categories *must* be done, but some things must be done. The determination of what must be done arises out of an analysis of human rights law and the nation's commitments to that law, as they relate to local circumstances.

The categories of respect, protect, facilitate, and provide are also useful for identifying the different kinds of things that nonstate actors can do in relation to food issues. However, unless there is some explicit provision set out in national law, these organizations are not legally obligated to do these things. Of course, they are obligated to respect others' rights just as much as any other individual or organization. But they have no special legal obligations beyond those that apply to all nonstate actors. Thus, an organization like CARE is not required to provide humanitarian assistance to anyone; it does that by choice.

Civil society organizations may feel a moral responsibility to help care for the needy, and they may do so directly. Human rights, however, are mainly about the obligations of national governments. After all, it is national governments, not private individuals or civil society organizations, that sign and ratify the international human rights agreements on behalf of the states they represent. Thus, it seems reasonable to say that organizations providing services directly, on their own initiative, are not doing human rights work. However, if they do that in collaboration with government in some way—perhaps under contract with the government—they may help the government to fulfill its obligations. Certainly an organization that presses government to recognize and carry out its obligations with regard to human rights is doing human rights work.

Some civil society organizations place great emphasis on building self-reliance among the poor. Though that certainly is of great importance, from a human rights point of view, it can go too far. Emphasizing individual and community self-reliance may tend to relieve governments of their responsibilities. Indeed, governments may sometimes advocate local self-reliance as a way of shirking responsibility. Just as exclusively top-down strategies of development are objectionable, so too are strategies based entirely on local self-reliance. There needs to be an appropriate balance, with both governments and local people carrying their appropriate burdens.

Similar points can be made about the roles of international agencies. The Office of the United Nations High Commissioner for Refugees (UNHCR), for example, plainly recognizes that its task is not to take over the work of delivering services to refugees directly. Instead, UNHCR favors a rights-based approach that

> underlines the legal obligations of States to meet the basic needs of the most vulnerable individuals (including refugees), and ensures that the work of humanitarian agencies such as UNHCR provides support to States in fulfilling their responsibilities, rather than being a substitute for State action (or inaction). (Jessen-Pettersen 1999, 32)

Thus, the primary function of nonstate actors in relation to human rights is to support states in meeting their human rights obligations. That is different from fulfilling people's needs through independent direct action.

There is widespread confusion regarding the relationships between humanitarian work and human rights work. Perhaps things would be clearer if we accepted that, for nonstate actors, humanitarian work is mainly about service delivery, and human rights work is mainly about advocacy. That advocacy is mainly about the behavior of states in relation to human rights law.

Questionable Charity

Efforts to help the needy can go wrong in many different ways. This section calls attention to three major concerns, centered on three different parties. First, assistance can be disempowering to its *recipients*. Second, assistance can be provided in ways that reflect arrogance and an inadequate understanding of recipients' needs on the part of the *provider*. Third, assistance can relieve *those who ought to be helping* from fulfilling their obligations.

Disempowering Assistance

If you feed people a few meals immediately following an acute disaster, such as an earthquake, you help them "get on their feet" quickly so that they can provide for themselves. However, if you continue feeding them day after day, they may lose the incentive to provide for themselves, and thus become disempowered, weakened by the help. In some countries, many people have come to depend on welfare schemes for much of their lives. Recall the old adage, "Give a person a fish and feed him for a day. Teach him to fish and feed him for a lifetime." Helping people to provide for themselves, empowering them, is likely to do them more good over the long run.

Those who design such programs should distinguish carefully between empowering and disempowering kinds of assistance. Assistance to the poor, for example, should not reward and reinforce poverty; rather, it should reward and reinforce the climb out of poverty. Thus, instead of structuring assistance as an unconditional grant, it should be provided under the terms of a performance contract, to reward those who move ahead. Of course, exceptions must be made for those who have diminished capacity or who do not have decent opportunities to pull themselves up.

Arrogant Assistance

Sometimes, we take the old adage about teaching people to fish too uncritically. Justo Gonzalez points out that it may oversimplify:

> The dictum implies that people don't have enough to eat simply cause they don't know how to fish or how to grow food. While technologies can improve food production, most fisherfolk know how to fish in their own waters much better than any outsiders no matter how technologically informed or how well meaning. Likewise, traditional cultures know more than we often acknowledge about their soils, their climate and the diseases that threaten their crops and livestock.
>
> The saying ignores a number of factors that cause hunger more often than ignorance or even lack of tools: Do the fisherfolk have free access to the lake? Is the lake polluted? Who is polluting it? Who controls the sale of hooks and lines? Is the lake overfished by industrial interests?
>
> The first thing we must do is realize that, more often than not, hunger is a political problem. "Politics," in the strictest sense, is the manner in which humans divide and distribute power and resources. People are not hungry in this country and elsewhere because they don't know how to raise food or are lazy. . . . They are hungry because they have no access to power, and therefore no access to food. . . .
>
> To those starving right now, with no possibility of fishing, we must provide a fish for the day and work for the day when they may fish. To those

who need hooks and lines, we should provide them. We must also work to make certain that those who live by fishing have guaranteed access to the waters by which they live. (Gonzalez 1986, 1)

Surely, educational programs should be offered when they are wanted and when they can in fact be useful and empowering in the concrete local circumstances. The caution here is simply that helpers should not approach the needy with an a priori assumption that their troubles arise out of their ignorance. Frequently, the more fundamental issue is that they lack decent opportunities to do meaningful, productive work. Often, subsistence producers remain at that level because they discover, through hard experience, that innovations are risky, and when they are successful in increasing their productivity, others come along to somehow reap the harvest. Assistance should be based on a careful and sensitive analysis of the situation, undertaken jointly by the providers and the receivers of that assistance.

Assistance Can Relieve the Primary Duty Bearers

Just as people who are fed may lose the incentive to provide for themselves, feeding someone who should be fed by another party may dissipate that other party's incentive to carry out his or her responsibilities. For example, if you regularly feed your neighbor's children, those neighbors may in time lose their sense of responsibility to feed their own children. Similarly, in some countries, the government does not adequately feed the people it has imprisoned. If the families of the prisoners then bring in food, that tends to reinforce the government's irresponsible behavior. The point here is not that the families should not feed their imprisoned relatives but that we should be aware that there is this disadvantage in what they are doing. They might want to consider campaigning to get the government to do the right thing and feed its prisoners.

Time magazine ran an advertisement soliciting contributions for charitable causes. It boasted:

> In America, you are not required to offer food to the hungry. Or shelter to the homeless. There is no ordinance forcing you to visit the lonely, or comfort the infirm. Nowhere in the Constitution does it say you have to provide clothing for the poor. In fact, one of the nicest things about living here in America is that you really don't have to do anything for anybody. (*Time*, May 5, 1997, p. HON2)

Is this absence of obligation a good thing? In 1964, Kitty Genovese was murdered in New York City while thirty-eight people watched without helping or calling for help. They were not under any legal obligation to help. Under the no-duty-to-rescue principle that prevails in the United States, bystanders are not required to come to the assistance of strangers in peril if they did not cause that peril.

This principle of no-duty-to-rescue is peculiarly American. In contrast, most European countries do impose a legal duty on individuals to come to the aid of an imperiled person where that can be done without risk of harm to the rescuer.

There is a well-established international duty to come to the assistance of the needy in the case of ships in distress on the high seas. Captains failing to meet this obligation have been prosecuted. However, there is no general duty of nations to respond to distress in other nations. The international community provides assistance in many different circumstances, but it is not required to do so. Should we continue to leave assistance—within countries or internationally—as a matter of charity and chance, or can we agree that at least under some circumstances there should be a limit to the depths to which we will allow human degradation to sink without intervening?

In *Sweet Charity: Emergency Food and the End of Entitlement*, Janet Poppendieck (1998) examined the impact of heavy reliance on charitable giving to the hungry in the United States. She found that the heavy emphasis on food pantries and similar private feeding initiatives has undermined the government's social safety net.

Charities generally have no legal obligations with regard to what they provide, and they have no legal obligations with regard to whom they provide. A privately run food pantry could, if it wished, limit its services to people of a particular faith or a particular ethnicity. Even where there is no overt discrimination, the supply system for food pantries often results in better services for better-off neighborhoods. "In Manhattan, for example, the borough's two wealthiest city council districts have more soup kitchens than the two poorest; the wealthy districts simply have churches and synagogues with the resources to sustain such programs. . . . [Standards of equity] cannot be applied to charity, precisely because the charitable giver has no responsibility to provide equitably" (Poppendieck 1998, 221–22, 229).

Many food pantries were started with the idea that they would respond to short-term emergencies, but then they found they were serving chronic needs (Poppendieck 1998, 259–62). Charity should be viewed as something that is appropriate mainly for short-term acute crises—what we usually think of as emergencies. We should see food pantries that stay in business endlessly as signs that there is something wrong with the basic structure of the society.

Surely, people always will be faced with unpredictable emergencies due to accidents, fires, sudden unemployment, and so on. In those situations, people should step in to help their neighbors "get back on their feet." But if a society has sustained problems—such as the United States, which always has one-fifth of its children living in poverty, or steadily widening gaps between rich and poor—this is a sign that there is something fundamentally wrong in the society, and a clear indication that the government is not fulfilling its obligations. It is entirely predictable that automobile accidents will occur on streets and highways, so governments everywhere understand that they have an obligation to provide ambulance services. Hunger among children is just as predictable, but in many countries they have no more than a very tattered safety net.

The emphasis on charity has "curtailed the legally enforceable claims that people in need may make upon the collectivity" (Poppendieck 1998, 5). Where there is an overreliance on charity, people's rights are not respected.

As was pointed out above, in human rights work, the emphasis is on clarifying the obligations of governments. Some things may be left to private charity, but at the same time governments should be expected to do some things. The specifics are subject to debate, but the basic starting principle is that governments do have an obligation to help the needy. Once that is accepted, the challenge is to work out the exact dimensions of that obligation.

It is important to make a clear distinction between humanitarian assistance work and human rights work. As was indicated earlier in this chapter, humanitarian assistance is mainly about service delivery, while human rights work is mainly about advocacy in relation to governmental actions. Human rights work involves clearly articulating and implementing the obligations of governments to help meet human needs. When a food pantry gives food to the poor, it is doing humanitarian assistance work, not human rights work. When it presses government to act on the problem, it is doing human rights work.

Some organizations combine humanitarian work and human rights work. For example, some food pantries provide food and also inform their clients about their entitlements under various government programs. Some also lobby for more vigorous action by government and for a strengthening of these entitlements. Such advocacy is human rights work.

The Community Food Resource Center in New York City demonstrated how organizations could work to ensure that their clients know their rights. It opened an "entitlements clinic," in which community workers helped people obtain the social services to which they were entitled. It then helped to create a traveling outreach team, the Food Force, that would go from pantry to pantry to help clients determine their eligibility for food stamps (Poppendieck 1998, 264).

There is a place for private charity, of course, but it is important to understand that charity can be excessive when it serves as a substitute for good government, filling in gaps that are allowed to continue because government has not done what it is obligated to do. As Poppendieck observes, "Emergency food programs do not function in a neutral environment in which any charitable activity undertaken is automatically a net addition to the well-being of the poor. They function in an environment in which there is another side, a group working to reduce the public safety net that emergency food was originally created to supplement" (Poppendieck 1998, 295).

Instead of simply adding to the well-being of the poor, the voluntary provision of food supplies to the poor by private parties may lead to the decline of public assistance and shift the costs of caring for the poor to the private sector. Some degree of shift in this direction may amount to wise economizing of the taxpayers' money, but it can also go to excess and allow government to avoid what it should be doing. The substitution of charity for entitlements may unwittingly further the conservative political agenda under which the needy are left to fend for themselves. "Programs that were created largely to compensate for the shortfalls of public entitlements are being used to further undermine them" (Poppendieck 1998, 296, 301–2).

Poppendieck points out that "apart from issues of individual performance or merit, people have moral claims on the collectivity" (1998, 47). Surely individuals have responsibilities, but there is also some form of obligation on the part of society as a whole. There must be at least some minimum level of support for the needy for which society, through its government, will take responsibility. The task of human rights work is precisely to articulate and ensure the fulfillment of these obligations, which are carried out primarily by government agencies on behalf of the collectivity.

It is not only private, voluntary agencies that need to be wary of going to excess in relieving duty bearers of their obligations. If government agencies feed my children when I am perfectly capable of doing so, the government is acting inappropriately. In the United States, the federal government sponsors many nutrition programs. As a result, many state and local governments feel that food insecurity is no longer their concern. Though it is often the voluntary actions of private agencies that tend to relieve duty bearers of their obligations, government agencies themselves sometimes do this. The problem does not arise only from acts of private charity.

CHAPTER 7

Accountability Mechanisms

A society of sheep must in time beget a government of wolves.
BERTRAND DE JOUVENAL

Varieties of Accountability

If the law says that people have a particular right (chapter 5), the law should assign the duty for ensuring the realization of that right to some specific agency of government (chapter 6). The law should also provide for some sort of accountability to ensure that the responsible agency does what it is supposed to do. That is the concern of this chapter.

Holding people or agencies accountable means finding ways to make sure that they do what they are supposed to do, fulfilling their duties. To illustrate, traffic police and courts are mechanisms for holding drivers accountable with regard to their duty to obey speed limits and other traffic laws.

Action intended to realize rights could go wrong in many different ways. For example, in programs intended to help alleviate malnutrition, income provided to families to be used for food might be diverted to other uses. People who are entitled to particular benefits might not know about them, or they might have difficulty accessing them. A child who is fed at a centralized feeding program might for just that reason get less to eat at home. Those managing an effective system would notice these problems and make constant course corrections to navigate the system toward the goal. The system as a whole would be refined over time until it worked well.

Social service programs usually reach only some of the needy some of the time. Governments may boast about the number of individuals served, but they tend to be silent about the number of people who are needy but not served. Accountability means paying attention to that shortfall. With regard to the human right to adequate food, the obligation is not simply to provide some food-related service to some people but also to ensure adequate food for all. Any government that really wants to achieve that goal should be willing to make itself accountable for meeting that challenge.

As indicated in chapters 4 and 5, a rights system can be viewed as a goal-seeking arrangement. The ultimate goal, overall, is the realization of all rights for all individuals. The rights represent the goals, and the obligation holder's implementation mechanisms provide the means for reaching the goals. The accountability mechanism is the rights system's means for making corrections in case there are deviations from the path toward the goal. It is the means for making sure that the government and other responsible parties meet their obligations. The accountability mechanism watches the implementation agency to make sure it does its job well.

Accountability is important not only with regard to rights but also with regard to all aspects of governance. Thus, governments have their legislative auditors and inspectors general to make sure government agencies stay on track. They may have ombudsmen to provide links between citizens and government agencies and help handle complaints against the government. All these different types of mechanisms can be used to help ensure that governments fulfill their responsibilities with regard to rights. In the United States, for example, there is a detailed compliance-monitoring procedure to ensure that the states provide disabled children with the services to which they are entitled under the law. In Hawai'i, the Children's Rights Coalition launched a suit against the state government in 1993 and obtained a consent decree ordering the state to provide the mandated services. If there were a right to adequate food on the law books, such a coalition also could bring action against the government for failing to ensure the realization of that right.

There should be explicit standards against which the accountability agency evaluates the performance of the implementing agency. If people's entitlements are not clear and widely recognized and accepted, it will be difficult to hold anyone to account for failures to fulfill them.

Accountability mechanisms have two distinct phases in their operations. One element is monitoring or *detection* to determine whether there is deviation from the standard, and to what degree. The second is *correction* through which something is done with the information obtained to restore the behavior to the zone of acceptability. In the sketch of the steam engine governor in chapter 4, the whirling balls detect the speed of the shaft's rotation. The rods linked to the valve accomplish the correction that is required.

In some cases, detecting and reporting on the deviation to the responsible actors may be sufficient to induce them to correct their own behaviors. Consider the example of controlling speeding drivers on the highway. In some cases, signs about speed limits may be sufficient. In other cases, it may be useful to have a large digital sign connected to a radar device that tells individual drivers how fast they are going. Or it could tell them by how much they are exceeding the legal speed limit. For some drivers, this would be sufficient. For others, it might be necessary to connect the radar to a police officer and court system that imposes fines and suspends drivers' licenses.

In the international human rights system, there is little capacity to actually pursue and punish human rights violators. However, there is a reasonably good system of detection, by both governmental and civil society agencies. Although not backed by powerful tools of correction, these alerting mechanisms do appear to have considerable effect.

Accountability mechanisms are institutional arrangements for providing feedback to the implementation mechanisms—the agencies designated with primary responsibility for ensuring the realization of rights—and also to other parties that may have some role in ensuring the realization of rights. An accountability mechanism functions by assessing the performance of the agencies responsible for the implementation of human rights, much as a police officer might monitor the speed of passing cars. The monitoring agent informs the responsible parties of those assessments to guide them toward improving that performance. In some cases, the accountability mechanism might also have the power to impose sanctions of different types, but in many cases they function on the basis of "constructive dialogue"—persuasion rather than punishment.

Accountability mechanisms might take several forms. With regard to national human rights performance, accountability from "above" comes from international organizations, particularly the United Nations treaty bodies. There is a kind of "horizontal" international accountability when one nation-state offers guidance to another, guidance that is between peers. That is, states are peers in principle, on the basis of their "sovereign equality." Guidance from "below" comes from within the nation, from the civil society through concerned organizations and the population as a whole, and most important, from the rights holders themselves.

When nations critically assess one another's human rights performance, that can be viewed as a kind of "external horizontal" accountability. There is also a kind of "internal horizontal" accountability when some government agencies monitor the performance of other government agencies. Though this has always been carried out in some measure, it is now becoming systematic. Later in this chapter, the section titled "Accountability through Public Action" describes several different kinds of national human rights agencies.

A well-developed rights system has distinct institutional arrangements created by government and dedicated to the function of making sure that rights are realized. Nevertheless, more informal means for holding governments to account can be of great importance. Many civil society organizations—especially those that identify themselves as human rights organizations, such as Amnesty International and Human Rights Watch—use publicity to highlight government wrongdoing with regard to human rights. News media often do similar exposés, but they do not do it as systematically as the nongovernmental human rights organizations. In some cases, there might be popular demonstrations and social movements. Action might even be taken to overthrow the government.

Sometimes, these challenges to government are explicitly based on references to international human rights law or to the corresponding national law. Often, however, there is no reference to the law, and the claim is simply that the government is obviously doing bad things. To illustrate, when evidence is found that a government has allowed its agents to torture private citizens, hardly anyone troubles to cite the particular law that is violated. When the suspension of food subsidies leads to food riots, little attention is given to the relevant law.

It may be difficult to judge whether popular social movements should be regarded as human rights actions, and thus as means for holding governments to account with regard to the human rights performance. The primary test is whether or not a basis for the claims of that movement can be found in the International Bill of Human Rights, which is discussed in chapter 2.

A good example of horizontal accountability may be found in the way in which the U.S. Department of State provides critical assessments of the human rights performance of other nations each year (http://www.state.gov/g/drl/rls/hrrpt/2003/index.htm). China typically responds with its own criticism of the United States' human rights performance (http://english.peopledaily.com.cn/200403/01/print20040301_136190.html).

China's critique is based primarily on published U.S. information sources, both governmental and nongovernmental. It uses material such as the U.S. Department of Agriculture's reports on food security in the United States, which is described in chapter 10, and it also uses the abundant criticism of the U.S. government that is easily accessed in the popular press. Although it is not China's intention, this demonstrates the positive value of the United States' openness and capacity for self-criticism. This informal, open self-criticism is an important means for holding governments accountable, whether by their own people or the people of other countries. Most countries do not keep their darker sides so open to examination.

Justiciability

Broadly, the justiciability question asks whether disputes relating to a particular kind of law can be settled by a court of law. Some say that certain kinds of law are, by their very nature, not appropriately addressed through judicial procedures. Some say that establishing a new international mechanism for adjudicating economic rights would not be practical (Dennis and Stewart 2004). Some say that a law that cannot be enforced in the courts is not really a proper law. Justiciability is about accountability through adjudication, that is, through court procedures.

Some people think of accountability in relation to human rights exclusively in terms of whether and how rights holders can make claims regarding their rights in the courts in national, regional, or global legal systems. However, accountability can be based on a much broader range of possible measures. As we have indicated, many different parties, both inside and outside the nation, can hold governments accountable. The means may be juridical (based on the use of judges and courts), or they may be administrative.

The question of justiciability is closely linked to what can be described as the *violations orientation* to human rights work. For those who focus on this approach, the central task is to identify violations, identify the violators, collect evidence, and "bring the violator to justice" through some sort of court procedure. War crimes tribunals are of this nature. The Convention on the Prevention and Punishment of the Crime of Genocide, for example, is quite emphatic, even in its title, about the need to punish violators.

Debates about the justiciability of human rights had already begun during the drafting of the Universal Declaration of Human Rights. In 1947, the British representative on the drafting committee complained that many proposed provisions, especially those involving social welfare, were not legally enforceable (Glendon 2001, 59). As we will see in chapter 10, this has been one basis of the United States' refusal to recognize economic rights.

At the international level, there is a great reluctance by some countries to allow human rights issues to be taken to an international court because of the fear that it could be used to interfere in the internal affairs of sovereign states. In the drafting of the Universal Declaration of Human Rights, by late 1947 it already had become clear that "the chief obstacle to unanimous approval of the Declaration was not going to be its content, but its potential for legitimating outside interference in a country's internal affairs" (Glendon 2001, 96). This same reasoning accounts for the United States' resistance to compulsory jurisdiction by the International Court of Justice in the Hague, and its resistance to the International Criminal Court beginning in the late 1990s. This argument, centered on maintaining the sovereignty of nations, is quite different from the one that says that certain kinds of laws, by their nature, have no potential for justiciability.

Those who focus on violations also tend to focus on specific events. Wrongs are seen to result from wrong*doing*, from specific acts. Bad outcomes are seen as resulting from bad people. From this perspective, it is difficult to see or to critically assess chronic conditions such as ongoing discrimination, poverty, or hunger as human rights issues. The violations approach, and thus the issue of justiciability, is oriented toward addressing distinct events of direct violence, not ongoing structural violence. To illustrate, far more harm to children arises from neglect than from abuse. Courts and other violations-oriented procedures are geared more to dealing with abuse than with neglect. They function best when a specific wrong act has been committed. They are not very effective in responding to failures to act appropriately. In legal terms, courts tend to focus on *malfeasance* rather than *nonfeasance*.

Bad outcomes such as hunger and poverty can occur without necessarily having bad people that caused them. Sometimes, the blame should be placed on particular social systems. Thus, winnowing out bad actors such as corrupt leaders or wrongdoing corporations will not change the way in which the market system steadily widens the gap between rich and poor. Focusing on bad actors tends to blind us to structural violence and the harms that result from and through social systems.

One should not confuse the task of identifying who is to blame for a bad situation with the task of identifying who has what duties to correct it. To illustrate, national governments have a duty to address the problem of poverty among their people even if that poverty is not due to the government's wrongdoing (International Council on Human Rights Policy 2003, 20). In chapter 16, the discussion of humanitarian assistance makes it clear that duties to assist people in life-threatening situations are not limited to those who caused those situations.

Adjudication is not the only violations-oriented approach to accountability. An important nonjudicial means for calling violators to account is *naming and shaming*, an approach favored by Human Rights Watch (Roth 2004). This also focuses on distinct violations and on the assignment of blame.

There is a need to constantly strengthen the institutional arrangements for accountability through adjudication. However, we should not view adjudication as if it were the only important mechanism of accountability. The human rights treaty bodies in the United Nations have no power of adjudication. Instead, they use a nonjudicial approach described as *constructive dialogue*, a softer approach intended to encourage errant states to take the right direction. They use well-established administrative procedures for obtaining information from national governments and from other sources, analyzing that information, and then responding to the governments. Details regarding the procedures used by the UN treaty bodies are available elsewhere (cf. Alston 1992b).

Some observers may feel that constructive dialogue is simply a default, an approach that the treaty bodies take as a result of their political weakness. However, it can be seen as the most realistic and appropriate approach to dealing with the widespread resistance to anything that looks like global governance. The constructive dialogue approach shows strong respect for national sovereignty, which is what the member nations demand of the United Nations.

Even when trial and punishment for violators are available, it may sometimes be unwise to pursue that option. To illustrate, where parents fail to take adequate care of their children, it may be more sensible to focus on making sure that the children are taken care of, and the parents are somehow helped so that they become willing and able to handle their responsibilities. Usually, punishing the parents is not likely to be very useful. The same may be said about weak states. If a weak government fails to ensure that its people get adequate food, the need is not to punish that government, but rather to find ways to help it to carry out its responsibilities. When a government allows a country to go hungry, there is a need for solutions, not punishments.

Thus, while the violations-oriented approach, emphasizing justiciability, has an important role to play, it is not always essential. Assigning blame for a problem is not the same as finding remedies for it.

Remedies for Rights Holders

The most important form of accountability mechanism is giving the rights holders themselves (or their representatives) a procedure for complaining and getting some remedy. Human rights in the law rests on the principle *ubi jus ibi remedium*—where there is a right, there must be a remedy. Article 8 of the Universal Declaration of Human Rights asserts that "everyone has the right to an effective remedy by the competent national tribunals for acts violating the fundamental rights granted him by the constitution or by law." The human right to adequate food along with all other rights should be articulated in the law, together with a description of the remedies that are available if even a single individual's rights are violated. Individuals who fail to get what they are entitled to under the law should have effective means available to them for pressing their claims. If there are no such remedies, there is no real right.

There are possibilities for bringing complaints at the international level. For example, under the "1503 procedure" (discussed in chapter 2, and further described at http://www.unhchr.ch/html/menu2/8/1503.htm), under certain conditions individuals can bring complaints to the Commission on Human Rights and also to the Committee on the Elimination of Racial Discrimination. Under an Optional Protocol to the International Covenant on Civil and Political Rights, individuals can, under certain conditions, bring complaints to the Human Rights Committee. A campaign has been launched in support of a similar Optional Protocol to the International Covenant on Economic, Social, and Cultural Rights. As indicated in chapter 2 (in table 2.2), individuals may bring complaints to most of the treaty bodies.

The regional human rights bodies also have procedures under which individuals can file complaints. Details may be found in Steiner and Alston (2000).

There are these possibilities for making complaints at the international level, but they have not been used much. The remedies at the global level, such as the 1503 procedure, are unknown and inaccessible to most people. There is broad agreement among human rights advocates that these mechanisms have not been very effective.

Until the recent efforts to create national human rights commissions, there has been a curious failure to develop strong remedies in national law. It seems that many human rights advocates had overlooked the fact that the primary locus of realization of human rights is within nations, not in the international setting. This may have resulted, in part, from an assumption that domestic court systems are adequate to the task, and no special remedies are needed with regard to human rights. However, the historical evidence contradicts that view. Most nations have no good institutional mechanisms for dealing with human rights violations, none apart from the capacity of their courts for dealing with those human rights that are explicitly covered in national law. The national human rights commissions that have been established vary a great deal in their capacities. Many have little or no ability to deal with complaints from individuals.

Remedies may take many different forms, but the most central and essential element is that the individual who feels that his or her rights have been violated should be able to do something about it. If, for example, your child is supposed to get a free lunch at school, there should be somewhere you can go to complain if she does not get it, and there should be some sort of correction and/or compensation. The mechanisms should be built into the design of the program. In some cases, the remedies can be quite clever. For example, in one country people were supposed to be able to buy a basic loaf of bread at a subsidized price. However, the bakeries through which they were provided often had inadequate supplies, and those who came for the subsidized bread were turned away. Then a new rule was passed. If the subsidized bread were not available, the customer would be entitled to buy any other loaf of bread in the bakery at the price of the subsidized bread. After that, the supplies of the basic bread became plentiful.

If needy citizens are entitled to a specific government service but are not told about it, that could hardly be regarded as a real and effective entitlement. In the United States, for example, one analyst found that "the major reason for failure to register for food stamps among the elderly and the working poor was simply lack of information about eligibility" (Eisinger 1998, 51). Often, many people entitled to particular services are not aware of it. The right to a particular service should be understood to include a right to appropriate information about that service. The most important mechanism of accountability in a properly functioning human rights system is the means of recourse available to the rights holders themselves. Obviously, if they are not aware of their rights, they have no recourse.

In properly functioning rights systems, rights holders must know their rights. And knowing their rights, the rights holders also must have and know about realistic possibilities for seeking remedies if they feel their rights have not been realized. Despite its centrality to rights systems, human rights advocates often neglect this requirement of basic knowledge about rights and about locally accessible remedies.

The remedies available to rights holders are essential elements of any properly functioning rights system. These remedies ensure that the individual will not be treated simply as a passive object. Human rights means recognizing people as active participants in helping to shape the circumstances in which they live, and recognizing that they have specific powers to make claims on the world in which they live.

National and Local Human Rights Agencies

Mechanisms for fulfilling obligations with regard to human rights and for holding national governments accountable vary a great deal. Many different branches of government may have responsibilities for carrying out the government's obligations, but only one or two specially identified agencies will have distinct responsibilities for holding the government accountable. This section describes agencies that have specific accountability functions.

Many national governments assign the accountability function to existing agencies in their national governments. In many cases, there is heavy reliance on the existing judicial system, and no special institutional arrangements are made for dealing with human rights issues. Executive or legislative agencies may also be assigned roles. In the United States, for example, the Department of Justice oversees the implementation of human rights within the country, whereas the Department of State has primary responsibility for its international dimensions.

In some cases, new agencies are created for the purpose of monitoring the national government's human rights performance. There has been a decisive trend toward the creation of national human rights commissions, demonstrated by the fact that about fifty countries now have such commissions. Website addresses for several of them are provided in this book's sources section.

There are not only national human rights commissions, but also, in many cases, similar bodies at subnational levels, including states, provinces, and municipalities. In many cases, they focus more on rights under local and national law than on human rights as set out in the major international human rights instruments. In Mexico, for example, the national human rights commission, the Comisión Nacional de los Derechos Humanos (CNDH), was created by the government in 1990. It was designed to serve as an independent agency within the Ministry of the Interior, with a mandate to investigate human rights abuses and make recommendations to the government. In 1998, a CNDH report highly critical of the Morelos state government contributed to the state legislature's initiating impeachment proceedings against the governor (U.S. Department of State 1998). More recent reports on the human rights situation in Mexico suggest that the Human Rights Commission of Mexico City plays a more active role than the national human rights commission. Another example of a subnational human rights commission is the Minnesota Department of Human Rights. However, rather than dealing with international human rights, its work centers on the Minnesota Human Rights Act, which deals mainly with issues of discrimination (http://www.humanrights.state.mn.us).

National human rights commissions have different sorts of functions and structures. In South Africa, for example, the creation of the Human Rights Commission was mandated in paragraph 181 of the constitution of 1996. Its functions are enumerated in paragraph 184:

FUNCTIONS OF THE SOUTH AFRICAN HUMAN RIGHTS COMMISSION

(1) The Human Rights Commission must

    (a) promote respect for human rights and a culture of human rights;

    (b) promote the protection, development and attainment of human rights; and

    (c) monitor and assess the observance of human rights in the Republic;

(2) The Human Rights Commission has the powers, as regulated by national legislation, necessary to perform its functions, including the power

    (a) to investigate and to report on the observance of human rights;

    (b) to take steps to secure appropriate redress where human rights have been violated;

    (c) to carry out research; and

    (d) to educate.

(3) Each year, the Human Rights Commission must require relevant organs of state to provide the Commission with information on the measures that they have taken towards the realisation of the rights in the Bill of Rights concerning housing, health care, food, water, social security, education and the environment.

(4) The Human Rights Commission has the additional powers and functions prescribed by national legislation.

South Africa's Bill of Rights is in chapter 2 of its Constitution. Its provisions include the statement in paragraph 27 that everyone has the right to have access to sufficient food and water. The reporting process has been systematized through the creation of "protocols" or questionnaires that guide the government agencies in the formulation of their responses. In parallel with its inquiries to government agencies, South Africa's Human Rights Commission has also conducted a systematic survey of the public's perceptions on the realization of socioeconomic rights (South African Human Rights Commission 1999).

In the United Kingdom, the Human Rights Unit is part of the lord chancellor's department. According to the Home Office, the unit includes a Human Rights Task Force, whose terms of reference are as follows:

FUNCTIONS OF THE BRITISH HUMAN RIGHTS TASK FORCE

1. The purpose of the Task Force is to

(i) help Departments and other public authorities prepare for implementation of the Human Rights Act 1998; and

(ii) increase general awareness, especially amongst young people, of the rights and responsibilities flowing from the incorporation of European

Convention on Human Rights and thus to help build a human rights culture in the United Kingdom.

2. The Task Force will maintain a dialogue between Government and non-governmental organisations on the readiness of public authorities for implementation. It will help identify, promote and support, as appropriate, a range of initiatives and opportunities to assist training and development, including the production and dissemination of appropriate guidance, good practice and publicity material.

In India, the National Human Rights Commission functions under the Protection of Human Rights Act of 1993. Its functions are as follows:

FUNCTIONS OF INDIA'S HUMAN RIGHTS COMMISSION

The Commission shall perform all or any of the following functions, namely:

(a) inquire, on its own initiative or on a petition presented to it by a victim or any person on his behalf, into complaint of

(i) violation of human rights or abatement thereof or

(ii) negligence in the prevention of such violation by a public servant;

(b) intervene in any proceeding involving any allegation of violation of human rights pending before a court with the approval of such court;

(c) visit, under intimation to the State Government, any jail or any other institution under the control of the State Government, where persons are detained or lodged for purposes of treatment, reformation or protection to study the living conditions of the inmates and make recommendations thereon;

(d) review the safeguards provided by or under the Constitution or any law for the time being in force for the protection of human rights and recommend measures for their effective implementation;

(e) review the factors, including acts of terrorism that inhibit the enjoyment of human rights and recommend appropriate remedial measures;

(f) study treaties and other international instruments on human rights and make recommendations for their effective implementation;

(g) undertake and promote research in the field of human rights;

(h) spread human rights literacy among various sections of society and promote awareness of the safeguards available for the protection of these rights through publications, the media, seminars and other available means;

(i) encourage the efforts of non-governmental organisations and institutions working in the field of human rights;

(j) such other functions as it may consider necessary for the promotion of human rights.

Apart from the national commission, many of the states of India have human rights commissions as well.

Several national governments (e.g., Norway, South Africa) now ask government departments to submit regular reports on their performance in relation to human rights. These internal reporting procedures are comparable to the reporting by states to the global treaty bodies. In some cases, these reports by government agencies are directed to the national human rights commissions. The commissions use this information in preparing their reports for the global treaty bodies. However, the most important function of these internal reports is their use by the commissions to provide feedback to the government agencies on the quality of their performance.

Some national human rights agencies appear to be rather weak, having only grudging support from their governments. However, the creation of human rights commissions generally is a good indicator that governments are taking human rights seriously.

Accountability through Public Action

Amartya Sen points out that there are far fewer famines in democracies. His view is that, while authoritarian rulers lack the incentive to take timely measures to prevent famines, "democratic governments, in contrast, have to win elections and face public criticism, and have strong incentives to undertake measures to avert famines and other such catastrophes" (Sen 1999, 16). He believes that "a government in a multiparty democracy with elections and free media has strong political incentives to undertake famine prevention" (pp. 51–52).

In democracies, the people hold the government accountable, not only through the press but also through their voting powers and, more generally, through their sustained and vigorous participation in public life. The observation apparently correlates with the democratic peace hypothesis, that democracies do not make war on one another, and are much less violent internally than undemocratic nations.

While Sen may be correct about democracies having few famines, the argument does not work so well in relation to chronic malnutrition, or as Sen's colleagues sometimes call it, "endemic" malnutrition:

> Even an active press, as in India, can be less than effective in moving governments to act decisively against endemic undernutrition and deprivation—as opposed to dramatically visible famines. The quiet persistence of "regular hunger" kills millions in a slow and non-dramatic way, and this phenomenon has not been much affected, it appears, by media critiques. There is need for an analysis here of what explains the difference. (Hussain 1995, 19)

Many factors account for the tendency of the media to emphasize episodic famines rather than chronic malnutrition, including, for example, their tendency to emphasize sudden-onset events over continuing phenomena. However, the major factor undoubtedly is that democracies are not as democratic as we sometimes assume (Banik 1998). Sen has come to acknowledge that there is chronic malnutrition in democracies (Massing 2003), but it seems he does not associate that with any possible defects in the qualities of their democracy.

Drèze and Sen (1989) speak of the importance of public accountability as a means for forcing governments to prevent famines from developing. The unfortunate fact is that in all societies, including democracies, governments tend to be more "accountable"—more responsive—to those who are more powerful. These are the constituencies that keep their leaders in power. This pattern is clearly visible in major democracies such as India and the United States. Thus, while Sen is correct in observing that acute famines are virtually nonexistent in democracies, he overlooks the fact that they continue to have extensive chronic malnutrition among their poor. Those who are politically weak tend to be ignored, except when those who are relatively powerful speak out in their behalf.

Democracies such as the United States and India do not have famines, but they do have widespread chronic undernutrition. We can explain this, and still save Sen's concept, by acknowledging that these democracies-as-lived are imperfect. There is government accountability to the people, but not uniformly. Like other political systems, democracies tend to be more responsive to those who are powerful than to those who are needy. We see this in their economic systems, their social systems, their educational systems—indeed, in every quarter of society. Even programs designed for the poor tend to favor the more capable among the poor. This pattern of democracy-as-lived may be described as elite democracy, to distinguish it from truly egalitarian ideal democracy.

Thus we come, at last, to the explanation for chronic malnutrition that was missing from the early chapters of this book. We can understand the persistent and widespread chronic malnutrition in the world, within countries and internationally, as a concrete manifestation of the persistent and widespread disparities in power in the world. Weaker people have weaker entitlements, and thus they will always have a disproportionately small share of the Earth's abundant produce. Some individuals will enjoy meals costing hundreds of dollars, and thus command the labor of many others, and at the same time other individuals will squat before nearly empty rice bowls.

The United Nations Development Program asserts that

> the primary purpose of government should be to promote sustainable human development in ways that reduce disparities in income, well-being, education and opportunity among all people without depriving future generations of, at the very least, similar levels of well-being, security and choice. (United Nations Development Program 1997, iii)

The United Nations Development Program also recognizes that human rights work is essential to the pursuit of the integrated complex of goals described in terms of good governance, democracy, and sustainable development (United Nations Development Program 1998).

Accountability through public action may occur not only within countries but globally as well. This is well illustrated by the separate studies by Human Rights Watch and Amnesty International of violations of the human right to adequate food in Zimbabwe (Human Rights Watch 2003; Amnesty International 2004). The research by Human Rights Watch was strongly supported by a nongovernmental organization food security network called FOSENET that systematically monitors food needs, availability, and access within the country (FOSENET 2003).

In May 2003 the Asian Legal Resource Centre, based in Hong Kong, launched a Permanent People's Tribunal on the Right to Food and the Rule of Law in Asia. It was founded on the understanding that holders of human rights should play an active role in holding their governments to account:

> When the state itself transgresses, people must either wait for government to correct itself or forge their own tools to reveal truth and condemn injustice. . . . Thus, the Tribunal articulates society's claim to human rights and highlights the state's failure to pursue justice. It calls for a more vigorous commitment to protecting human dignity. However, its salient contribution is not decrying abuse, but investigating and explaining which human rights are denied, how and why. (Asian Legal Resource Centre 2003, 2)

The tribunal made a major contribution to a study of violations of the human right to adequate food in Burma, prepared by another international group based in Thailand (Burmese Border Consortium 2003).

Just as many national governments are not very responsive to the weaker segments of their populations, the international community tends to give little attention to the weaker nations of the world. Explicitly stated human rights, affirmed in the law, accompanied by distinct institutional mechanisms of implementation and of accountability, would contribute to counterbalancing this bias in social systems. Thus, both within nations and globally, a well-developed human rights system is not an add-on luxury; it is an integral part of any social system that aspires to be truly egalitarian. It is essential to good governance.

PART III Applications

CHAPTER 8

India

The website of the Indian Embassy in Washington describes the country's "Agriculture & Rural Developments" as "A Saga of Success." It boasts, "From a nation dependent on food imports to feed its population, India today is not only self-sufficient in grain production, but also has a substantial reserve" (Embassy of India 2002).

It is true that the country now produces enough food to feed all of its people. When there are rapid increases in hunger in some parts of India, it is now usually attributed to short-term natural events such as hurricanes or droughts, not to food shortage or poverty. Hunger "outbreaks" are described as transitory, episodic events, temporary deviations from the norm. India no longer suffers through large-scale famines, as it has in the past.

However, this upbeat version of the food situation in India neglects the reality of widespread chronic malnutrition in the country. In the period 1999–2001, India was estimated to have 213,700,000 undernourished people, more than any other country in the world, and more than all the countries of Sub-Saharan Africa taken together (Food and Agriculture Organization 2003, 31). Temporary disruptions in the food system by natural calamities are disastrous for so many people only because they live so close to the edge of disaster under normal conditions. India could feed all of its people, but it does not. The chronic conditions—the conditions that are normal—for many millions of people in India are unacceptable in terms of the basic requirements for human dignity.

The problems are not rooted in the vagaries of natural phenomena but in deeply embedded political and economic patterns. There are massive governmental programs—or "schemes" as they are called—for feeding poor children, providing subsidized foods, and so on—but still the problems persist. Enormous amounts of money are spent on such programs. Yet, somehow, the benefits do not reach the people who need them most.

The central government of India has been storing many millions of tons of grain while people are starving. That is not new. What is news is that a human rights organization in India, the People's Union of Civil Liberties, has challenged this practice in the country's Supreme Court. Light is being shined into places that had been well hidden, and the scandal is being thoroughly aired in India's media.

The case was tried on the basis of India's Constitution and its federal and state laws, especially its famed Famine Code. This chapter shows how the case fits into the framework of international human rights law, and specifically the human right to adequate food. Viewing the case in this larger context, we can see that it is relevant to food assistance programs in every country, and to international humanitarian assistance as well.

The Supreme Court Case

On April 16, 2001, the People's Union of Civil Liberties submitted a "writ petition" to the Supreme Court of India asking three major questions:

> 1. Starvation deaths have become a National Phenomenon while there is a surplus stock of food grains in government godowns. Does the right to life mean that people who are starving and who are too poor to buy food grains free of cost by the State from the surplus stock lying with the State particularly when it is lying unused and rotting?
> 2. Does not the right to life under Article 21 of the Constitution of India include the right to food?
> 3. Does not the right to food which has been upheld by the apex Court imply that the State has a duty to provide food especially in situations of drought to people who are drought effected and are not in a position to purchase food.

Article 21 of the Constitution, titled "Protection of Life and Personal Liberty," says, in its entirety, "No person shall be deprived of his life or personal liberty except according to procedure established by law."

As a result of the ongoing proceedings, the Supreme Court has been issuing orders calling upon government agencies to identify the needy within their jurisdictions and to ensure that they receive adequate food. For example, on July 23, 2001, the court said, "In case of famine, there may be shortage of food, but here the situation is that amongst plenty there is scarcity. Plenty of food is available, but distribution of the same amongst the very poor and the destitute is scarce and non-existent leading to malnourishment, starvation and other related problems."

On September 3, 2001, the court directed that sixteen states and union territories that had not identified families below the poverty line must do so within two weeks, so that those families could be provided with food assistance. After two weeks, on September 17, 2001, the court reprimanded them, saying, "We are not satisfied that any such exercise in the right earnestness has been undertaken." They were then given another three weeks to comply with the order.

All state governments were directed to take their "entire allotment of food-grains from the Central Government under the various Schemes and disburse the same in accordance with the Schemes." Further, the court required that "the Food for Work Programme in the scarcity areas should also be implemented by the various States to the extent possible."

On November 28, 2001, the court issued directions to eight of the major schemes, calling on them to identify the needy and to provide them with grain and other services by early 2002. For example, for the Targeted Public Distribution Scheme, "The States are directed to complete the identification of [below poverty level] families, issuing of cards, and commencement of distribution of 25 kgs. grain per family per month latest by 1st January, 2002."

Further details on the vigorous right to food campaign that was triggered by the Supreme Court's decisions may be found at the campaign's website (http://www.righttofoodindia.org). Broader accounts of India's situation with regard to the right to food may be found in Dev (2003) and in a case study on India issued by the Food and Agriculture Organization (http://www.fao.org/righttofood/en/highlight_45377en.html).

The orders clearly establish that the court understands the right to life, affirmed in article 21 of India's Constitution, as implying the right to food. Though the court was guided entirely by national law, it could also have drawn on recent advances made in understanding the human right to adequate food at the global level, as described throughout this text. As we have shown, the primary responsibility of national governments is to facilitate, which means ensuring that there are enabling conditions for people to provide for themselves. However, where people are not able to feed themselves adequately, governments have some obligation to provide for them.

Although international law does not specify the character or level of assistance that is required, it is clear that, at the very least, people must not be allowed to go hungry. Article 11 of the International Covenant on Economic, Social, and Cultural Rights recognizes "the fundamental right of everyone to be free from hunger." Paragraph 6 of *General Comment 12* explains, "States have a core obligation to take the necessary action to mitigate and alleviate hunger as provided for in paragraph 2 of article 11, even in times of natural or other disasters." Paragraph 14 adds, "Every State is obliged to ensure for everyone under its jurisdiction access to the minimum essential food which is sufficient, nutritionally adequate and safe, to ensure their freedom from hunger." Paragraph 17 says, "Violations of the Covenant occur when a State fails to ensure the satisfaction of, at the very least, the minimum essential level required to be free from hunger." There is no ambiguity here.

Starvation Is Not the Problem

The core definition of the human right to adequate food, as that is understood in international human rights law, was highlighted in chapter 3: "The right to adequate food is realized when every man, woman and child, alone or in community with others, has physical and economic access at all times to adequate food or means for its procurement." It is clear that this goal has not been achieved in India. Perhaps even more important, at this stage, is the fact that the realization of the right to food has not been clearly established as the government's goal.

Much of the debate in India has centered on the question of whether there have in fact been large numbers of starvation deaths. Those who say no, and thus defend the government, take a narrow view of the meaning of "starvation." They take it to mean deaths directly attributable to an extreme lack of food, and they focus on adult deaths. In fact, most deaths associated with malnutrition are due to a combination of malnutrition and disease. The immediate, final cause of death, the phrase written on the death certificate, is usually some disease, often an infectious disease, rather than starvation or hunger as such.

UNICEF estimates that in 2000, about 2,420,000 children in India died before their fifth birthdays. This was the highest total for any country. It was estimated that for the same year about 10,929,000 children died worldwide before their fifth birthdays. Thus, more than a fifth of the child mortality worldwide occurs in India alone. The international agencies estimate that about half of these deaths of children under five are associated with malnutrition. Thus we can estimate that more than a million children die in India each year from causes associated with malnutrition. To that number must be added a large but unknown number of adults who succumb for the same reason.

International agencies such as UNICEF and the World Health Organization do not keep records on starvation deaths. No one does. Even in the worst of times, few people die immediately and directly from starvation. They die more slowly, from malnutrition in combination with disease. Yes, if one takes a narrow view of the meaning of starvation, there are few starvation deaths in India. But using this trick of language to suggest that there is no serious problem of malnutrition in a country like India borders on the criminal.

India's government agencies at both the central and state levels have trouble seeing the massive hunger that characterizes their country. For instance, this is apparent in the working agenda of the National Institute of Nutrition in Hyderabad. The institute occupies itself with minor technical questions, and it does experimental studies on questions that can be addressed quite adequately in developed countries, while practically ignoring the deep and widespread hunger all around the country. Technical research avoids facing up to the problem, which is deeply political, not technical. There is no hope of solving the hunger problem if the government and its agencies refuse to see it.

In developed countries, hunger may be hard to see. But in developing countries, the suggestion that there is no hunger can only be a matter of deliberate denial. Some in government in India are suggesting that the poor have no serious problems, while many of the poor are in such deep despair that they are committing suicide.

The Missing Piece in India's Rights System

As a party to the International Covenant on Economic, Social, and Cultural Rights and the Convention on the Rights of the Child, India supposedly has committed itself to honoring the right to adequate food. In response to a question raised in Parliament in 1993 regarding the status of children's nutrition rights, the Department of Women and Child Development answered by listing the country's numerous programs for child care and feeding. The department apparently failed to grasp the distinction between having feeding programs and having a right to food. What is that right, and where is it elaborated in the law? Whose right is it? To what extent is this right realized? And what are the mechanisms of accountability for ensuring that the right is realized?

We have argued that in any rights system there are three major elements: the rights holders, the duty bearers, and the agents of accountability. The task of the agents of accountability is to make sure that those who have the duty do indeed carry out their obligations to those who have the rights. The rights holders themselves must have effective remedies through which they can complain and have the government's behavior corrected. This is the missing piece in India's system for addressing the right to food. Where there are no effective remedies, rights are not effective.

Intervention by the Supreme Court is a mechanism of accountability, but it is not normally available to ordinary people on a local basis. The Supreme Court case in India became necessary because there were no effective mechanisms of accountability available to ordinary people at the local level. Until local people know their rights and know that they have effective means through which to exercise them, there will be no effective system for ensuring the realization of the right to adequate food in India.

The Tamil Nadu Integrated Nutrition Project

The design of rights-based mechanisms of accountability can be illustrated by showing how a particular scheme, such as the Tamil Nadu Integrated Nutrition Project (TINP), could be adapted to acknowledge that its clients have specific rights to its services. In the 1970s, it was recognized that malnutrition was particularly severe in India's state of Tamil Nadu. At the time, about twenty-five different nutrition programs were operating in the state. About three-quarters of the state's funding for nutrition programs was devoted to the school meal program. All together, these programs reached only a small fraction of the groups identified as most vulnerable, and were of limited effectiveness. In response to these problems, TINP was launched in 1980.

The overall goal of the project was to improve the nutritional and health status of preschool children, primarily those six to thirty-six months old, and pregnant and nursing women. Four targets were specified: (1) a 50 percent reduction in protein-energy malnutrition from a level at appraisal of about 60 percent; (2) a 25 percent reduction in the infant mortality rate, then about 125 per 1,000 births; (3) a reduction in vitamin A deficiency in children under five from about 27 to 5 percent; and (4) a reduction in nutritional anemia of pregnant and nursing women from about 55 to 20 percent. Informal project targets for service delivery called for 80 to 90 percent coverage of target populations.

The package of services provided to accomplish these objectives included nutrition education, primary health care, growth monitoring, supplementary onsite feeding, education for diarrhea management, administration of vitamin A, and deworming. The program operated through a network of about 9,000 Community Nutrition Centers.

Growth monitoring was the key means for targeting interventions to problem cases, thereby controlling program costs. It provided a simple, objective way to decide when supplemental feeding and other services were called for. Growth monitoring also was viewed as an important educational tool, to explain to mothers why some children received services while others did not, and to provide mothers with feedback on how well they were doing in caring for their children.

TINP's design set out clear objectives based on measurable outputs. It identified its intended target population and reached a large proportion of that population. Growth monitoring provided an effective means for assessing the effectiveness of the services. There were explicit rules, based primarily on weight gain patterns, for determining when supplementary feeding should begin and when it should end. Outreach was vigorous, with community nutrition workers going to individual homes to persuade mothers if they did not bring in their children on their own. The costs per beneficiary were modest, and lower than that for other less sharply targeted nutrition programs.

Several deficiencies were found in TINP. Only about 77 percent of the eligible children were enrolled. Though the program's design called for the enrollment of children at six months of age, the mean enrollment age was higher than that. Although coverage was supposed to be provided until thirty-six months of age, many children exited much earlier. Enrolled children were supposed to be weighed once a month, but weighing was skipped quite often. Prenatal care was generally poor and fell short of the target levels. Community involvement in TINP was judged to be deficient. Communications with participants were good, but the project's reach beyond the participants was minimal. Boys participated and benefited more than girls. Scheduled-caste children had low rates of participation. The community had little involvement in monitoring the project. Overall, it was judged that health service delivery was below target and uneven.

An evaluation of TINP by the World Bank focused on improvements in nutritional status among children who were enrolled in the project. It gave little attention to the substantial numbers of children who were eligible but not enrolled. Apparently, there has been no systematic analysis of why some did not enroll. There were some cases in which people refused to participate, but most nonparticipation probably would be explained in terms of obstacles, and perhaps biases, in the recruitment process.

The original TINP operated until March 1989. The follow-on project, TINP-II, extended the area of coverage. Many modifications were made to correct deficiencies in TINP-I. TINP-II came to a close on December 31, 1997, but some of its activities are continuing as part of the Integrated Child Development Services and the Woman and Child Development Project.

Even in its first version, TINP had many qualities of a rights-oriented program. In the view of Dr. Anuradha Khati Rajivan, formerly collector in the Pudukkottai District:

> In the State of Tamil Nadu, India, it is now possible to think of the feeding programs for children as entitlement programs. Here the term entitlement is being used in the sense of a right, something accepted by the society and political leadership and which is unlikely to be questioned for reasons of resource constraints.... Budgetary pressures have not led to cutbacks for the feeding program.... The noon meal program now has a first call on the state budget along with food subsidies of the public distribution system and electricity subsidies.

Adequate food still is not a hard right in Tamil Nadu, because there are no explicit laws ensuring children of this entitlement, and there are no laws and institutional arrangements to make corrections when the right is not fulfilled. It would not be difficult to make those improvements.

Projects like TINP can be strengthened through the incorporation of human rights principles. For example, the basic criteria for delivering some of the services could be transformed into entitlements. With minor modifications, TINP's criteria for supplementary feeding could have been formulated as follows:

- Every child from birth to twelve months old who fails to gain at least 300 grams per month for two months is entitled to supplementary feeding, and the child's parents are entitled to associated educational programs.
- Every child twelve to thirty-six months of age who fails to gain at least 300 grams per month for four months is entitled to supplementary feeding, and the child's parents are entitled to associated educational programs.
- Every child assessed to be severely malnourished is entitled to a double ration.
- Once begun, feeding is to continue once a day for a minimum of three months.
- If a child gains 500 grams or more within three months, supplementary feeding is to cease. If not, the child is to be referred to the health subcenter, and feeding continued until adequate weight gain is recorded.

Further specifications would have to be made to define various terms, and to specify the quality and character of the basic ration in feeding, and where and how it is to be obtained. A technical definition of severe malnutrition would have to be supplied. "Adequate weight gain" would have to be defined. It could be described in numerical terms, be left to the judgment of a health professional, or some combination of criteria might be used. The point here is not to propose a specific service protocol but to suggest a form of language that could be used to provide *assurances* regarding the conditions under which specific services would be provided. People need to know what commitments have been made to them.

In a rights-oriented service program, a complaints procedure would have to be established, to be called upon when it appeared that commitments have not been fulfilled. A group could be assigned the *ombudsman* function, taking complaints and seeing that they are acted upon. Over time, the ground rules for this complaint service would need to be articulated, and its performance should become a matter of public record.

With such modifications, nutrition projects such as TINP could remain much the same as they had been, except that parents would be informed that under the specified conditions these were services they had a right to claim for their children. If they were turned away, they would know where they could go to complain, and they would have reason to expect that the situation would then be corrected. There might be a requirement that those who do not get services to which they are entitled must be compensated in some way, perhaps with extra food rations. These rights should be stated in the law and implemented through mechanisms described in the law. These arrangements should also be specified in the rules of operation of the project itself.

CHAPTER 9

Brazil

The preceding chapter on India illustrated an application of the right to adequate food in a nation with a well-established, stable government. However, the story here about Brazil centers on efforts to make the transformation to an acceptable form of government. The movement for recognition of the right to adequate food in Brazil exemplifies the sort of social mobilization described in the section titled "Informal Civil Society" in chapter 2. The movement in Brazil originated with what Stammers would describe as a "pre-institutionalized, non-legal" form (Stammers 1999, 997).

Brazil has made steady progress toward democratization and human rights-based governance, propelled by civil society since the early 1970s. Workers' strikes in the late 1970s were decisive in breaking the grip of the authoritarian state and creating a space for public action. The early 1980s were marked by demonstrations for direct elections. The federal constitution was rewritten in 1988. The first democratically elected president, Collor de Mello, was impeached in 1992 for corruption, providing clear evidence that the voice of the people was being heard (Valente et al. 1999).

Following the impeachment, in early 1993, the Movement for Ethics in Politics called for an end to corruption, hunger, poverty, and social exclusion. The civil society organization Ação da Cidadania (also known as Citizenship Action Against Hunger, Poverty, and for Life; or just Citizenship Action) was created. Its basic principles called for strong rights-based action against hunger.

BASIC PRINCIPLES OF CITIZENSHIP ACTION

1. The non-acceptance that a fellow human being could be dying of hunger at your doorstep. Something should be done immediately while we look for a mid or long term solution.
2. Having access to quality food, according to their cultural preferences, is a right of all human beings. Food cannot be used as a political weapon to submit people to the interests of the donors. Any donation, therefore, must be associated with mechanisms that empower people to be able to feed themselves as soon as possible.
3. The need to give name and address to the hungry and in need, to make possible immediate action (hunger mapping).
4. The responsibility of overcoming poverty and hunger as a responsibility of every citizen. As long as human beings do not have their humanity

fulfilled, no human being can fully enjoy our own humanity. Only with continuous solidarity can exclusion be overcome.

5. The State does not have the out-reach nor the needed agility to face alone—with its traditional mechanisms—the seriousness and breadth of the human problems posed by structural socioeconomic "apartheid".

6. New governance mechanisms are needed through administrative and financial decentralization; increased civil society participation in the management of public policies and programs, at all levels; the identification of new mechanisms of partnership among civil society organizations, market and governmental institutions; and broad solidarity among the people.

7. The State has the obligation to provide public funds to facilitate these partnerships and provide conditions—through appropriate public policies—for people to develop their own capacity to overcome exclusion. (Valente et al. 1999, 15)

Citizenship Action had about 7,000 local committees, and it involved more than 30 million people, or about 20 percent of Brazil's population. Alone or in partnership with government agencies, these committees undertook many different kinds of actions, such as food distribution, capacity building, urban vegetable gardens, income- and job-generation projects, professional training, reintegration of street children, support for agrarian reform, literacy programs, and popular education.

The vigorous mobilization of civil society contributed to the creation, also in 1993, of the National Food Security Council (CONSEA), which was composed of ten state ministers and twenty-one representatives selected by civil society. Its head, a representative of civil society, reported directly to the nation's president. Early in 1993, the president launched the new Plano de Combate à Fome e a Miséria, the Plan to Combat Hunger and Poverty.

CONSEA and Citizenship Action jointly proposed measures to use public food stocks to feed the poor, generate jobs and income, speed up agrarian reform, promote administrative and financial decentralization, coordinate actions against malnutrition and infant mortality, combat corruption, and undertake many other initiatives.

In 1994, CONSEA and Citizenship Action organized the first National Food Security Conference. This conference, which was funded by the federal government and preceded by state-level conferences, drew more than 2,000 delegates from all walks of life to discuss the eradication of hunger, poverty, and social exclusion. The conference agreed that food and nutritional security means "guaranteeing the right of everyone to feed oneself and to become a fully empowered human being, and that food and nutritional security should be one of the centrepieces of the national social and economic development strategy." However, at this stage, this thinking was not embedded into the framework of global human rights.

In 1995, the newly elected government discontinued CONSEA, and in its place created the Comunidade Solidária council. It incorporated CONSEA's experience and values in a new agency within the government for establishing partnerships with civil society. Combating hunger and poverty was one of its main goals, and for this purpose it worked to develop a new national food security policy.

In 1996, the National Human Rights Program was established. Like comparable initiatives in other countries, it focused on civil and political rights. It has not given substantial attention to economic, social, and cultural rights.

The first steps toward merging the food security movement and the human rights movement in Brazil occurred in the context of preparations for the World Food Summit of 1996. In that broad consultative process, Citizenship Action established conceptual links between the right to food in particular and human rights generally, and it discussed ways in which these rights could be implemented through the nation's food and nutrition security policy.

Comunidade Solidária was the focal point for the national follow-up for the World Food Summit. Its Executive Secretariat coordinated a broad-based ongoing national discussion of the ways in which the food security movement and the human rights movements could be joined together.

In early 1998, Brazil's Ministry of Health reviewed the National Food and Nutrition Policy. Draft proposals were examined in a two-day conference involving representatives of many different elements of civil society. There was a clear consensus on the recognition of the human right to adequate food. A special working group was established, with broad representation from government and from civil society, to draft a new policy. There was a widely shared understanding that Brazil's national food and nutrition policy should be based on human rights (Valente et al. 1999).

Leaders of the movement drew out some of the key lessons learned from the Brazil experience. They formulated four key points regarding state–society partnership:

- Citizenship Action Against Hunger, Misery and for Life did not characterise itself as opposition, nor as situation, gathering people from all parties and without parties, whose actions essentially aimed at improving peoples' lives. These facilitated the adhesion of millions of individuals who were mobilised by the values of partnership and solidarity;
- Government leaders showed themselves open to dialogue with society, creating negotiation fora, liberating resources (financial, human and material) for the financing of Citizenship Action;
- Communication media, non-governmental institutions, entrepreneurs, artists and others mobilised themselves based on the core understanding that links the deepening of democracy to the fight against hunger. It was defended that the fight against hunger should be faced not

only as a socio-economic question, but above all ethical: after all, the hunger of millions of people obscures the dignity of a whole nation. If its causes were due to historical processes, then its continuation would also be sustained by the indifference of those who share the same roads and cities as the indigent. Thus, the fight against hunger would be equally a fight to raise societal awareness, solidarity and partnership being the basic values to be strengthened;

- Understanding grew that the State alone could no longer adequately solve the problems of hunger and poverty in the country: only the union of the efforts of State and Society would be capable of making available the resources required to revert the social injustice situation in Brazil. This argument gained strength with the understanding that partnership meant equality of status for the partners and their free association, without subordination, as much in the elaboration as in the implementation and monitoring of public policies. (Valente et al. 1999, 20–21)

In July 2002, Flavio Luiz Schieck Valente was appointed national rapporteur on the human rights to food, water, and land, with his mandate to start immediately after national elections on October 27, 2002. The election of Luiz Inácio Lula da Silva as the new president of Brazil moved the effort into high gear, as newspapers headlined "Ending Hunger Tops New Leader's Agenda" (Lehman 2002).

The path to ending hunger in Brazil, as in the world as a whole, is full of obstacles. Even before Brazil's election results were reported, the naysayers talked about President "Lula" (as he is widely known) "snatching defeat from the jaws of victory." One critic argued that the greater hopes were likely to be dashed because "the policies implemented by Lula or any other incumbent must necessarily conform to the interests of global investors and not to those of Brazilian voters" (Bunzl 2002, 1). Many Brazilians have decisively rejected this sort of defeatism (Coitinho 1999; Valente 2000).

There have been administrative problems in getting the program started (Rohter 2003). However, as Lula and Valente would agree, optimism is an essential foundation of progressive political action. One of Lula's campaign slogans was "Hope Vanquishes Fear."

The program has gotten off to a strong start. Projeto Fome Zero (Project Zero Hunger) combines programs that provide immediate relief with a long-term strategy to attack the root causes of hunger. Needy families receive electronic cash cards to purchase food to meet their immediate needs. There are also programs that provide free or low-cost meals through schools, workplaces, and "people's restaurants." The long-term strategy addresses poverty, unemployment, and landlessness, and it includes programs to establish a minimum wage, agrarian reform, and a minimum income for needy households with school-age children. Projeto Fome Zero is overseen by the National Food Security Council, with participation from both government and civil society organizations (Food and Agriculture Organization 2003, 22). The UN's special rapporteur on the right to food visited Brazil in March 2002, and on that basis described Brazil as a promising example of promotion of the right to food (United Nations, General Assembly 2003).

CHAPTER 10

The United States

Some human rights go unrecognized and unrealized in the United States. Malnutrition can be found not only in poor countries but in rich countries as well. Sometimes rich countries are slow to discover it. In the 1960s, a local television station in the United States "uncovered the fact that 1,000 persons living in tar paper shacks surrounding the city dump relied upon the food they scavenged there for survival (Citizens' Board of Inquiry into Hunger and Malnutrition in the United States 1968, 26). It was not until 1973 that the U.S. Senate formed a Select Committee on Nutrition and Human Needs and concluded that more than 12 million Americans were malnourished. In June 1983, the U.S. Conference of Mayors issued a report titled *Hunger in American Cities* that said all cities had experienced significant increases in the demand for emergency food, but most were unable to meet the increased demand. The mayors described hunger as "the single greatest problem facing American cities." In the 1980s, several nongovernmental observers estimated that about 20 million people in the United States are chronically malnourished (Physicians Task Force on Hunger in America 1985; Brown 1987; Brown and Pizer 1987).

After many years of neglect of the issue, the U.S. government, through the Department of Agriculture (USDA), now undertakes serious and systematic assessments of food insecurity and hunger in the country. In 1999, the USDA reported that some 31 million Americans were food insecure, in the sense that they did not have ensured access at all times to enough food for an active, healthy life (Andrews et al. 1999). More recently, the USDA found that the prevalence of food insecurity in the United States rose from 10.7 percent in 2001 to 11.1 percent in 2002, and the prevalence of food insecurity with hunger rose from 3.3 to 3.5 percent (U.S. Department of Agriculture 2003a). It remained at essentially the same level in 2003 (U.S. Department of Agriculture 2004).

These figures should be interpreted with caution because they are based on methods of estimation very different from those used by international organizations (*Insight* 1988). If international measures and standards were to be used (FIVIMS 2002), it would be found that there is little malnutrition in the United States in comparison with developing countries. However, in comparison with other industrial countries, the United States' performance is quite poor.

The USDA's findings are reported at its website (http://www.ers.usda.gov/briefing/foodsecurity). A nongovernmental organization, the Food Research and Action Center (http://www.frac.org), also provides a good deal of useful information on the situation in the United States. Data also appear in the U.S. government's *Morbidity & Mortality Weekly Report* (2000) and elsewhere (Andrews et al. 1999; America's Second Harvest 2001; Brown 1987; Brown and Pizer 1987; Eisinger 1998; New York City Welfare Reform and Human Rights Documentation Project 2000). Because our purpose here is to focus on the right to adequate food, rather than the general problem of food and nutrition in the United States, we can simply summarize the USDA estimates: about 11 percent of U.S. households are food insecure, and in about 3 percent of U.S. households (3.1 million households), people were hungry at times during the year because there was not enough money for food. The problem is real, but certainly not as serious as in many other countries.

Obesity is also a major problem in the United States. Between 1986 and 2000, obesity approximately doubled. Severe obesity quadrupled during that period (Sturm 2003).

There are many different kinds of programs in the United States to respond to food and nutrition problems, from both governmental and nongovernmental agencies. The lead agency in the federal government responsible for these programs is the USDA's Food and Nutrition Service, which administers many different national food and nutrition programs, such as the Food Stamp Program; Special Supplemental Nutrition Program for Women, Infants, and Children (WIC); school meals programs; and nutrition programs for the elderly.

According to the USDA, every day, one out of six people in the United States receives assistance from one or more of the Food and Nutrition Service programs. In fiscal 2000, these programs cost the U.S. government $32.6 billion. More than half of this—$17.1 billion—was devoted to the Food Stamp Program alone.

The food and nutrition programs are only a small part of the broad array of assistance programs offered by the U.S. government. The U.S. Department of Health and Human Services catalogs 1,425 federal programs and activities that provide assistance or benefits to the public. Apart from these federal programs, there are also many different programs sponsored by state and local (county, city) governments. And beyond these, a wide variety of food and nutrition services are offered by private organizations.

Serious questions have been raised about both the *reach* and the *targeting* of the federal programs. To illustrate, in September 1997, the Food Stamp Program reached only about 62 percent of those who were eligible. In principle, all who met the eligibility criteria had a right to these services, but many did not get them. The issue of reach has to do with the adequacy of coverage of the pool of people who are eligible. To its credit, the Food and Nutrition Service has been studying the reasons for the shortfalls in enrollment in the Food Stamp Program, and it has been devising new methods of outreach, with positive results (U.S. Department of Agriculture 2001). The targeting questions center on the concern that the benefits may reach only the better off among the poor (e.g., the recently unemployed), and fail to reach the most needy (e.g., the chronically unemployed). Another targeting issue arises in connection with the school lunch program.

More than half the schoolchildren in the United States receive subsidized school lunches, including many who have not been determined to be needy. One could reasonably ask whether the funds spent to subsidize middle-class children's lunches might instead be spent to address other more urgent needs.

People who meet the criteria can benefit from a broad variety of programs and services. However, their rights are very limited. As Janet Poppendieck points out:

> Food stamps are the only food assistance program that might be expected to prevent hunger across the board. None of the other programs is a general entitlement. Most are limited to specific groups, children or the elderly, for example. Several, like the wic program, are limited by available funding, they are not entitlements at all. (Poppendieck 1999, 18–19)

The Food Stamp Program's being an entitlement program means that if a family meets the eligibility requirements, it must be allowed to participate. The entitlement character of the program was highlighted by a lawsuit brought in early 2002, which called on the federal government to provide food stamps for thousands of people in New York City who had been denied them (Bernstein 2002). The background on the situation in New York and on the organization that filed suit may be found in the Urban Justice Center's report, *Hunger Is No Accident: New York and Federal Welfare Policies Violate the Human Right to Food* (New York City Welfare Reform and Human Rights Documentation Project 2000).

In early 2002, Senator Richard Lugar of Indiana called for an investigation into the prospects of converting the wic program into an entitlement program (National wic Association 2002). The Center on Budget and Policy Priorities released an analysis of the issues involved in making it an entitlement (Clark 2002). Currently, the wic program and most of the other food and nutrition programs provided at federal, state, and local levels are not entitlements, which means that eligible people can be turned away, and they would have no basis for lodging complaints and no legal recourse. Thus, though there are some specific entitlements, there is nothing in U.S. law that says people have a right to adequate food (Good 1984). The fact that there are many food and nutrition programs in place does not in itself mean that the government has a commitment to the right to adequate food.

There is deep ideological resistance to economic rights in the United States (cf. Pasour 1976). The U.S. government has consistently expressed its opposition to the idea of the right to food. For example, in 1996, the United States explained its interpretation of the World Food Summit's concluding document, the *Rome Declaration and Plan of Action*, by saying that it interprets the right of everyone to have access to safe and nutritious food "to mean that governments should not interfere with the effective opportunity or ability of their citizens to obtain safe and nutritious food" (U.S. Department of Agriculture 1996, 1). In other words, the United States recognizes only the first level of obligation, *respect*, and agrees only that governments must not interfere with people's efforts to provide for themselves. There is no commitment to *protect, facilitate,* or *provide,* in the sense that these obligations are described in chapter 6. At the same time, the United States also explained that it believes that the right to adequate food or the right to be free from hunger "is a goal or aspiration to be realized progressively that does not give rise to any international obligations nor diminish the responsibilities of national governments toward their citizens" (p. 1). As one observer put it, "The United States Government has been in the forefront of the movement to characterize these, not as rights but as objectives to be progressively pursued by governments" (Butcher 1987, 197).

While the U.S. government's opposition to the right to food has been consistent, there have been anomalies. On the heels of the World Food Conference of 1974, resolutions on the right to food were introduced in both houses of the U.S. Congress in 1975. On World Food Day in 1998, President Bill Clinton, echoing President Franklin Delano Roosevelt's call in 1941 for freedom from want, described the right to food as the most basic human right. However, it appears that that was nothing more than a rhetorical flourish, perhaps the result of inadequate briefing of the president. On April 4, 2002, an *Aide-Memoire* from the government asserted that

> the United States recognizes the right of everyone to have access to food. This right is part of a country's commitment to ensure that its citizens enjoy a standard of living adequate for health and well-being as set out in the Universal Declaration of Human Rights.

Although this statement from President Clinton, and this *Aide-Memoire,* may have provided momentary hope that the U.S. government would change its position, they were completely out of step with the well-established pattern of U.S. resistance to recognition of the right to food.

At a meeting of the Commission on Human Rights on April 20, 2001, the United States was the only country to vote against a resolution (E/CN.4/2001/L.12) on the right to food. According to the UN's report on that meeting, the representative of the United States said that it could not accept the idea that "individuals had the right to be provided food directly by their Governments."

U.S. resistance to any comprehensive understanding of the human right to adequate food was reaffirmed at the World Food Summit: five years later, held in 2002. In reference to paragraph 10 of the final declaration (described in chapter 3), the United States stated its reservation:

> The United States believes that the issue of adequate food can only be viewed in the context of the right to a standard of living adequate for health and well-being, as set forth in the Universal Declaration of Human Rights, which includes the opportunity to secure food, clothing, housing, medical care and necessary social services. Further, the United States believes that the attainment of the right to an adequate standard of living is a goal or as-

piration to be realized progressively that does not give rise to any international obligation or any domestic legal entitlement, and does not diminish the responsibilities of national governments towards their citizens. Additionally, the United States understands the right of access to food to mean the opportunity to secure food, and not guaranteed entitlement. (Food and Agriculture Organization 2002b, 1; also see Rosset 2002)

This opposition to the right to food was affirmed again during meetings of the UN General Assembly's Third Committee in November 2002. In discussion of a resolution on the right to food, the United States stated that it "believed that the attainment of the right to food was a goal to be reached progressively that did not involve any national responsibilities on the part of the Government" (United Nations, General Assembly 2002, 11).

Once again, in 2004, the United States was the only country to vote against a resolution on the right to food (E/CN.4/2004/L.24). Using terminology that is by now quite familiar, the representative from the United States explained:

> The United States was the largest donor of food aid in the world. His Government's commitment to provide food and end hunger was unquestionable. The United States supported the progressive realization of the right to adequate food as a component of the right to an adequate standard of living. The attainment of that right was a goal to be realized progressively—it did not give rise to international obligations or domestic legal entitlements. His Government could not in any way recognize, support or commend the work of the Special Rapporteur on the right to food. His delegation requested a recorded vote and would vote against the text. (United Nations 2004, 7)

It is useful to examine this statement in detail:

- In the first sentence ("The United States was the largest donor of food aid in the world"), while large donations of food are appreciated, this is not an effective means for ending sustained hunger and malnutrition in the world. Bulk food donations make most sense in short-term emergencies.
- In the second sentence ("His Government's commitment to provide food and end hunger was unquestionable"), one should not suggest that providing food and ending hunger are the same things. In some cases, providing food may systematically delay the ending of hunger. The United States' commitment to ending hunger in the world is questionable.
- In the third sentence ("The United States supported the progressive realization of the right to adequate food as a component of the right to an adequate standard of living"), how can one support "the progressive realization of the right to adequate food as a component of the

right to an adequate standard of living" without supporting the human right to adequate food?

- In the fourth sentence ("The attainment of that right was a goal to be realized progressively—it did not give rise to international obligations or domestic legal entitlements"), (1) what is the point of saying "The attainment of that right was a goal to be realized progressively"? Is the United States suggesting here that hunger and malnutrition in the world should not be ended as rapidly as possible? (2) Is the United States here supporting "the attainment of that right," and thus acknowledging the existence of that human right? (3) Why is it suggested that a human right's being a goal to be realized progressively somehow implies that it does not give rise to obligations either externally or internally? What is the connection between the two parts of the sentence?
- In the fifth sentence ("His Government could not in any way recognize, support or commend the work of the Special Rapporteur on the right to food"), why did the United States raise this point? The resolution was not about the special rapporteur; it made only passing mention of him.

The United States has consistently resisted not only the human right to adequate food but also the more comprehensive human right to an adequate livelihood. Even before the Universal Declaration of Human Rights was adopted by the UN General Assembly in December 1948, Eleanor Roosevelt told that body that the U.S. government did not consider economic, social, and cultural rights to "imply an obligation on governments to assure the enjoyment of these rights by direct government action" (Glendon 2001, 186). The United States' failure to ratify either the International Covenant on Economic, Social, and Cultural Rights or the Convention on the Rights of the Child in part reflects its sustained resistance to the idea of economic and social rights.

The United States' understanding of the human right to adequate food contrasts sharply with the understanding presented in this book. There is nothing in the right that says governments must feed people on a regular basis. Rather, the core of the concept is that under normal conditions, governments must ensure that there are enabling conditions for people to provide for themselves. It is only when people are unable to provide for themselves that there is an obligation of government to feed people directly. For example, people who are living under the care of the government, perhaps in a prison or a hospital, must be fed adequately. In fact, the U.S. government does feed people in such situations. It also feeds people with low incomes under the Food Stamp and other programs. All these programs have precise, explicit criteria of eligibility. The United States' practice shows that it does agree that the government should feed some people under some conditions.

If there are no accepted national obligations, there is no meaningful right. Moreover, contrary to the view presented in chapter 5—that all rights represent goals—the U.S. position assumes that characterizing something as a goal or objective somehow precludes its being viewed as a real right. Apparently, to the U.S. government, something can be a right only if it is immediately achievable. The position taken here, and elaborated in chapter 6, is that all human rights are aspirational, and most of them require time and effort to ensure their realization.

The USDA's publication, *U.S. Action Plan on Food Security: Solutions to Hunger*, includes dissenting statements from civil society. With regard to the right to food, the USDA's Food Security Advisory Committee explained (emphasis in original):

> Endorsing the right to food does not oblige governments to provide everyone with three meals a day. Rather, governments must respect everyone's right to have access to adequate food, protect that right from encroachment by others, facilitate opportunities to enjoy that right, and only in the last instance fulfill the right to food for those unable to do so by themselves. The Advisory Committee strongly urges the U.S. Government to support global efforts, in accordance with Objective 7.4 of the World Food Summit Plan of Action, "to better define the rights related to food . . . and to provide ways to implement and realize these rights. (U.S. Department of Agriculture 1999, 7)

While the food *status* of most people in the United States is quite good, the situation with regard to the *right* to adequate food is quite bad. There is no general right to adequate food in U.S. federal law. The U.S. government resists recognition of the human right to adequate food not only domestically but also internationally, because it does not want to accept any obligations relating to that right, either internally or externally. It is not clear how one could hope to end hunger and malnutrition, whether within the United States or globally, without recognizing and actively working to realize the human right to adequate food.

CHAPTER 11

Feeding Infants

The feeding of infants generally goes smoothly, particularly with the advice of appropriately trained health workers. Lactation counselors can help to overcome many problems encountered in breast-feeding. However, there are times when the difficulties are so serious and so extensive that they must be viewed as problems of society. The most widespread and sustained of these issues to catch the public consciousness has been the improper marketing of breast milk substitutes. There also have been problems in finding ways to accommodate mothers doing income-generating work so that they can feed their infants. There have been controversies over whether breast-feeding in public is permissible. In several countries, there have been court cases on the question of whether a mother diagnosed as HIV-positive should be permitted to breast-feed her infant. All of these are political issues, issues that can raise serious concerns about human rights.

The parties to infant feeding are, most obviously, the mother and the child. But there are many others with some interest and some influence in the situation. There are the father and siblings. There is the extended family. There are friends. There is the local community. There are also doctors, nurses, and other health professionals. Employers are affected. The local government may be concerned in some way, possibly the national government, and even some international organizations. And there are also a variety of commercial interests.

Each of these parties has some interest in the infant feeding relationship. All of them may feel, or claim that they have, an interest in the health and well-being of the infant, but they have other interests as well. The mother is, and should be, concerned with her own health and comfort. Siblings may be jealous because of the attention paid to the newcomer. Some fathers may feel jealous as well. Both father and mother may be concerned about the mother's being drawn away from work in the field or the factory, or from the work of caring for other family members. Employers may be concerned with the ways in which breast-feeding takes the mother away from work, whether for minutes, hours, days, or months. They may be concerned that publicly visible breast-feeding will distract other workers.

Health professionals are concerned with the well-being of the infant and the mother, but they also have other concerns. They may have only limited time and other resources for preparing the new mother for breast-feeding. Their incomes may be affected by the new mother's choice as to whether to breast-feed or not. Commercial interests may want to sell products, either to support breast-feeding, such as breast pumps or special clothing, or for alternatives to breast-feeding, such as bottle-sterilization equipment. Government officials may be swayed in different directions, depending on which of these parties has the greatest influence on them.

These parties can influence one another's decisions in many different ways, through education, persuasion, money, and affection. The least influential of them is the infant. The infant does have some influence, because its birth and its behavior affect the mother's hormones and provide a positive stimulus for breast-feeding. Beyond that, the interests of the infant may have an impact if surrogates (i.e., others who have some capacity in the situation and who choose to speak and act in the infant's behalf) represent him or her. Nevertheless, the infant has relatively little power in the relationship. It is particularly because of this extreme asymmetry in the power relationships that it is important to articulate the rights of the infant.

Breast-Feeding Rights

The idea of breast-feeding as a human right is ambiguous; it can refer to the rights of the infant or of the mother. We may normally think of them as bonded so closely that they are one, with no imaginable conflict between them. Perhaps that is usually the case, but we must acknowledge that sometimes there can be differences between them. Certainly, they do not always "agree" on when to start or when to stop feeding. The infant may be insensitive to the inconvenience or even pain that he or she may sometimes cause. The mother may also be unhappy about being drawn away from work, from her husband, from her other children, or from rest. There sometimes can be real differences in interests between mother and child.

The question of human rights in relation to infant feeding is a practical one. A great deal of attention has been given to the issue of maternity protection, which is concerned with ensuring that working mothers, whether salaried or self-employed, have accommodations for feeding their infants. This may come as paid maternity leave and also accommodations in the workplace, in the form of modified work schedules and appropriate spaces for infant feeding. In 2000, the International Labor Organization completed its revision of the Maternity Protection Convention 183 (which may be accessed at http://www.ilo.org/ilolex/cgi-lex/convde.pl?C183).

Women's right to breast-feed at their workplace has frequently been challenged. In a case in California, for example, a schoolteacher wanted to breast-feed her infant during her free hour. The Circuit Court held that the woman had a constitutional right to breast-feed but that the state could abridge that right if there was a compelling state interest in doing so. The state was allowed to prevent her from breast-feeding because it had an interest in running efficient schools (New Mexico Breastfeeding Task Force 2003).

There have been many issues about breast-feeding in public, especially in the United States (a detailed review of the issues and the current status of legislation may be found at http://www.lalecheleague.org/LawBills.html). Typically, the states of the United States that have adopted such laws assert that a mother is allowed to breast-feed her child in any location, public or private, where she is otherwise allowed to be.

The human rights questions are especially stark in cases in which the mothers are imprisoned. Should imprisoned women have the right to breast-feed their infants? Do their infants, who have committed no crime, have the right to be breast-fed by their mothers? In one case, the court held that breast-feeding could interfere with the efficient running of the prison and thus could be curtailed. In another case, a woman was allowed to breast-feed during visiting hours but was not provided with facilities to store her milk at the prison (New Mexico Breastfeeding Task Force 2003). Thus, it is clear that work needs to be done to clarify and strengthen rights in relation to infant feeding.

Infants' Human Right to Adequate Food

The human right to adequate food described earlier in this book, especially in chapter 3, applies to everyone, but of course the law and principles may require some adaptation as they are applied to infants. Article 24, paragraph (e), of the Convention on the Rights of the Child specifically mentions breast-feeding. It says that states parties shall take appropriate measures

> [t]o ensure that all segments of society, in particular parents and children, are informed, have access to education and are supported in the use of basic knowledge of child health and nutrition, the advantages of breastfeeding, hygiene and environmental sanitation and the prevention of accidents.

Also, article 24 says that states parties shall "take appropriate measures to diminish infant and child mortality."

Several nonbinding international declarations and resolutions help to shape the emerging international consensus on the meaning of the human right to adequate food in relation to infants. The major initiatives include the following:

- In response to concerns about inappropriate marketing and promotion, the World Health Assembly adopted the International Code of Marketing of Breastmilk Substitutes in 1981. The assembly approved a series of resolutions in subsequent years to further clarify and strengthen the code (World Health Organization 1981).
- On August 1, 1990, the Innocenti Declaration on the Protection, Promotion, and Support of Breastfeeding was adopted by participants at a meeting on breast-feeding in the 1990s held at the International Child Development Center in Florence. The declaration stated a variety of

specific global goals, including the goal that "all women should be enabled to practice exclusive breast-feeding and all infants should be fed exclusively on breast-milk from birth to 4–6 months of age." In 1991, the UNICEF Executive Board passed a resolution (1991/22) saying that the Innocenti Declaration would serve as the "basis for UNICEF policies and actions in support of infant and young child feeding." In May 1996, the World Health Assembly passed a resolution on Infant and Young Child Nutrition (WHA49.15), in which it confirmed its support for the Innocenti Declaration.

- The World Summit for Children held in 1990 called for the "empowerment of all women to breast-feed their children exclusively for four to six months and to continue breastfeeding, with complementary food, well into the second year."

- In 1992 the World Declaration and Plan of Action for Nutrition, agreed upon at the conclusion of the International Conference on Nutrition in Rome, pledged "to reduce substantially within this decade . . . social and other impediments to optimal breastfeeding." The Plan of Action asserted, in article 30, "Breastfeeding is the most secure means of assuring the food security of infants and should be promoted and protected through appropriate policies and programmes." Article 33 stated that "[g]overnments, in cooperation with all concerned parties, should . . . prevent food-borne and water-borne diseases and other infections in infants and young children by encouraging and enabling women to breast-feed exclusively during the first four to six months of their children's lives." Article 34 provided a detailed call for action on promoting breast-feeding.

- In 1995, the Platform for Action that came out of the Fourth World Conference on Women in Beijing called for promoting public information on the benefits of breast-feeding, implementing the International Code of Marketing of Breastmilk Substitutes, and facilitating breast-feeding by working women.

- In 1996, the World Food Summit's Plan of Action, in objective 1.4, called on governments to "enact legislation and establish institutional structures that provide opportunities for youth and enhance the special contribution that women can make to ensuring family and child nutrition with due emphasis on the importance of breast-feeding for infants."

- In 2003, the World Health Organization released a report titled *Global Strategy for Infant and Young Child Feeding*. It said, "As a global health recommendation, infants should be exclusively breastfed for the first six months of life to achieve optimal growth, development and health. Thereafter, to meet their evolving nutritional requirements, infants should receive nutritionally adequate and safe complementary foods while breastfeeding continues for up to two years of age or beyond" (World Health Organization 2003, 7–8).

As was indicated in chapter 1, there is an increasing recognition at the international level that good nutritional status depends not only on good food but also on good health services and good care. Health services consist of a broad range of measures for the prevention and control of disease, including the maintenance of a healthy environment. Thus, infant feeding is not simply a matter of the physical transmission of nutrients. There should be a strong component of caring in it, through the closeness and contact that can be provided during feeding. Breast-feeding can be regarded as a kind of health service because of the fact that it immunizes the infant against a broad variety of diseases.

Because of their immediate and direct dependence on their mothers, the nutrition status of infants is determined not only by the quality of the food, health services, and care they receive directly but also by the food, health service, and care received by the mother herself. The infant's nutrition status at birth depends on the quality of the mother's health status and prenatal care, and whether she has had a good diet in general and has been protected from iron deficiency anemia in particular.

Mothers, and fathers as well, should be entitled to particular services not only because of their own rights but also because of their obligations to provide for their children. Mothers should receive good prepregnancy and prenatal care, and parents should be well informed about the risks and benefits of all alternative means for feeding their infants because, like everyone else, their infants have a human right to adequate food.

Principles

What does the human right to adequate food mean for infants in particular? At a forum of the World Alliance for Breastfeeding Action (WABA) held in Thailand in 1996, a number of specialists formulated a statement on infant feeding and human rights. WABA's views were elaborated further in its 1998 *Quezon City Declaration, Breastfeeding, Women and Work: Human Rights and Creative Solutions.*

Reservations were later voiced about the WABA statements, especially with regard to the question of whether the infant should be regarded as having a right to be breast-fed. This was seen as problematic, because such a right would limit the mother's freedom of choice.

A group of interested specialists agreed to discuss the issues through e-mail on the Internet. The group took its task to be the articulation of a list of agreed-on principles related to human rights and infant nutrition. After a long, hard discussion, from May 1, 1999, to January 19, 2000, this online "Consultation on Human Rights and Infant Nutrition" formulated the following Consensus Statement Regarding the Nutrition Rights of Infants, based on the participants' understanding of international human rights law and principles (Kent 2001):

1. Infants have a right to be free from hunger, and to enjoy the highest attainable standard of health.
2. Infants have a right to adequate food, health services, and care.
3. The state and others are obligated to respect, protect, and facilitate the nurturing relationship between mother and child.
4. Women have the right to social, economic, health, and other conditions that are favorable for them to breastfeed or to deliver breastmilk to their infants in other ways. This means that women have the right to:
    a. Good prenatal care.
    b. Basic information on child health and nutrition and the advantages of breastfeeding, and on principles of good breastfeeding and alternative ways of providing breastmilk.
    c. Protection from misinformation on infant feeding.
    d. Family and community support in the practice of breastfeeding.
    e. Maternity protection legislation that enables women to combine income-generating work with nurturing their infants.
    f. Baby-friendly health facilities.
5. Women and infants have a right to protection from factors that can hinder or constrain breast-feeding, in accordance with:
    a. The Convention on the Rights of the Child,
    b. The International Code of Marketing of Breastmilk Substitutes and related World Health Assembly resolutions,
    c. The International Labor Organization's Maternity Protection Convention Number 103 and its subsequent revisions, and
    d. The Innocenti Declaration on the Protection, Promotion, and Support of Breastfeeding.
6. States, represented by their governments, have an obligation to:
    a. Protect, maintain, and promote breastfeeding through public educational activities,
    b. Facilitate the conditions of breastfeeding, and
    c. Otherwise assure that infants have safe access to breast milk.
7. No woman should be prevented from breastfeeding.

Some participants in the consultation initially viewed the exercise as one of polling the participants to identify the most favored positions. However, this was not a contest to determine which positions were most popular. Rather, it was a task of determining what seemed the most reasonable interpretation of existing international human rights law and principles. Personal preferences had their influence, of course, but the major objective was to interpret currently prevailing human rights.

Although this consensus statement seemed useful, it did not resolve the most troubling question: whether or not infants had the right to be breast-fed. At the second WABA forum, held in Arusha, Tanzania, in September 2002, a Workshop on Human Rights and Infant Nutrition formulated the following:

Draft Statement on THE HUMAN RIGHT
OF THE INFANT TO BE BREASTFED

Arusha, 27 September 2002

In view of the fact that almost all countries have ratified the Convention on the Rights of the Child which affirms two fundamental principles: "the best interests of the child," and "children's right to survival and development," and the overwhelming body of evidence that breastfeeding provides unparalleled nurturing, nutrition and protection against disease, we recognize the human right of the infant to be breastfed.

This means that parties such as mothers, fathers, families, communities, governments and the international community have duties to respect, protect and facilitate the right of the infant to be breastfed. This is in accordance with the Innocenti Declaration on the Protection, Promotion and Support of Breastfeeding (Florence, Italy, 1990).

In order for the relevant parties to fulfill their duties, their capacities must be strengthened where necessary. None of the parties can or should be held solely accountable for the realization of the right of the infant to be breastfed.

The way to assure the realization of the rights of infants is to assure the realization of the rights of all women. Coercion may not be used to press a mother to breastfeed. It is the duty of fathers, families, communities, governments and the international community to respect, protect and facilitate the mother to breastfeed in the framework of her own human rights.

Note: There are exceptional cases where breastfeeding is proven not to be in the best interests of the infant. (World Alliance for Breastfeeding Action 2004, 105)

The WABA Steering Committee did not adopt the statement. Thus, the core question remains unresolved. Though many individuals have their own strong, clear positions, there is no widely accepted consensus. The following section suggests one possible method for resolving the question.

Women's Right to Breast-Feed versus
Infants' Right to Be Breast-Fed

The major question that remains is: *Do infants have a right to be breast-fed?* What is the relationship between the mother's interest in breast-feeding and the infant's interest in being breast-fed? How are the mother's rights related to the infant's rights?

At times, the mother and the infant may have conflicting interests in relation to feeding. The conflict is raised in clear relief when it is argued not only that the infant has a right to be well nourished but, more specifically, that the infant has a right to be breast-fed. Such a right could clash with the woman's right to choose how to feed her infant.

Article 3 of the Convention on the Rights of the Child says, "In all actions concerning children . . . the best interests of the child shall be a primary consideration." Combining this with the observation that breast-feeding is better for infants' health than alternative methods of feeding, some argue that infants have a right to be breast-fed.

Although it is true that decisions must include consideration of the best interests of the child, that need not be the only factor considered. Moreover, it is assumed that normally the parents judge what is in the child's best interests. The position taken here is that the state should interfere in the parent–child relationship only in extraordinary situations, when there is extremely compelling evidence that the parents are acting contrary to the best interests of the child. This point is elaborated further in the following chapter.

Those who press the view that the infant should be viewed as having the right to be breast-fed center their argument on the point that breast-feeding is almost always best for the health of the infant. I do not dispute that. In my view, the difficulties arise out of a misunderstanding of the nature of human rights and the proper role of government. Human rights generally are not intended to prescribe optimal behavior, but rather to place outer limits, saying it should not go beyond certain extremes. Thus, people are allowed to smoke and eat unhealthy food, and to buy their children cheeseburgers, even though these things are not best for them.

By definition, human rights are universal. The law and principles do not vary from country to country, from place to place. However, national and local legislatures are free to formulate legal requirements appropriate to their particular local circumstances, provided they do not conflict with general human rights law and principles.

The infant has great interests at stake, but few resources to be used to press for preferred outcomes. Given the infant's powerlessness, it is sensible to use the law to help ensure that the best interests of the infant are served. However, though it is surely appropriate to use the law to protect the infant from outsiders with conflicting interests, it is not reasonable to use the law to compel an unwilling mother to breast-feed, or to prevent a willing mother from breast-feeding. The view here corresponds to that offered in the *Journal of Human Lactation*:

> Mothers are not mandated to breastfeed, but governments are mandated to educate mothers, to support their use of education, and to assume that they will act in the best interest of their children. Governments have the responsibility to inform so that parents can make informed choices for their children. (Bar-Yam 2003, 359; also see Kent 2004)

Thus, for the purposes of framing appropriate law, the woman and infant can be viewed as generally having a shared interest in the infant's well-being. From the human rights perspective, the major concern is with protecting the woman–infant unit from outside interference.

Mothers should remain free to feed their infants as they wish, in consultation with other family members. In normal circumstances, outsiders should refrain from doing anything that might interfere with a mother's freely made, informed decision. Mothers should have appropriate and accurate information available to them so that they can make informed decisions. This is the approach taken in the International Code of Marketing of Breastmilk Substitutes. The code is not designed to prevent the marketing or use of formula, but to assure that parents can make a fully and fairly informed choice on how to feed their infants. The main task is not to prescribe to women what they should do but to remove all the obstacles to feeding their infants in accordance with their own well-informed choices.

Thus, the solution to the dilemma proposed here is that the mother and child together should be understood as a dyad, having a type of group rights. *Breastfeeding is the right of the mother and the infant together.* This might be expressed in an additional principle, to be added to the seven formulated by the online Consultation on Human Rights and Infant Nutrition:

8. Infants have the right to be breast-fed, in the sense that no one may interfere with women's right to breast-feed them.

This means that the pair taken together have rights in relation to outside parties, such as rights to certain kinds of information and services and the rights to be protected from undue influences from outside interests. It does not say that women are obligated to breast-feed their infants. It does not invite the state to intervene in the relationships between women and their infants.

The eight principles proposed here do not give priority to the woman or to the child but instead try to forge a sensible balance between their interests. They are based on the concept that women should not be legally obligated to breast-feed, but rather women should be supported in making their own informed choices as to how to feed their infants. Women should be enabled to make their choices with good information, and with the elimination of obstacles to carrying out their choices.

There is widespread concern that mothers might make unwise choices with regard to feeding their infants. We then have two basic options: Either have society override the mother's choice, or find ways to support the mother so that she makes wise choices. In my view, the first approach is disempowering, while the second is empowering for women. If women are given good information, and have all the obstacles to breast-feeding eliminated, they are likely to make a good choice.

Rather than have the state make decisions for them, citizens in a democracy prefer assurances that nothing impedes them from making their own decisions. To the extent possible, we should be free to choose, and that includes being free to some extent to make what others might regard as unwise or suboptimal decisions.

CHAPTER 12

Feeding Infants of HIV-Positive Mothers

The preceding chapter discussed the application of the human right to adequate food in the special case of infants. Here we examine a still more special case, the right as it applies to infants of mothers who have been diagnosed as having the human immunodeficiency virus (HIV). There has been serious debate regarding the feeding of such infants, arising out of the fact that under some circumstances the dangers of breast milk substitutes may outweigh the risk of being infected with HIV through breast-feeding.

Official Guidance on HIV/AIDS and Infant Feeding

There is a risk of transmission of HIV from mother to child in the uterus during pregnancy, during the birth process, or through breast-feeding. The risk of transmitting the virus through breast milk has raised concern about whether mothers who are HIV-positive should breast-feed their infants. If there is some chance that HIV can be transmitted through breast-feeding, how should mothers who are HIV-positive feed their infants? How does this relate to the human rights of the mother and of the infant?

In 1998, the World Health Organization published three manuals titled *HIV and Infant Feeding* (World Health Organization 1998). They provided a comprehensive overview of the issues but focused on the objective of preventing HIV transmission through breast-feeding. With qualifications, the approach advocated in these manuals centers on finding ways to provide breast milk substitutes to infants of HIV-positive mothers, possibly with the support of government subsidies. The health risks and the economic plausibility of this approach were not assessed. The manuals remain the basis for policymaking at the international level.

In October 2000, the World Health Organization convened an interagency task team to review recent data on mother-to-child-transmission and formulate new recommendations. They were approved in January 2001 (World Health Organization 2001). The major recommendation was that "when replacement feeding is acceptable, feasible, affordable, sustainable and safe, avoidance of all breastfeeding by HIV-infected mothers is recommended," and "otherwise, exclusive breastfeeding is recommended during the first months of life." The policy was restated in a resolution of the World Health Assembly in May 2001 (World Health Assembly 2001, paragraph 10).

In 2003, the UN agencies published a new brochure titled *HIV and Infant Feeding: Framework for Priority Action* (World Health Organization 2003b). It reiterated the recommendation developed in 2001.

Issues

The call for the use of replacement feeding in the context of HIV/AIDS reinvigorated old debates about the merits of formula feeding. A journal in South Africa ran a special issue on the question (*Special Report on Infant Feeding, Sid-Afrique* 1997). On July 26, 1998, the *New York Times* ran a front-page article, "AIDS Brings Shift in U.N. Message on Breast-Feeding," which began:

> Countering decades of promoting "breast is best" for infant nutrition, the United Nations is issuing recommendations intended to discourage women infected with the AIDS virus from breast-feeding.

It added:

> In its directive, the United Nations said it was deeply concerned that advising infected mothers not to breast-feed might lead many mothers who are not infected to stop breast-feeding. To reduce that possibility, it is advising governments to consider bulk purchases of formula and other milk substitutes, and to dispense them mainly through prescriptions. (Altman 1998, 1)

The Steering Committee of the World Alliance for Breastfeeding Action issued a statement, *WABA Position on HIV and Breastfeeding*, which said, in part:

> WABA is concerned about what appears to be recent changes in the WHO, UNICEF and UNAIDS policy regarding breastfeeding and HIV. We are especially concerned that these changes appear to put major stress on the use of infant formula and less on alternative feeding methods. (World Alliance for Breastfeeding Action 1998, 1)

The statement closed by saying that "extreme caution must be shown in involving the commercial firms that have direct economic interests in the outcome of such policy deliberations."

In a letter to the British medical journal *The Lancet*, Michael Latham and Ted Greiner, experts on breast-feeding, said that they were troubled by "the new proposals to conduct large-scale trials in several developing countries to replace breastfeeding with formula feeding in HIV-1 positive mothers." They went on to say:

> We are concerned that WHO and UNICEF will invest major resources in formula feeding and few into alternatives, such as modified breastfeeding, heat treatment of expressed breastmilk to kill the virus, wet nursing, donation (or even sales) of breastmilk, and use of animal milks or homemade

formulas. These options are preferable to the use of infant formulas in poor communities. None of them are easy, nor ideal, but they warrant careful study. Much of the successful work over the years to stem the use of commercial breastmilk substitutes in poor countries is now threatened. The involvement of the commercial infant formula industry, both in deliberations leading to the new policy and also in offering to make their products available, is troubling. (Latham and Greiner 1998, 737)

The debate over how infants of mothers diagnosed as HIV-positive should be fed is related to several major dimensions of concern. These include the likelihood of transmission, the likely consequences of infants' HIV infection via breast-feeding, the knowledge of infant's HIV status, the need to clarify and assess alternatives, and the problem of responsibility.

The Likelihood of Transmission

The brochure *HIV and Infant Feeding: Framework for Priority Action* says that 5 to 20 percent of infants born to HIV-positive women acquire infection through breast-feeding (World Health Organization 2003b, 1). Though that is a reasonable estimate of the range, the likelihood of transmission varies for different subpopulations in different kinds of circumstances. For example, the likelihood of virus transmission through breast-feeding may depend on whether the mother was infected before or after the infant was born (Dunn et al. 1992). Also, the transmission likelihood may be influenced by different kinds of micronutrient deficiencies (Friis 2002; Dreyfuss and Fawzi 2002).

There may also be differences depending on methods and timing of breast-feeding. A mother in advanced stages of disease may be more likely to transmit the virus through breast-feeding. In addition, because of her illness, she may be less able to sustain breast-feeding and less able to care for her infant, whether the infant is infected or not. There may be differences in the virus content of colostrum and early human milk compared with later milk.

Likely Consequences of Infants' HIV Infection via Breast-Feeding

Much of the research on HIV/AIDS and infant feeding is preoccupied with the question of how to reduce the likelihood of the transmission of the virus. However, under some circumstances, it might be better to breast-feed, risking transmission of the virus, because the health risks of alternative feeding methods are even worse. This is implicitly recognized in the UN agencies' statement, "When replacement feeding is acceptable, feasible, affordable, sustainable and safe, avoidance of all breast-feeding by HIV-positive women is recommended." The primary objective should not be to minimize the rate of transmission of HIV but to obtain the best possible health outcome for the infant.

For the purpose of formulating feeding advice, it is actually not necessary to know the likelihood of virus transmission via breast-feeding. To guide policy as to whether HIV-positive mothers should breast-feed or use some other feeding method, we need to know and compare the consequences, in terms of the infant's health, that are likely to result from taking each of these courses of action. The *feeding method* is the key independent variable, and the *health outcome* is the key dependent variable. Research on the biological mechanisms of virus transmission (e.g., Kourtis et al. 2003) are of scientific interest, but for the purpose of guiding the choice of feeding methods, research is needed on the likely health consequences for the infant of different feeding methods.

The preoccupation with the risk of transmission of the virus through breast-feeding apparently results from the fact that many people assume the worst, believing that infection means almost certain death. Some studies explicitly assume that the mortality rate is 100 percent by the age of five years (Bertolli et al. 2003). However, the data that are available indicate that the risk of mortality due to HIV infections contracted through breast-feeding is well under 100 percent; HIV infection is not always fatal. For example, one study indicated that about 22 percent of the HIV-positive children studied progressed to AIDS or death by ten years of age (European Collaborative Study 2002). Another review found that "early cohort studies have shown that 20-25% of children infected with HIV-1 progress rapidly to AIDS or die during infancy" (HIV Paediatric Prognostic Markers Collaborative Study Group 2003). This figure is for HIV infection generally, regardless of the transmission pathway. As a result of the protective effective of breast-feeding, the mortality rate for infants infected through breast-feeding is likely to be lower than it is for infants infected during pregnancy or in the birth process.

The issue is further complicated by the fact that drug treatments can reduce the mortality associated with HIV infection. One study of a group of children in the United Kingdom and Ireland who were HIV-infected through transmission from their mothers showed that about 20 percent died before their tenth birthdays. However, "while the number of perinatally infected children in follow up has increased steadily over time, the annual number of deaths declined markedly after 1996." They added, "From 1997 onwards we have seen reductions of about 80% in mortality" (Gibb et al. 2003, 1022, 1023). As drug treatments progressively reduce the risk of death resulting from HIV infection, the breast-feeding option becomes relatively more attractive because of the advantages of breast-feeding over the use of breast milk substitutes.

One study in a resource-poor setting found that mortality in breast-fed and formula-fed infants was similar, "suggesting that not breastfeeding may increase morbidity and mortality in the early years even while reducing HIV infection" (Coutsoudis et al. 2003, 890). Another showed that infants of mothers diagnosed as HIV-positive who were fed with breast milk substitutes had a higher rate of hospitalization than those who were breast-fed (Phadke et al. 2003). Such studies support the thesis that, at least under some conditions, breast-feeding may be better than using breast milk substitutes for infants of mothers diagnosed as HIV-positive.

There is no doubt that the morbidity and mortality rates associated with HIV infection are unacceptably high. In resource-rich settings, morbidity and mortality rates are likely to be lower than in resource-rich settings, no matter what feeding methods are used. However, the issue under discussion here is not whether these rates are high or low but whether, in any particular setting, they are significantly different with one method of feeding rather than another. There is remarkably little hard evidence on this question.

Outside the HIV/AIDS context, there is clear and consistent documentation showing that, with rare exceptions, compared to the "gold standard" of exclusive breast-feeding, all other methods of feeding yield inferior results in terms of the health of the infant (Oddy 2002). Even in cases in which breast milk is tainted by pathogens such as viruses or heavy metals, the infant is practically always better off being breast-fed (Lawrence and Lawrence 1998).

Does this pattern hold when mothers are diagnosed as HIV-positive, or does that constitute an exception to the prevailing pattern? There is evidence suggesting that the dominant pattern may hold even in these cases.

Breast-feeding is a form of immunization against a broad variety of diseases, including diseases for which the pathogens are transmitted via breast milk (Goldman, Chheda, and Garofalo 1998). Because breast-feeding transmits immunological properties from the mother to the infant, it could be especially beneficial to breast-feed infants believed to be at risk of immune deficiency. The health benefits resulting from the immunological properties of breast milk could outweigh the health risks of virus transmission through breast milk.

Breast-feeding increases the likelihood of the transmission of HIV, but at the same time it also provides important protection against the diseases that can result from HIV. That is, apart from any effect on transmission of the virus, breast milk may inhibit the virus's activity (Morrison 1999). A recent study posed the question of whether breast milk is a "vector of transmission or vehicle of protection" with regard to HIV (Kourtis et al. 2003), but the answer undoubtedly is *both*. This study considered the possibility that HIV antibodies that are present in breast milk may reduce the likelihood of transmission of the virus. Apparently, it did not consider the benefits that breast milk could provide if the virus has been transmitted. To see this, one must give attention to health outcomes and not just virus transmission rates.

For infants who are not infected at birth, the risk of HIV infection that might come from breast-feeding must be weighed against the risks of depriving the infant of the advantages of breast-feeding and at the same time exposing the infant to the risks of alternative feeding methods. Many people have strong opinions about how these considerations balance out, but in the final analysis these are empirical questions. The researchers have not given these questions the attention they deserve.

TABLE 12.1. MOTHER-TO-CHILD TRANSMISSION RATES OF HIV

		RATE OF INFANT HIV INFECTION (%)					
				Months			
Study	Group	At birth	6 weeks	3	6	15–18	24
South Africa	Breast-fed (n = 394)	6.9	19.9	21.8	24.2	31.6	—
	Formula (n = 157)	7.6	18.0	18.7	19.4	19.4	—
Kenya	Breast-fed (n = 191)	7.0	19.9	24.5	28.0	—	36.7
	Formula (n = 193)	3.1	9.7	13.2	15.9	—	20.8
Brazil	Breast-fed (n = 168)	—	—	—	—	21.0	—
	Formula (n = 264)	—	—	—	—	13.0	—

Note: A dash indicates data is not available. Infants were categorized either as breast-fed (predominantly mixed breast-fed) or fed formula (never breast-fed). *Source*: Coovadia and Coutsoudis (2001).

Knowledge of Infant's HIV Status

When infants are diagnosed as HIV-positive, it is difficult to determine whether the virus was transmitted during the pregnancy, the birth process, or breast-feeding. It is commonly assumed that increases in viral load over time in breast-fed infants are attributable to the breast-feeding. However, the viral load in the infant can increase after birth even in the absence of breast-feeding. Consider table 12.1, on the rates of virus transmission for breast-fed and formula-fed infants in several different studies.

In the South Africa and Kenya studies, not only the breast-fed infants but also the formula fed infants appear to have had increasingly high rates of infection over time. Comparable data on increasing infection after birth in never-breast-fed infants may be found in Coutsoudis and others (1999, table 2).

What can this mean? One possibility is that the infants who supposedly were not breast-fed actually were breast-fed. In the Kenya study, infants who were mixed feeders (some breast-feeding and some formula) were supposed to be placed with the breast-feeding cohort (Nduati et al. 2000; Kent 2002). Though that was the intent, about 25 percent of the women who were assigned to the formula feeding group were reported to have also been given breast milk (Coovadia and Coutsoudis 2001). This could account for infection of some infants after birth.

Another possibility is that there is a latency effect. It may be that when the actual transmission of the virus occurs during pregnancy or delivery, the resulting biological activity does not rise to the level of detectability until some weeks or months after birth. If this is the case, the share of mother-to-child transmission attributable to breast-feeding might be much lower than has been supposed. According to this table, at six months the rate of HIV infection for breast-fed infants in South Africa was only 4.8 percent higher than the rate for formula-fed infants. Because there might well be a significant time-lag between transmission of the virus and the onset of measurable infection, there is no good way to know the exact moment of transmission, and thus no good way to determine which infections are due specifically to breast-feeding.

It is important to distinguish between transmission and infection. As we see in table 12.1, the onset of infection can appear several months after birth, even for cases in which there is no breast-feeding. The most plausible explanation is what we can call a *latency effect*: The virus was transmitted before birth, but the infection did not rise to a detectable level until several months after birth.

There are ambiguities regarding the very meaning of HIV infection. The terminology that emphasizes virus transmission suggests that if a small number of "copies" of the virus pass from mother to infant, that infant is thereby infected, by definition. However, some analysts emphasize the importance of "seroconversion," the change in the blood stream that can result from the activity of the virus. Transmission is instantaneous, but seroconversion, the process of infection, apparently can take weeks or even months. The evidence of seroconversion is the presence of antibodies in the bloodstream. It is important to distinguish infection in the first sense (presence of the virus) from infection in the second sense (seroconversion), because the first does not always lead to the second.

Coovadia and Coutsoudis (2001, 5) say "the only data that we have currently available to estimate transmission in the first 6 months is to calculate the rate of new infections between 6 weeks and 6 months." However, they do not make a clear distinction between transmission and infection, and they do not acknowledge that there might be a significant time delay between the two.

The Need to Clarify and Assess Alternatives

There are many different possible means of feeding infants, including not only alternatives *to* breast-feeding but also alternative methods *of* breast-feeding. Breast milk can be provided in many different ways, and many of these variations can make a difference in the context of HIV/AIDS. Exclusive breast-feeding is different from breast-feeding combined with other liquids or solids. Breast milk can be delivered directly from the source or indirectly. Wet nurses, relatives, or friends can provide direct breast-feeding. Or the mother's breast milk can be provided indirectly by being expressed, heat treated to inactivate the virus, and then supplied to the infant with a cup.

The use of commercial formula may itself be managed in a variety of ways. For example, some proposals call upon national governments to pay for the formula and provide it free to HIV-positive mothers. Some express the hope that there will be international subsidies. And some call for using generic labels on formula containers to minimize the promotion of particular brands. It is generally agreed that the use of commercial formula should be in conformity with the

International Code of Marketing of Breastmilk Substitutes and subsequent clarifying resolutions of the World Health Assembly.

All plausible options should be fairly assessed. For example, whereas the large-scale banking of breast milk may have been deemed impractical in the past, in the context of HIV/AIDS there should be renewed interest in its potential. Even commercial milk banking, with appropriate safeguards, might be feasible (Rao 1977).

Responsibility

The agencies that discuss the question of feeding strategies by HIV-positive mothers are cautious. Instead of providing clear instructions, they say mothers "might want to consider" using breast milk substitutes rather than breast-feeding, and they qualify their positions with numerous cautionary remarks. Despite the agencies' cautions and qualifications, their persistent expression of alarm over the risk of virus transmission tends to lead health workers and mothers to only one conclusion: HIV-positive mothers should not breast-feed. Surely, if the international agencies interviewed health workers and mothers, they would find that their cautions and qualifications have been lost by the time they reach the ground. *HIV and Infant Feeding: Framework for Priority Action* says:

> To help HIV-positive mothers make the best choice, they should receive counseling that includes information about both the risks and benefits of various infant feeding options based on local assessments, and guidance in selecting the most suitable option for their situation. (World Health Organization 2003b, 2)

Unfortunately, good information about "the risks and benefits of various feeding options based on local assessments" simply is not available. Similarly, there is no established basis for determining when replacement feeding is acceptable, feasible, affordable, sustainable, and safe (the so-called AFASS criteria), and it appears that in many cases health workers make no serious effort to make judgments on this.

Mothers are urged to make informed choices, but they are not provided with the means required to do that. The agencies avoid responsibility by saying the choice must finally be made by the mother herself, but they fail to meet their responsibility to assure that mothers are provided with the information they need.

A Court Case

The rights of HIV-positive mothers and their infants faced a hard test in Eugene, Oregon. On September 17, 1998, Kathleen Tyson, then six months pregnant, was told that her blood tests indicated that she was HIV-positive. Her son, Felix, was born on December 7. He appeared to be healthy in every way. Less than twenty-four hours after his birth, Kathleen was pressed by a pediatrician to treat Felix with AZT, an antiretroviral drug, and to not breast-feed him. Having studied the issue along with her husband, David, she declined to accept that advice. Within hours, a petitioner from Juvenile Court came to her hospital room and issued a summons for her to appear in court two days later. She and her husband were initially charged with "intent to harm" the baby, but the petition, dated December 10, said that the child "has been subjected to threat of harm." When the Tysons appeared in court, they were ordered to begin administering AZT to Felix every six hours for six weeks and to stop breast-feeding completely. The court took legal custody of the infant, but it allowed the Tysons to retain physical custody as long as they obeyed the court's orders (Tyson 1999).

A court hearing was held in Eugene from April 16 to 20, 1999. There were three main lines of argument for the Tysons. First, their advocates questioned the validity of the blood tests used as the basis for diagnosing Kathleen Tyson as HIV-positive. Expert witness Roberto Giraldo, who has published extensively on the uncertainties surrounding the tests, supported this. Second, they raised questions as to whether it has really been clearly demonstrated that HIV causes AIDS. This was the view advanced by expert witness David Rasnick, a leading challenger of conventional thinking about the causes of AIDS. Third, I was to be the expert witness regarding the human rights dimensions of the case.

I wanted to argue that the basic principle underlying health care decision making normally is that patients themselves are to make the final decisions regarding their care, on the basis of informed consent. The function of health care workers is to provide the information needed, and to give advice, but not to make the final decisions. Though there are exceptional cases in which the state may override this principle and the patient may be treated coercively, the conditions required to justify such an exception were not met in this case. The published scientific evidence available at that time did not justify the state's presumption that breast-feeding by a woman diagnosed as HIV-positive, but otherwise asymptomatic, would be subjecting that child to excessive risk by breast-feeding. The literature was full of assumptions and questionable arguments about likely health outcomes, not hard evidence. Where the scientific findings are controversial, it is the mother's interpretation that should prevail, not the government's.

Moreover, I wanted to show that United Nations agencies and the U.S. government had repeatedly reaffirmed the principle that HIV-positive women should not be coerced. Their official policies say that the treatment of HIV-positive women should be based on their informed consent.

After I was sworn in, and the Tysons' lawyer explained that he was going to ask me about the human rights dimensions of the case, the judge intervened and said these matters were irrelevant. I then had to step down.

Just hours later, the judge gave his decision: The Tysons lost. Thus, the state retained legal custody of Felix. The Tysons retained physical custody on the condition that, as ordered, Felix would not be breast-fed.

On June 8, 1999, the court reviewed the case and decided that the state would continue to retain legal custody and give physical custody to Felix's parents. A similar review on December 10 led to the same conclusion. However, on December 29, the state returned full custody to the parents. During this time, neither the mother nor the infant showed any signs of AIDS.

The physicians who took the state's side in the case against the Tysons sincerely believed that the Tysons were endangering Felix. In my view, however, the scientific community had failed to meet its responsibility to produce the strong and clear scientific knowledge that would be needed to guide individuals in situations like the one faced by the Tysons. If the Tysons had been presented with clear, hard evidence that breast-feeding Felix would be likely to harm him, they would have decided accordingly. The physicians' beliefs were strong, but they did not have scientifically sound studies of the sort they themselves claim to require. Where information is inadequate, resort to coercion is not the appropriate remedy.

Both the Tysons and the cause for realization of the human right to adequate food lost in this case. Nevertheless, this case helps us to appreciate that it is as important for health care workers and policymakers to understand the relevant human rights as it is for them to understand the technical and scientific dimensions of health care. The argument that I would have liked to make in court, summarized here, is available in more extended form in Kent (1999). A somewhat different perspective is provided in Wolf and others (2001).

Informed Choice

It is widely agreed that medical and other decisions related to health care generally should be made on the basis of the principle of *informed choice,* or *informed consent.* Human rights law is explicit about the requirement of consent only in relation to medical experimentation, in article 7 of the International Covenant on Civil and Political Rights: "no one shall be subjected without his free consent to medical or scientific experimentation." However, *General Comment 14,* subtitled *The Right to the Highest Attainable Standard of Health,* speaks about "supporting people in making informed choices about their health" (United Nations, Economic and Social Council 2000, para. 37). More specifically, it says, "Reproductive health means that women and men have the freedom to decide if and when to reproduce and the right to be informed and to have access to safe, effective, affordable and acceptable methods of family planning of their choice as well as the right of access to appropriate health-care services that will, for example, enable women to go safely through pregnancy and childbirth" (para. 12).

The principle of informed consent is widely recognized as being applicable not only in the context of experimentation but also with regard to health care generally. To illustrate, the American Medical Association's ethical guidelines (at http://www.ama-assn.org/ama/pub/category/8488.html) state that the patient's right of self-decision can be effectively exercised only if the patient possesses enough information to enable an intelligent choice. The patient should make his or her own determination on treatment. The physician's obligation is to present the medical facts accurately to the patient or to the individual responsible for the patient's care and to make recommendations for management in accordance with good medical practice. The physician has an ethical obligation to help the patient make choices from among the therapeutic alternatives consistent with good medical practice.

This means that while health care workers and government agencies may offer information and advice, it is the patient herself or himself who makes the final decision. The common understanding is that parents are to make these decisions on behalf their children, at least until they become competent to make their own decisions.

Although the informed-choice approach is widely accepted, it is also recognized that there may be exceptions. There are some who argue that it is not appropriate in relation to infant feeding. Some say not only that informed choice should be suspended in the HIV/AIDS context, but that it is not an appropriate basis for determining infant feeding methods in general. They feel that because the advantages of breast-feeding are so great, it should be recognized that infants have a right to be breast-fed, and therefore that their mothers are obligated to breast-feed them. The mother should not be free to choose. The analysis here, however, is grounded on acceptance of the principle of informed choice.

In the infant-feeding situation, as in others, there are two types of possible violation of the principle of informed choice. One is that there may be violations of the "choice" part, through attempts to coerce the mother to take a particular course of action. There have been cases, like the Tyson case, in which government agents have prevented mothers diagnosed as HIV-positive from breast-feeding their infants, based on the fear of transmission of HIV through the breast milk. There is also the possibility of violation of the "informed" part. That is the central concern of this chapter.

The position taken here is that, if possible, mothers, in consultation with their families, should be free to make informed choices, but that freedom is of little value when the information available is inadequate. Governments have responsibilities related to the quality of our health care and the quality of our food, and they also have responsibilities to provide information and education to ensure the quality of our knowledge about these things. Thus the core question of how to feed infants in the context of HIV/AIDS raises serious human rights issues.

The human right to adequate food is closely linked to the human right to adequate information about our food. Thus, campaigns for labeling purchased foods with details regarding their ingredients and their nutritional values are largely based on the premise that consumers have a right to thorough information so that they can make informed choices about the foods that they eat. This approach has become prominent in debates about genetically modified food. Many argue that in the face of scientific uncertainties about their health effects, foods that contain genetically modified components should at least be labeled as such, so that consumers would have the opportunity to avoid them if they wished.

The principle of informed choice may sometimes be suspended, as when the individual is not competent to make informed choices, or when the risks to individuals or to the society as a whole warrant suspension of the principle. However, the informed choice approach is clearly implied by article 24 of the Convention on the Rights of the Child, which says that states parties shall "ensure that all segments of society, in particular parents and children, are informed, have access to education and are supported in the use of basic knowledge of child health and nutrition [and] the advantages of breastfeeding."

One careful analysis of the ethical dilemmas involved argued that in the Tyson case, the evidence *might* have warranted suspension of the normal right to make an informed choice (Wolf et al. 2001). The analysis is flawed, however, because it fails to take into account the absence of relevant evidence on likely health outcomes, and it did not take notice of the explicit policy statements of United Nations agencies and the U.S. government to the effect that mothers diagnosed as HIV-positive should not be coerced in regard to the choice of treatment of their infants. The argument here is that at present there is no scientific or policy basis for suspension of the principle of informed choice for situations in which mothers diagnosed as HIV-positive are faced with the challenge of deciding how to feed their infants.

Even if the woman herself does not make the feeding choice, there are health care workers, policymakers, or ministers of health who will have to make choices. The HIV/AIDS epidemic inescapably requires that choices must be made at some level. No matter who makes them, these should be well-informed choices.

Choices should be based on good information. Beyond that, to the extent feasible, choices should be made by those most directly affected, rather than by distant authorities that presume to make choices on their behalf. Mothers should receive information about the risks and benefits of different possible approaches to feeding their infants, weigh the alternatives, and make their own decisions.

Under some circumstances, there may be compelling reasons for governments to override individual freedom of choice. For example, there may be situations in which individuals may be quarantined, or compelled to accept examinations or treatments in order to control an epidemic (De Cock, Mbori-Ngacha, and Marum 2002). Currently available evidence does not justify any such coercion in relation to choosing methods of feeding infants of women diagnosed as HIV-positive.

Principles

The position advocated here is that the principles regarding the rights of infants presented in the preceding chapter should continue to apply in the context of HIV/AIDS; they should not be suspended. This means, for example, that even HIV-positive mothers have a right to breast-feed. If any country were to prohibit HIV-positive mothers from breast-feeding, that would violate both their and their infants' human rights.

Particular attention should be given to the obligation to assure that the infants' parents are well informed with regard to their infant feeding choices. This is the major idea underlying the International Code of Marketing of Breastmilk Substitutes (1981; available at http://www.ibfan.org/english/resource/who/fullcode .html). The code does not prohibit marketing or use of formula, but it insists that promotion activities for the products must be conducted in ways that are fair rather than skewed to favor commercial products. Article 24, paragraph 2e, of the Convention on the Rights of the Child goes directly to the point. It calls upon states parties "[t]o ensure that all segments of society, in particular parents and children, are informed, have access to education and are supported in the use of basic knowledge of child health and nutrition, the advantages of breast-feeding, hygiene and environmental sanitation and the prevention of accidents." This is a legally binding obligation on all states parties to the convention (all countries except Somalia and the United States), and a strong moral obligation on those that are not.

These points can be formulated as fundamental principles on the human rights of infants with regard to adequate food where there is significant risk of HIV infection through breast-feeding. These principles, to be added to those listed in the preceding chapter, can be stated as follows:

- Regardless of their HIV status, women are entitled to be informed of the full range of infant feeding alternatives and their advantages and disadvantages in their local circumstances.
- Women in their childbearing years are entitled to accessible voluntary testing and counseling regarding HIV/AIDS. This counseling must include information about the limitations, validity, and meaning of the test, and about the benefits and risks of various feeding alternatives in the local circumstances.
- Testing should be confidential, in the sense that no one apart from the woman herself is entitled to know the results without the woman's consent.
- Women are entitled to expect that their governments will help to make quality feeding alternatives available, including expressed and heated breast milk, or breast milk from others obtained through wet nurses, milk banks, or other comparable arrangements.

- Women are entitled to expect that their governments will seek to obtain and provide unbiased information regarding the benefits and risks of alternative feeding methods in the context of HIV/AIDS.

In other words, as a consequence of the infant's human right to adequate food, parents are entitled to good information about a broad range of feeding alternatives. The right of informed choice implies a right to good information. Women have a right to expect that governments and international agencies will develop that information and deliver it to them. These principles should be considered in preparing policy at the global level, and also in drafting national legislation and national policies relating to HIV/AIDS.

CHAPTER 13

Water

The Household Water Problem

Water serves us in many different ways, as a medium for sanitation, for transport, for irrigation, and for producing fish and other products. Water is an essential component of our diets. This chapter focuses on the simple fact that we must have potable water as part of our bodily intake, and also for sanitation. There are reasonable substitutes for many other things we consume, but there is no substitute for water. Many people find it difficult to get water, and in many cases it is becoming increasingly difficult over time. Water is a central factor in many conflicts, including many conflicts that erupt into violence.

Many people get sick and die because they do not have adequate water. According to the World Health Organization (1999b, 6), an estimated 5.3 percent of all deaths are associated with inadequate water and sanitation. Many women and children in developing countries devote much of their lives to fetching water. It has been estimated that "on average women and children travel 10–15 kilometers, spending eight or more hours per day collecting water and carrying up to 20 kilos or 15 liters per trip" (UNIFEM 2004, 1).

Not only the poorer countries of the world have water problems. It has been estimated that one in seven of the 870 million people in Europe do not have access to safe water, and many who are connected to piped water are supplied irregularly (*The Lancet* 1999).

Many studies of water issues are preoccupied with identifying water-short countries. This neglects the many millions of people who do not have adequate water despite the fact that their countries do have adequate water supplies in the aggregate. Just as in the case of food, we should not rely so much on averages but should focus more on the plight of individuals.

In 1999, the International Committee of the Red Cross published the study *War and Water* as the first in its new Forum series (International Committee of the Red Cross 1999). There is evidence that "contrary to the Geneva Convention, the U.S. government intentionally used sanctions against Iraq to degrade the country's water supply after the Gulf War," contributing to the high postwar mortality among Iraqi children (Nagy 2001). Water politics is a major factor in international politics (Elhance 1999). However, those struggles are mostly over property rights in relation to water. The focus here is on the struggles to realize individuals' human right to adequate water.

We must pay attention not only to the overall availability of water but also to the issue of access. Food and nutrition specialists learned the importance of making this distinction after observing that in many famines, overall food supplies have been adequate, and in some famines exports of food have even increased. As was pointed out in chapter 1, it is now recognized that the hunger problem is due not so much to inadequate food supplies as to failures of entitlements: People cannot make adequate claims on the food around them, mainly because they are too poor (Sen 1981; Drèze and Sen 1989). Often, the same is true for water.

Increasing population leads to increasing pressure on available water supplies. Improved technology in waterworks has generally allowed governments to keep pace by making better use of already accessible water and by drawing water in from broader catchment areas. However, the character of water supply problems is beginning to change. There is a steadily increasing trend toward the privatization of what had been public water supplies:

> In the now-infamous case of Cochabamba, Bolivia, the Government sold off the public water to Aguas del Tunari, a subsidiary of the transnational corporation Bechtel, in 1999. The company immediately announced an increase in water prices by up to 35 per cent, which for many Bolivians meant that water was no longer affordable. . . . A public outcry led to broader civil unrest, and the government declared martial law to control the protests, but finally revoked the water privatization legislation. (United Nations, General Assembly 2003, para. 36)

Privatization results in increased marketing of water both at the high end (bottles of Perrier) and low end (from tank trucks or limited access rivers, lakes, or spigots).

The steady movement toward commodification is indicated by the marketing of bottled water in poor countries. Critics worry that the success of this bottled water among the better-off poor could ease pressure on governments to improve local water infrastructure, to the disadvantage of those who cannot afford even inexpensive bottled water (Beck 1999).

Thus there is concern not only with the shrinkage of the per capita supply of water but also with the movement of whatever supply is available toward those most able to pay for it. Even if there are no wars over water (Postel 1999), the absence of these wars will not mean that everyone gets the water they need.

There are already many good studies on the technical, economic, and political problems of obtaining safe drinking water. Our concern here is the human rights aspects of the issue. The introduction pointed out that a strong distinction should be made between this statement:

> Everyone should have adequate food.

and this one:

Everyone has the right to adequate food.

The meaning of the human right to adequate food is to be found in the difference between these two statements. Taking a similar approach here, consider the following two statements:

Everyone should have adequate water.
Everyone has the right to adequate water.

The first of these statements is wholly transparent and needs no analysis or argument. The task here is to explore the meaning of the second of these statements. It is easy enough to proclaim that water is a human right, but the proclamation is empty—merely a rhetorical flourish—if we do not pursue its implications. What does it mean? Is it in fact true? If water is indeed a human right, what can be done to ensure that all human beings do in fact realize that right?

There is no explicit mention of water in the Universal Declaration of Human Rights and the two covenants. However, article 24 of the Convention on the Rights of the Child says that states parties shall take appropriate measures

(c) [t]o combat disease and malnutrition, including within the framework of primary health care, through, inter alia, the application of readily available technology and through the provision of adequate nutritious foods and clean drinking-water, taking into consideration the dangers and risks of environmental pollution;

In the Convention on the Elimination of All Forms of Discrimination Against Women, article 14 says women have the right

(h) [t]o enjoy adequate living conditions, particularly in relation to housing, sanitation, electricity and water supply, transport and communications.

Although water is not mentioned often in international human rights law, it should be understood that, as in the case of the human right to adequate food, the human right to adequate water does not rest entirely on explicit references to those words. Rather, it rests on a deeper commitment. As was shown in chapter 3, international human rights law explicitly states that all human beings have a right to an adequate standard of living. There can be no doubt that the human right to an adequate standard of living necessarily includes the human right to adequate water.

Water Rights Are Different

As an important element of the human diet, the human right to adequate water takes on many of the characteristics of the human right to adequate food. However, water has two features that distinguish it from other foods. First, water is irreplaceable. There is no adequate substitute for it. It is quite possible to live a long and healthy life without eating, say, fish. Even if you had in the past depended on fish for particular nutrients in your diet, it is at least technically possibly to find other sources of those nutrients. Because it is not essential, one cannot argue that people generally have a human right to eat fish. We do not have human rights to any specific food commodity. However, because water is an essential element in an adequate diet, there is a human right to water.

The second major distinctive feature of water of concern here is the traditional assumption of free or nearly free access to water. Most foods in most societies are distributed through the marketplace. It is understood and accepted that it takes work and effort to produce food, so people generally have to pay for the food they obtain. With regard to water, however, the prevailing assumption in many societies is that it is not a marketed good but is and should remain something to which all people have free, or nearly free, access. The increased privatization of previously open access water supplies and the increasing popularity of bottled water are rapidly undermining that assumption. Thus, though we are comfortable with the idea that the human right to adequate food means access at reasonable prices, we may want to claim that the human right to adequate water means a right to free or nearly free water.

Clearly, there is a cost to providing water. Even if the commodity itself is viewed as free, there is always a cost for delivering it. Waterworks must be built, sometimes at great expense. Measures must be taken to ensure that the water that is delivered, by whatever means, is safe. Because water costs something to provide, and we generally expect it to be provided free or nearly free to the consumer, it follows that there is an expectation that the state, through the government that represents it, will see to making the necessary arrangements. In other words, it is generally assumed that governments have immediate and direct responsibility for ensuring that people under their jurisdiction have access to adequate water. Many of us have come to assume a right to water even if it is not yet articulated as such in our national or local laws.

It is not always necessary for the state to directly subsidize water supplies. An alternative approach is semiprivatization. The state could issue a contract to a semiprivate corporation to run the waterworks, functioning as a public utility. In exchange for this monopoly, it could be required to devise a pricing system through which larger and wealthier users pay higher prices, and thus subsidize the lower prices that are established for poorer users. In this approach, there would be no need for the government to fund the operations through the public treasury. The pricing system could in effect serve as a method of taxation to ensure the realization of the human right to adequate water for all.

Several large corporations, such as Suez, have promoted privatization for the development of water in poor countries. As in the case in Bolivia, the companies often have operated in highly exploitative ways, resulting in increased costs to poor consumers (Center for Public Integrity 2004). Many have now withdrawn, having found that these operations were not sufficiently profitable (Hall 2003a,

2003b; Mestrallet 2002). Nevertheless, the semiprivatization of water, carefully controlled by government, remains a plausible approach. A well-designed system could be self-financing and not require significant capital from outside. While semiprivatization has at times been done badly, it could be done well. It should be designed primarily to ensure that the poor get adequate water, rather than to provide for high levels of profit taking.

General Comment 15

Historically, a great deal of attention has been given to the institutional and legal bases for managing water. There are many analyses of property rights over water, and of state rights to water in the context of international disputes. However, little attention has been given to human rights in these discussions. The UN's Committee on Natural Resources, for example, has given a great deal of attention to property rights relating to water, but it has not considered the human right to adequate water. Similarly, studies on freshwater resources for the UN's Commission on Sustainable Development have not considered the human right to adequate water. International agreements relating to water have not taken notice of the right. The pattern was repeated in the legally binding protocol on water and health that was opened for signature in June 1999 in Europe. There was no mention of the human right to water or to health (United Nations, Economic and Social Council 1999b). Until recently, there has been practically no analysis and no recognition of the human right to water.

The situation has changed. In November 2002, the Committee on Economic, Social, and Cultural Rights issued its *General Comment 15* on the right to water (United Nations, Economic and Social Council 2002b). It formulates clear principles regarding the obligations of states everywhere for the assurance of adequate water supplies to all. It builds on the foundations set out in *General Comment 12* on the right to food, issued in May 1999 (United Nations, Economic and Social Council 1999d).

It would be useful to formulate a framework law at the national level to plainly articulate the human right to adequate water and to ensure its realization. This could be combined with the framework law on the human right to adequate food. In doing this work, it would be useful to study current national and local laws related to water in countries in which there is an explicit right to water, and also those countries in which there is a presumed or implicit right to water. What are the terms under which one's local board of water supply (or equivalent) supplies its customers? What commitments are made regarding the quality of service that will be provided? What mechanisms of complaint are available to consumers who feel they are not getting proper service?

In some cases, there are mechanisms of accountability to higher levels of government. In the United States, for example, the Environmental Protection Agency's 1998 regulations require local water supply agencies to provide annual reports to their customers on the quality of their local drinking water. The annual reports list different possible contaminants, their actual levels, and the maximum level allowed. Though this is good as far as it goes, it is not clear what customers might do if the report is somehow unsatisfactory. Having a right to information about the quality of service is not quite the same as having a right to good service.

Details of the commitments required to ensure the realization of the human right to water will vary according to local circumstances, but they should be based on the principles set out in *General Comment 15*. The essential point is that governments are obligated to ensure that all the people have access to enough water to ensure that they do not get sick or die because water supplies are inadequate in quantity or quality. This can be accomplished in many different ways. Governments must provide water, or provide an enabling environment, so that people can arrange to get adequate water for themselves on reasonable terms.

A major World Water Forum took place in Kyoto, Japan, in March 2003. Human rights advocates were greatly disappointed with the fact that its concluding Ministerial Declaration did not acknowledge the human right to water, especially when this followed so soon after the release of *General Comment 15* on that right (Amnesty International 2003). Other opportunities will have to be found to advance the recognition and realization of the human right to adequate water.

CHAPTER 14

Trade

Issues

Trade (understood here to mean international trade) can produce substantial benefits, but it can also result in various kinds of harm. In particular, though trade in food products frequently strengthens food security, under some circumstances it can harm food security. To illustrate, fish is one of the most highly traded food commodities:

> The developing countries are also taking a growing share of the international trade in fish and fishery products. This may have both benefits and drawbacks. While the exports earn them valuable foreign exchange, the diversion of fish and fish products from local communities and developing regions can deprive needy people, including children, of a traditionally cheap, but highly nutritious food. (Food and Agriculture Organization 2002c, 1)

The possibility of diversion of food products away from the needy is a serious matter. One should also give attention to the distribution of economic benefits. The fact that "developing countries are also taking a growing share of the international trade in fish and fishery products" does not necessarily mean that the poor are getting an increasingly large share of the benefits. In many cases, it is rich countries—or, more important, rich companies—that harvest the benefits, doing it through, but not for, poor countries and poor people.

Export-oriented food production generally works to higher standards of quality and safety. This sometimes results in improvements in the quality of domestic supplies as well. However, the local impacts also can be negative. In Kenya, for example, measures taken to meet the European Union's food safety requirements have resulted in more intermediaries between the fishing areas and the centralized collection points, reducing the incomes to the fishers. The costs of the new safety measures make the final product too expensive for the domestic market. Furthermore,

> the drive to earn foreign exchange means that all resources available to the fisheries sector are spent to meet export market conditions. Little effort goes to setting and enforcing domestic-market standards. Thus, the costs of producing high-quality fish for export largely fall to local communities, while they also bear the cost of consuming unwholesome fish. (Abila 2003, 18)

TABLE 14.1. DIRECTION OF FOOD TRADE
BY VALUE, 1999 (MILLIONS OF DOLLARS)

	DESTINATION	
Origin	Developed Market-Economy Countries	Developing Countries
Developed market-economy countries	211,587 (49.2%)	55,582 (12.9%)
Developing countries	76,850 (17.9%)	56,466 (13.1%)

Note: Centrally planned economies are excluded. *Source*: United Nations Conference on Trade and Development (2001, A-6).

Food trade can harm those who work in food and related industries, especially if they are displaced from their customary employment. It can harm food security in entire communities when it results in deterioration in the quantity or the quality of local food supplies. It can harm the food security of the poor in particular if the foods on which they had depended become unavailable or unacceptably expensive because of trade.

Like everything else in the marketplace, food tends to move toward those who can pay for it. Food follows this pattern both within countries and internationally. Most food trade is between developed countries. There is relatively little trade among developing countries. In the trade between developed and developing countries, on balance the flow of food is from developing to developed: The poor feed the rich (Kent 1982, 2002). Table 14.1 shows the global pattern.

In 1999, the total value of world food trade was $429,648,000,000. Of this, table 14.1 shows that 17.9 percent of it went from developing to developed countries, while 12.9 percent went from developed to developing countries. Thus, in terms of value, developing countries provided 1.4 times as much food to developed countries as developed countries provided to developing countries.

There is a net flow of food from developing to developed countries. Whether this should be viewed as problematic remains a matter for debate. As advocates of the free market would point out, the poor nations are paid for this food, and they would not engage in this production and export unless they saw it as advantageous. More specifically, those who feel the pattern of food trade is not problematic would point out the following:

- A large share of the international trade in food products is composed of high-value products (e.g., shrimp) that are of little interest to consumers in the poorer nations.
- Most food trade is among developed nations.
- Foreign exchange earnings from the export of high-value food products can be used to import much larger volumes of low-cost foods, with a large net nutritional gain.

- There is no systematic evidence that export-oriented nations suffer from higher levels of malnutrition.
- Food trade yields substantial foreign exchange earnings for the exporting nations.

Critics of the trade would raise different points:

- Excessive production for foreign markets can lead to environmental damage, depleting agriculture lands, fish stocks, and water resources.
- Export-oriented food production may divert resources such as labor and capital away from production for local communities.
- Export-oriented food production may interfere with food production for local communities.
- Although earnings from exports conceivably could be used to import cheap food for those most in need, usually they are not used that way. The poor are not the ones who decide how foreign exchange earnings are spent.
- The benefits of trade between parties of uneven power will be distributed unevenly, with the result that the gap between them widens steadily.
- The volume of exports from developing nations, and even the price, may not be a good indicator of the extent to which the people of those nations draw economic benefit from the trade. Many food production operations in developing nations are owned by people from developed nations.
- Excessive promotion of exports can lead to weakening commodity prices, to the disadvantage of exporting nations.

In some ways, both the advocates and the critics of food trade are correct. Increasing foreign exchange earnings is of particular interest to governments and to the rich people within poor nations. When a nation shifts to increasing export orientation in its food production, the benefits are likely to shift from poorer toward rich people within the nation. Thus such a shift can result in a net gain of benefits to the nation as a whole but a net loss to the poor. In principle, it is possible to compensate for this negative effect with transfer payments to those who are harmed. The difficulty is that the poor, being politically weak, have limited ability to press for such transfer payments.

There is an unfortunate tendency to look only at broad patterns while ignoring specific situations, as is illustrated by recent case studies on the relationships between agricultural trade and food security (Food and Agriculture Organization 2000). With highly aggregated studies that look only at broad patterns, it becomes difficult to see that particular kinds of cases may deviate from the dominant pattern. The poor may become worse off even while average incomes go up.

Proposed trade arrangements should be assessed not only for their net economic benefits but also for all their effects, including those on the environment.

There is no reason for a blanket condemnation of food trade, but by the same token the trade should not be promoted indiscriminately, without regard to its impact on food security.

The Human Right to Adequate Food in Relation to Trade

As was shown in chapter 3, the foundation of the human right to adequate food in international law lies in article 11 of the International Covenant on Economic, Social, and Cultural Rights. We repeat that article here, adding emphasis to show its international dimensions:

> 1. The States Parties to the present Covenant recognize the right of everyone to an adequate standard of living for himself and his family, including adequate food, clothing and housing, and to the continuous improvement of living conditions. The States Parties will take appropriate steps to ensure the realization of this right, recognizing to this effect the essential importance of *international co-operation based on free consent.*
> 2. The States Parties to the present Covenant, recognizing the fundamental right of *everyone* to be free from hunger, shall take, individually *and through international co-operation*, the measures, including specific programmes, which are needed:
> (a) to improve methods of production, conservation and distribution of food by making full use of technical and scientific knowledge, by disseminating knowledge of the principles of nutrition and by developing or reforming agrarian systems in such a way as to achieve the most efficient development and utilization of natural resources;
> (b) *taking into account the problems of both food-importing and food-exporting nations, to ensure an equitable distribution of world food supplies in relation to need.*

Paragraph 2, on taking measures through international cooperation, should be read in conjunction with article 28 of the Universal Declaration of Human Rights, which says, "Everyone is entitled to a social and international order in which the rights and freedoms set forth in this Declaration can be fully realized." The last subparagraph, 2(b), makes it clear that countries that have ratified this covenant are obligated to consider the impacts of international trade on food security.

Opening a country to increasing trade is likely to accelerate its economic growth. Often, this means betting on the strong sectors and sacrificing the weaker ones. Though promoting trade may have an overall net positive effect, some are likely to be hurt in the process. Competition is a race that produces losers as well as winners.

The system can work well over time if the losers are able to adapt and find new opportunities, but some may not be able to adapt. Some may simply become worse off. Unlike economics, which generally deals with averages and aggregates, and promises of net future benefits, human rights is concerned with individuals, including those who are hurt by "development" and have meager alternatives. Those who are hurt might be a small minority, but from a human rights perspective, that does not matter. The human rights approach calls for giving attention to individuals and not just to averages.

Reconciling Different Frameworks

The World Trade Organization (WTO) takes the leading role at the global level for overseeing the management of international trade. Its primary mandate is trade liberalization, based on the steady reduction of tariffs and other barriers to free trade. The organization has no substantive powers of its own; rather, it serves to facilitate the implementation of agreements among its member states. The WTO has a comprehensive website (http://www.wto.org), and its publication *Understanding the WTO* (World Trade Organization 2003) provides a good overview of the organization and its operations.

Although the WTO has not given much attention to the issue of food security, it is evident that it places its faith in trade liberalization as the means for achieving food security (World Health Organization and World Trade Organization 2002; Mendoza 2002). As demonstrated by the breakdown of the WTO ministerial meeting at Cancún, Mexico, in September 2003, many critics do not agree that this will work (cf. Madeley 2000a, 2000b; Oxfam 2002; Phillips 2001).

Some argue that the trade framework and the human rights framework are inherently incompatible (Right to Education Project 2003). A good case can be made that human rights takes precedence and that trade should be viewed as a means for the realization of human rights (United Nations, Economic and Social Council 1999a). The tension between trade policy and human rights is especially serious with regard to the human right to adequate food (Ritchie 1999).

Debate over whether one normative framework should take precedence over another is meaningful only to the extent that there are important incompatibilities among them. There can be no doubt that food trade sometimes harms food security. However, on closer examination we see that *at the level of principle* there are no important incompatibilities between the human right to adequate food and present rules regarding trade within the WTO framework. Six concerns need to be noted. First, the Marrakech Agreement, establishing the WTO as the final act of the Uruguay Round of multilateral trade negotiations, made it clear that trade was not to be pursued for its own sake but as a means for development. In the preamble, the parties recognized that "their relations in the field of trade and economic endeavour should be conducted with a view to raising standards of living, ensuring full employment and a large and steadily growing volume of real income and effective demand, and expanding the production of and trade in goods and services, while allowing for the optimal use of the world's resources in accordance with the objective of sustainable development, seeking both to protect and preserve the environment and to enhance the means for doing so in a manner consistent with their respective needs and concerns at different levels of economic development." The parties recognized the need for "positive efforts designed to ensure that developing countries, and especially the least developed among them, secure a share in the growth in international trade commensurate with the needs of their economic development." (World Trade Organization 1996).

Second, the General Agreement on Tariffs and Trade includes article XX, "General Exceptions." The article says:

> Subject to the requirement that such measures are not applied in a manner which would constitute a means of arbitrary or unjustifiable discrimination between countries where the same conditions prevail, or a disguised restriction on international trade, nothing in this Agreement shall be construed to prevent the adoption or enforcement by any contracting party of measures: . . . (b) necessary to protect human, animal or plant life or health.

Surely, food security is necessary to protect human life.

Third, at the WTO's ministerial meeting at Doha in 2001, it was agreed that "special and differential treatment for developing countries shall be an integral part of all elements of the negotiations . . . to enable developing countries to effectively take account of their development needs, including food security and rural development" (World Trade Organization 2001). Work on the Framework Agreement on Special and Differential Treatment is under way in WTO.

Fourth, decision making in WTO is supposed to be by consensus. Fifth, the fundamental principle of national sovereignty remains intact. The WTO is not supposed to be a world government. Membership in the WTO is optional; it is possible to withdraw if participation is viewed as harmful. And sixth, the WTO framework is only one of several relevant normative frameworks. There is no reason to assume that its perspectives must prevail over all others.

A study titled *Human Rights and Trade*, prepared by the Office of the UN High Commissioner for Human Rights for the WTO Ministerial Conference in Cancún, explained that, in terms of law,

> all WTO Members have undertaken obligations under international human rights law. This means that WTO Members should promote and protect human rights in the processes of negotiating and implementing trade law and policy. For example, of 146 members of the WTO, all have ratified at least one human rights instrument. 113 WTO Members have ratified the International Covenant on Economic, Social and Cultural Rights (ICESCR) and all but one have ratified the Convention on the Rights of the Child. Further, those areas of human rights law recognized as customary international law take on universal application, which means that trade rules should be interpreted as consistent with those norms and standards whatever the treaty commitments of States in trade matters. (United Nations, Office of the High Commissioner for Human Rights 2003, 4)

At the level of principle, wto rules and human rights standards are wholly compatible. However, principle and political realities are different matters. The excessive and trade-distorting use of agricultural subsidies, for example, does not result from wto principles. Pressures of various kinds have been put on developing countries to comply with the wishes of developed countries in the wto, so the decision-making process has not been open and democratic in practice (United Nations Development Program 2002, 118–121; Jawara and Kwa 2003). The point here is that the *principles* on which the wto was founded do allow national governments to assert control over their food security situations.

The possibility for developing countries to stand up to the developed countries was indicated by Brazil's challenge to the United States' heavy subsidization of its cotton farmers. Brazil claimed this drove down world cotton prices and thus made it increasingly difficult for cotton producers in Brazil, West Africa, and elsewhere to make a living. In April 2004, a wto panel issued an interim report supporting Brazil. Though Brazil had the strength to challenge the United States, one cannot imagine Benin, Burkina Faso, or Mali doing so.

Power differentials have a great impact on trade. Some poor countries seem to imagine that they can become players in the world trading game if they just agree to join the wto and lower their trade barriers. However, rich countries with a far greater capacity to reach outward are likely to gain far more benefit from liberalized trade. It is the rich that will penetrate the poor; not the other way around. In the 1990s, when Haiti removed its restrictions on agriculture imports, it was flooded with subsidized rice from the United States. What could Haiti do about it? Relative power has a strong impact on international trade, but that is not because wto principles say that it should, and it is not something that originates with the wto. The difficulties arise not out of the wto's stated principles but out of the fact that in practice the wto serves the strong much more than it serves the weak. This follows from the simple fact that open trade is of greatest benefit to those that have the greatest capacity to take advantage of it.

It is possible to imagine new and different rules for trade that would level the playing field somewhat (Hines 2004). However, the prospects for the adoption of such proposals will remain slim until the weaker countries assert themselves more decisively.

Food Sovereignty

The views of trade advocates and of those who are concerned with the human right to adequate food may be reconciled through appreciation of the principle of *food sovereignty*. National sovereignty has been the fundamental principle of the nation-state system since the Treaty of Westphalia of 1648. Sovereignty means that all nation-states are equal in the eyes of the law; there is no legal authority above nation-states, except with their consent; and outsiders may not interfere in their internal affairs without their consent. In their international relations, states are represented by their national governments. Sovereignty is based on the premise that normally national governments are the best judges of what is good for their people.

An essential component of national sovereignty is food sovereignty. Though various interpretations of the concept have been proposed, the core element is that all national governments have a permanent responsibility for their nation's food security. Because national governments have a fundamental legal and moral obligation to ensure their people's food security, they must have the right to make their own decisions on food security. That responsibility cannot be relinquished through, or overridden by, international agreements of any kind.

The issues can be illustrated by the dumping of heavily subsidized corn from the United States into Mexico under the aegis of the North American Free Trade Agreement (NAFTA). This has hurt small-scale corn producers in Mexico, who cannot compete with the subsidized corn that comes in from the north. Their income has fallen so sharply that their food security has declined (Audley et al. 2003; Oxfam 2003). Some observers blame NAFTA itself. However, it is important to recognize that the government of Mexico accepted NAFTA because it anticipated considerable gains from exporting other kinds of goods to Canada and the United States.

It is reasonable for national governments to make international agreements that produce some harm to one sector if that is outweighed by large gains in another sector. Of course, some enterprises and individuals may be hurt in the process. In some cases, it might be possible to shift people and resources around so that, apart from temporary dislocations, most people end up better off. However, we know that the reality is that many people are not able to adjust by changing jobs or learning new skills. Under changing economic arrangements, some people are marginalized. The change that benefits some sectors of the economy may result in serious harm to other sectors. National trade policy should be based on the premise that it will do no sustained harm to the very poor. Trade liberalization should not come at the expense of the poor. It should be for the benefit of the poor.

When governments make deals in a way that results in substantial deterioration in food security, that action violates the human right to adequate food. Such deals might be acceptable if the government took measures to ensure that those who were harmed were adequately compensated or were effectively supported in shifting to other means of livelihood. However, if this is not done, the government violates the human rights of the poor. The obligation to respect and protect the people's human right to adequate food falls primarily on their national governments, not on any international organizations.

Although the primary responsibility rests with national governments, international organizations do have obligations to act in support of the human right to adequate food and all other human rights. This will be discussed more fully in chapter 17.

CHAPTER 15

Refugees

What are the obligations of the international community with regard to humanitarian assistance? This question is explored here specifically with reference to refugees and in broader terms in the following chapter.

Although many countries use their own definition in their immigration laws, the most widely accepted definition of a refugee is that provided in the Convention Relating to the Status of Refugees of 1951 and its Protocol of 1967:

> [A]ny person who ... owing to well-founded fear of being persecuted for reasons of race, religion, nationality, membership of a particular social group or political opinion, is outside the country of his [or her] nationality and is unable or, owing to such fear, is unwilling to avail himself [or herself] of the protection of that country.

The issue of the international community's obligations to assist the needy may be seen with special clarity in relation to refugees because, by definition, refugees are not under the protection of their home states.

Human rights law implies that the nations of the world have obligations to refugees, but these obligations are not very concrete. There is a need for clarification, not only with reference to the obligations of particular states (e.g., the state of first asylum) but also with regard to the obligations of the international community taken as a whole.

Issues in Refugee Nutrition

There is a Refugee Nutrition Information System in place, established in 1993, that is managed by the United Nations System Standing Committee on Nutrition. This system provides an analytical framework and periodic data on nutrition status that can be used as the basis for work on the human right to adequate food as it applies to refugees. Its reports may be found at the commission's website (http://www.unsystem.org/scn/Publications/html/rnis.html).

Although these data clearly show that refugees suffer from serious and sustained nutrition problems, they do not lay out all the dimensions of the problem. In one refugee camp, for example, it was found that unaccompanied minors had very low cash incomes and were therefore obliged to sell a portion of their rations in order to obtain other needed items. The result was that many of them faced acute hunger (Save the Children Fund UK 1997).

In 1999, a *Los Angeles Times* story titled "Relief Camps for Africans, Kosovars Worlds Apart" highlighted "the enormous difference between the newly sprouted camps in Europe and existing facilities in Africa" (Miller and Simmons 1999). It reported:

> The Office of the U.N. High Commissioner for Refugees is spending about 11 cents a day per refugee in Africa. In the Balkans, the figure is $1.23, more than 11 times greater. Some refugee camps in Africa have one doctor for every 100,000 refugees. In Macedonia, camps have as many as one doctor per 700 refugees—a ratio far better than that of many communities in Los Angeles.

The *Times* article noted the differences in food supplies:

> World Food Program officials say both European and African refugees are getting about 2,100 calories a day of food rations. But for the Kosovo Albanians, those calories come in the form of tins of chicken pate, foil-wrapped cheeses, fresh oranges and milk. In some ready-made meals, there is even coffee and fruit tarts. . . . That contrasts with Africa, where refugees are far less likely to get ready-made meals and have to make most of their food from scratch—a practice reflecting the simpler lifestyles of the area, say U.N. officials. Instead of meals, the refugees are given basic grains such as sorghum or wheat.

The major issues, then, are the many instances of inadequacy of nutrition services for refugees, and beyond that, the question of whether these services are provided in ways that are just.

Explanations and Justifications for Uneven Services

Having established that there was an enormous difference between the treatment of refugees in Europe and Africa, the *Los Angeles Times*'s writers try to explain it:

> The most common explanation for the gap in resources is culture. U.N. officials and aid workers say they must give European refugees used to cappuccino and CNN a higher standard of living to maintain the refugees' sense of dignity and stability. (Miller and Simmons 1999)

The writers then acknowledge that it may be a matter of racial discrimination:

> Others offer a blunter assessment: They say wealthy donors in the developed world and the aid agencies they support feel more sympathy—and reach deeper into their pockets—for those with similar skin tones and backgrounds. Andrew Ross, a refugee worker who came from Africa to the Balkans last month, called the camps in Macedonia "far superior" to those in Africa. "What's the difference?" Ross asked. "There's white people here."

Some suggest that the differences in treatment are both explained and justified by the differences in the refugees' prior living standards:

In Africa, where many refugees eke out an existence in seminomadic tribes, the bare provisions of shelter and health care offered by the refugee camps are a step up in life for many. But in Europe, where many of the refugees from Kosovo, a southern province of Serbia, the main Yugoslav republic, had two cars, a city apartment and their own business, a night in a canvas tent with cold food is misery. "You've got to maintain people's dignity," said Bob Allen, a camp manager who has worked in both Africa and Europe for the relief agency CARE. "The life in Africa is far more simple. To maintain the dignity and lifestyle of Europeans is far more difficult."

This reference to dignity resonates with human rights thinking. It suggests that in assuring the right to an adequate livelihood, "adequate" may have to be understood differently in different circumstances.

The justification for providing no more than simple, traditional African food to the Africans and richer western meals to the westerners might be tested by imagining that both groups would be offered both kinds of meals. If the Africans consistently chose the African food and the westerners consistently chose the western food, then the cultural argument would be vindicated. But if, given the opportunity, the Africans chose the western foods, that would suggest that they had traditionally consumed the African diet out of necessity, not out of choice. To make up for the Africans' prior deprivation, maybe it would be fairer to feed the westerners with simple grains, while providing richer meals to the Africans! Of course both groups might be healthier with the simpler diet, but that is another matter.

Should those who are used to having more get more in emergency situations? Before answering too quickly, we should recall that in many assistance programs in developed countries, emergency assistance is explicitly designed to allow people to maintain the lifestyle to which they had been accustomed. A middle-class person who loses his home in a fire will get various forms of assistance that are not made available to homeless people.

Also, it might be argued that richer people should get more generous assistance because their countries probably have contributed more to the supply of resources used for assistance. A contrary argument would be that richer people in trouble should get less from the global agencies because they have better prospects for getting help from other sources.

Maybe it does cost less to save poor people. Does this mean we should spend less on them, or does it perhaps means that we should save more of them? It is not clear what arguments should prevail. Moreover, it is not clear who should decide what arguments prevail. Should the donors dominate the policymaking as to how humanitarian assistance is to be allocated? Should the receivers of assistance be represented in policymaking? The discrimination among different categories of refugees may arise not from the assistance agencies themselves but from the donors behind them who supply the resources:

> All the attention focused on the Balkans has frightened refugee officials and charity groups in Africa, who fear that the continent's already meager resources will be further drained by the Balkan crisis. For instance, the World Food Program has a fund-raising goal this year of $98.5 million for the area around Africa's Great Lakes—Rwanda, Burundi, Tanzania, Uganda—where long-simmering, though often ignored, conflicts have created hundreds of thousands of refugees. So far, the food agency has received 22% of that amount. In Liberia, the situation is even worse. The agency made an appeal for $71.6 million. It received $500,000. That compares with the situation around Kosovo, for which the agency has requested $97.4 million and received more than 70% of that amount already, with a "large number of commitments" now under negotiation, Davies said. "Africa is just being eclipsed by this," said Fitzgerald of Refugees International. Refugees in Eritrea "are just being ignored for the large part because of Kosovo," she said. "Everybody is focused on Kosovo, because it's a serious situation, and because of peer pressure." (Miller and Simmons 1999)

How should donated food be distributed? In the abstract, we might imagine a large-scale funneling operation in which there is first an allocation to continents, then to host countries, then to camps, and then to individual persons within camps. At each stage, there would be a question of what allocation mechanisms and principles are in fact in place, and what mechanisms and principles should be in place. On the principle that those with equal needs should get equal assistance, the first-order guideline might be that all refugees should get equal rations. However, it would quickly be seen that other considerations must be taken into account as well. Some people have greater needs than others. Some resourceful individuals are able to provide for themselves, at least in part. Some camps or some individuals may not be accessible. Corrections may have to be made for unauthorized redistribution that occurs within camps. And so on.

Of course, this funneling-down image is not appropriate because there is not one central pool of resources to be allocated. Most donor contributions are tied contributions, in the sense that they are designated ("earmarked") for particular situations. Donors might not be willing to contribute as much if they did not get to decide where their contributions would be used. Donor bias may be an accurate *explanation* of the skewed distribution of assistance, but it need not be accepted as a *justification* for those facts.

Even where good clear standards are set regarding appropriate food supplies and nutrition-related services, these standards frequently remain unmet. The reasons are described succinctly by Mears and Young (1998, 16–17): "The reasons for gaps in supply and shortfalls in rations received are manifold and often context-specific. However, the more important causes can be grouped as follows":

- Restricted access to the affected population for reasons of remote locations, insufficient infrastructure (roads, transport networks, etc.), seasonal closures, and possible insecurity.
- Lack of resources and variable donor commitment.
- Disagreement over accuracy of beneficiary numbers linked with registration.
- Erratic distribution system.
- Erratic monitoring of distribution and complaints.

Donor countries provide much of the food supplied to refugees, either through direct commodity supplies or through the provision of funds to purchase foods on local markets. In addition, there is considerable self-provisioning by resourceful individual refugees. Self-provisioning may be based on gardening, raising small animals, or purchasing food in local markets. Trading outside of refugee camps can increase or decrease the total food supply within them.

The Human Right to Adequate Food

Although refugees are not under the protection of their home governments, in principle they retain all their human rights. The obligation to ensure their realization falls on the international community, taken as a whole. The international community is obligated to act to ensure the realization of the human rights of refugees in much the same way as states are obligated to act to ensure the realization of the human rights of all people living under their jurisdictions.

How these obligations ought to be carried out is not yet clear. Refugees' human right to adequate food derives from the more general human right to adequate food described throughout this book. This right must be understood and then interpreted in accordance with the particular circumstances of refugees.

Like all other human rights, the human right to adequate food should be recognized and realized because it is the right thing to do. However, taking the human rights approach can also provide "value added." The Office of the UN High Commissioner for Refugees (UNHCR) has articulated benefits that are of particular importance in relation to refugees (Jessen-Petersen 1999, 33): "UNHCR fully favours the adoption of a rights-based approach in the refugee protection and assistance context. Its added value lies in the fact that a rights-based approach":

- Ensures that humanitarian action is based on the rights of the beneficiaries and is not simply a gratuitous act of charity.

- Calls for treating the refugee as an "active claimant" and not merely a "passive recipient," thereby giving the refugee a voice and power with which to participate to seek to meet their own basic needs.
- Underlines the legal obligations of states to meet the basic needs of the most vulnerable individuals (including refugees), and ensures that the work of humanitarian agencies such as UNHCR provides support to states in fulfilling their responsibilities, rather than being a substitute for state action (or inaction).
- Helps provide a principled, predictable, and structured framework within which humanitarian work can be undertaken and this, in turn, will help to define both the objective and content of humanitarian aid more clearly—particularly in the development and implementation of policy and programs.
- Places humanitarian action within a rights-based framework which serves to define more clearly the respective areas of expertise and the responsibilities of the many different humanitarian actors (e.g., UNHCR and the World Food Program have signed a memorandum of understanding which covers cooperation in the provision of food aid to refugees, returnees and, in specific situations, internally displaced persons).
- Provides a stronger incentive for donor support for humanitarian efforts as traditional donor States (and their constituencies) often have a well-developed awareness of human rights as a basis for government action and by moving the debate away from charity (where the usual arguments of compassion fatigue and prioritization are invoked) to the language of rights and duties, the imperative for donor support can be made more forcefully.

Food and nutrition programs for refugees could be designed to more explicitly acknowledge their human right to adequate food. Such programs might be more efficient and effective than current ones. But even if they were not more efficient and effective, as a matter of principle, it is important that rights of refugees in regard to adequate food and other matters are clarified and honored.

The Adequacy Question

In studying the human right to adequate food, we must ask about the meaning of *adequate*. Basic standards for nutrition have been worked out in several different contexts. Some focus on food requirements, while others consider food as only one part of a broader set of services. Food-based standards take forms such as recommended daily allowances. In contrast, a broader, service-based set of standards is illustrated by the "nutrition minimum package" for children designed by the program called BASICS—Basic Support for Institutionalized

Child Survival (Sanghvi and Murray 1997). The Sphere Project has formulated detailed minimum standards for nutrition and food aid in humanitarian assistance (Sphere Project 2000). For refugees in particular, the World Food Program and UNHCR (1999) have established *Guidelines for Calculating Food Rations for Refugees.*

Biologically, the basic *nutrient* requirements are roughly the same for all human beings of about the same size. Thus, it might seem that what constitutes "adequate food" could be addressed as a purely technical question, with answers differentiated only on the basis of data on the individual's age, gender, and body weight. Standards for refugees might reasonably be adapted from other sectors such as the military (Committee on Military Nutrition Research 1999). The concern with establishing basic minimum standards on the basis of technical considerations alone leads naturally to the design of some sort of standardized meal that could be packaged in a factory and distributed in mass quantities. Thus we now have the standard Humanitarian Daily Ration, comparable to the U.S. military's "Meals Ready to Eat."

This purely technical perspective is much too narrow. Human rights advocates recognize that the feedlot approach to nutrition violates human dignity. It fails to recognize that food is only one element in the broader context of the human right to an adequate livelihood, and that right in turn is embedded in the entire human rights framework. The human right to adequate food must be realized in a way that does not violate the individual's other human rights. *General Comment 12*'s paragraph 7 acknowledges that "the precise meaning of 'adequacy' is to a large extent determined by prevailing social, economic, cultural, climatic, ecological and other conditions" (United Nations, Economic and Social Council 1999d). Paragraph 8 explains that the core content of the right to adequate food implies:

> The availability of food in a quantity and quality sufficient to satisfy the dietary needs of individuals, free from adverse substances, and acceptable within a given culture; The accessibility of such food in ways that are sustainable and that do not interfere with the enjoyment of other human rights. (United Nations, Economic and Social Council 1999d)

These elements are explained further in *General Comment 12*'s subsequent paragraphs. Paragraph 11, for example, explains, "Cultural or consumer acceptability implies the need also to take into account, as far as possible, perceived non-nutrient-based values attached to food and food consumption."

Thus, there is no suggestion that all individuals—or all refugees—must be treated identically. There is a difference between treating people equitably (fairly) and treating them identically. Hardly anyone would argue that everyone should be paid the same regardless of what work they do, but we should all insist that people are treated equitably with, for example, equal pay for equal work. Making everyone eat the same thing (as in a prison) might be equal treatment, but it would be far more equitable and dignified to recognize that there are differences among people, and give them all some appropriate choices.

There is a serious practical problem that would arise if all refugees were treated identically. If refugees everywhere were to be provided with the same standard of service—somewhere between that provided to the Europeans and that provided to the Africans—there would be enormous management problems. Europeans would be dissatisfied. In Africa, people might rush to be identified as refugees and try to get into refugee camps because that would make them materially better off than they had been. Because people and their circumstances differ, there is no reason to believe that treating everyone identically, regardless of their circumstances, would contribute to maintaining reasonable standards of human dignity. The answer must lie somewhere between the highly skewed treatment described in the *Los Angeles Times* story and the mechanistic ideal of treating everyone the same, without consideration of their particular circumstances.

A human rights approach to the design of programs for the nutrition of refugees could be based on the guidelines for infant feeding in emergencies proposed by the Emergency Nutrition Network (Ad Hoc Group on Infant Feeding in Emergencies 1998). The World Health Organization's manual *Management of Severe Malnutrition* is generally useful, and its chapter 8 provides suggestions specifically for the management of malnutrition in disaster situations and refugee camps (World Health Organization 1999a).

In setting standards of adequacy, the focus should be more on the results obtained than on the character of the inputs. That is, instead of concentrating narrowly on food supplies and nutrition status, consideration should be given to the broader concept of adequate livelihood. A basic measure here would be survival. The core objective of food and nutrition programs for refugees should be to minimize morbidity and mortality associated with malnutrition. The level of nutrition-related services required to achieve this should be viewed as the minimum requirement.

From this perspective, any enhancement of nutrition-related services beyond the level that would reduce morbidity and mortality could be viewed as a luxury. Because European refugees would not die if they were not given fruit tarts, perhaps they should not be given fruit tarts. Of course, if they found a way to bake or buy tarts with the basic resources provided to them, that would be their choice to make.

The concern here is with the minimum obligations of the international community and its representatives, such as the World Food Program, UNHCR, and the International Federation of Red Cross and Red Crescent Societies. Other parties might want to provide extra rations for particular refugees because of cultural affinities, shared religions, kinship, or other reasons. They should be free to do so. For example, in the humanitarian assistance it provides, Saudi Arabia should be free to favor other Muslim countries. But that assistance should be provided

directly rather than through global intergovernmental organizations such as
UNHCR and the World Food Program. The intergovernmental agencies should be
obligated to provide assistance without discrimination based on the recipients'
religious, cultural, or other characteristics.

The adequacy issue may be further clarified by posing a dilemma. Suppose
that the cheapest way to provide the basic nutrients that would keep people alive
is through mass-produced pellets, optimized in the way an animal feedlot manager would calculate the most cost-effective mix of feed components. Deviating
from this standardized pellet to accommodate special needs would be costly. If
the money available for food is limited, we face a hard question: Should we dis-
tribute the pellets to as many needy people as possible, thus maximizing the
number of lives saved? Or should we accommodate special needs, allowing people to live with at least some measure of human dignity, even if that means fewer
lives are saved?

My answer is to refuse to accept this formulation of the problem. With appropriate enabling conditions, people are producers of food and not just consumers. People are smarter and more industrious than cattle. People must be respected and treated as capable human beings. Instead of investing effort into
designing the best possible pellet, we should be finding ways to enable people to
move progressively toward providing for themselves as they would in a normal,
healthy society. As was argued in chapter 3, moving toward feedlot types of operations moves us toward the wrong kind of governance, whether in refugee camps
or in other social situations. Though highly standardized rations might be sensible for a short period in acute crisis situations, creating sustained dependency on
feed pellets or prepackaged rations would disempower people. In all circumstances, people must be treated in ways that empower then.

Although there are serious problems of obtaining and allocating scarce resources, some of what is required is not so scarce. Nutrition status depends not
only on food supplies but also on health services and on care, especially for children. For small children, who are most vulnerable to malnutrition, the critical issue may not be food supply as such but the supply of appropriate health and care
services. For example, conditions supportive of proper breast-feeding can make
a very big difference. Refugees themselves can participate in the production,
preparation, and distribution of food, and they can participate in the delivery of
health and care services. In other words, refugees themselves can be viewed as
assets, as resources for addressing the issues of concern to them.

Specifying the Obligations

Useful guidance for the management of humanitarian assistance has already
been provided in various forms. For example, *The Fundamental Principles of the
International Red Cross and Red Crescent Movement* (International Federation of
Red Cross and Red Crescent Societies 1996a) speaks of the principles of hu-

manity, impartiality, neutrality, independence, voluntary service, unity, and universality. There is also the *Code of Conduct for the International Red Cross and Red Crescent Movements and NGOs in Disaster Relief* (International Federation of Red Cross and Red Crescent Societies 1994). A great deal of work has already been done to specify appropriate nutrition standards in humanitarian assistance programs.

Specifying what food and nutrition services refugees ought to get is useful, but more than that is required to ensure the actual realization of their human right to adequate food. There is a need for appropriate and effective institutional arrangements. The different pieces can be brought together systematically through the explicit use of the rights framework. As was indicated above, any rights system has three distinct parties: the rights holders, the duty bearers, and the agents of accountability. The task of the agents of accountability is to make sure that those who have the duties carry out their obligations to those who have the rights.

Specifying what refugees ought to get, perhaps framed as minimum standards, is not enough. It is also necessary to establish institutional arrangements that will ensure that the standards are met. The specific obligations of the host state and of the international community must be spelled out, and suitable accountability mechanisms must be put in place.

Careful distinctions must be made between the obligations of host states and the obligations of the international community. In general, host states are obligated to recognize the rights of refugees as equivalent to the rights of others under their jurisdiction. Because many host states have a limited capacity to provide the resources needed for refugees or for their own people, the international community must be viewed as the backup, the provider of last resort.

The rights and the corresponding obligations need to be concretized. For example, the position taken might be that "every refugee has a right to consume at least 1,900 calories per day" or "every refugee under five years of age has a right to be at least 80 percent of his or her standard weight." If the international community accepts this, it is then obligated to do whatever needs to be done to ensure the realization of that right.

Both the host state and the international community have four levels of obligation with regard to refugees' human right to adequate food. The following reproduces the characterization of these obligations provided by *General Comment 12*, but it adds, in capital letters, a few words to highlight the role of the international community:

- *respect*—"The obligation to respect existing access to adequate food requires States Parties AND THE INTERNATIONAL COMMUNITY not to take any measures that result in preventing such access."
- *protect*—"The obligation to *protect* requires measures by the State AND THE INTERNATIONAL COMMUNITY to ensure that enterprises or individuals do not deprive individuals of their access to adequate food."

- *fulfil (facilitate)*—"The obligation to *fulfil (facilitate)* means the State AND THE INTERNATIONAL COMMUNITY must pro-actively engage in activities intended to strengthen people's access to and utilization of resources and means to ensure their livelihood, including food security."
- *fulfil (provide)*—"Finally, whenever an individual or group is unable, for reasons beyond their control, to enjoy the right to adequate food by the means at their disposal, States AND THE INTERNATIONAL COMMUNITY have the obligation to *fulfil (provide)* that right directly. This obligation also applies for persons who are victims of natural or other disasters."

It must be emphasized that the words in capital letters are not in *General Comment 12*. They have been added here and are open to discussion.

Limiting the Obligations

The international governmental agencies that assist refugees are constrained because they only pass through resources provided by donors; they have no resources of their own. The obligations fall ultimately on the nations of the world, not on the agents that administer the resources. In time, it may be feasible to create a form of international taxation so that all members of the international community contribute their fair share. However, if taxation is not feasible, the question is whether donors would be willing to make concrete long-term commitments, accepting them as obligations. Are the donor nations of the world willing to commit themselves to, say, ensuring that all refugees will have at least some specified quantity and quality of food and some basic package of services?

It is possible for international commitments to be open-ended. With regard to security issues, for example, the UN Security Council frequently authorizes members to "take all necessary measures" to achieve a given objective. With regard to issues of humanitarian assistance, however, the international community tends to be more cautious. Those who are obligated to assure the realization of rights will resist if there is no clear limit to those obligations. For example, if a commitment were made to provide 1,900 calories a day to all refugees, and there were no fixed limit to the number of refugees, that would be an open-ended commitment. Entitlements must somehow be capped. Entitlements to food or to nutrition services should be stated in terms of concrete rules specifying what categories of people are entitled to what sort of goods and services under what conditions. There must be clarity not only with regard to their entitlements but also with regard to their limits.

Whether or not the donors are willing to make firm commitments, the agencies could adopt human rights principles to guide the allocation of whatever resources are available to them. For example, it could be said that no matter what total amount of food is provided to a particular camp, each individual in the camp is entitled to a share of it, or that children must have their needs fulfilled before others.

The objective of a rights-based approach to assistance is not necessarily to demand that more resources should be provided. Rights are also important to ensure that whatever resources are available are used effectively for meeting needs. The argument to the donors is that under this approach they would not necessarily be spending more; they would be spending better. The human right to adequate food can provide a means for introducing effective performance accountability and thus for increasing the efficiency and effectiveness of refugee nutrition programs.

The Work Ahead

It would be useful to have a clear statement of principles or guidelines regarding refugees' human right to adequate food, the obligations of host states and the international community, and the mechanisms of accountability. This should be worked out with participation from representatives of the refugees themselves, the assistance agencies (both governmental and nongovernmental), the donor agencies, and human rights agencies. To launch the effort, guidance should be drawn not only from international human rights law but also from the different statements of principle that have been formulated to guide humanitarian assistance activities.

In a very preliminary way, we can suggest some of the basic principles to be considered. For example, there should be a principle of nondiscrimination. This does not mean that everyone should be treated identically. Rather, it means that no groups should be singled out to be treated in ways that are harmful to them or that put them at a disadvantage. To the extent feasible, assistance should be provided through means that are empowering and that respect the dignity of those who receive that assistance. Nutrition services, and not just food, should be provided in culturally appropriate ways.

The helplessness that appears to overwhelm many refugees comes in part from the ways in which they are treated (Soguk 1999). As in any normal society, refugees themselves should have ample and steadily increasing opportunities to participate in providing their own food and meeting their other needs. Means must be found to increasingly involve refugees themselves in making the decisions and taking the actions that affect their situations.

Human rights work means much more than setting standards. There is a need to acknowledge that refugees have specific human rights in relation to food. The corresponding obligations should be plainly identified, and there should be a system for holding accountable those who carry the obligations. Most important, refugees themselves should know to what services they are entitled, and they or their representatives should have effective means for holding those responsible to account. Where there are no effective remedies, there are no effective rights.

Refugees' human right to adequate food, and indeed all the human rights of refugees, are not special. Refugees are not a distinct species with distinct incapacities. Their circumstances of the moment may be special, but their rights as human beings are not. They are entitled to the same things as everyone else who is human, and this means they have a right to live a life that is as normal as possible. They must be enabled to grasp increasing control over the shape of their own lives. They must be increasingly enabled to provide for themselves.

The primary obligation for ensuring the realization of human rights rests with the state. When that obligation is not or cannot be carried out, for whatever reason, specific obligations then fall on the international community. These obligations of the international community with regard to human rights need to be acknowledged, clarified, and carried out.

CHAPTER 16

International Humanitarian Assistance

Issues

Refugees, discussed in the preceding chapter, represent just one type of situation in which people desperately need help. Many people around the world suffer as a result of armed conflict, genocide, exploitation, and disasters of different kinds. In many cases, the international community provides humanitarian assistance in the form of food, health care, and shelter to alleviate their suffering. The system under which international humanitarian assistance (IHA) is provided has become increasingly effective, significantly reducing the misery. However, there is room for improvement, especially with regard to the targeting of IHA. In a world full of people with many different kinds of needs, where should the resources that are available for humanitarian assistance be used? Who should be helped? It is argued here that the system for providing international humanitarian assistance would be more effective if it were based on application of human rights principles. In certain circumstances, some people should be recognized as having specific rights to assistance.

The concern here is not with the radical social change that might be needed to prevent suffering in the world but rather with the need to relieve suffering immediately. Humanitarian assistance is about symptomatic relief, not about trying to get at the roots of problems. The premise is that while we work to forecast and prevent future crises, we should not neglect the many severe crises that are currently ongoing.

At the global level, the lead agency for IHA is the United Nations Office for Coordination of Humanitarian Assistance, formerly the Department of Humanitarian Affairs. Other global organizations are also heavily involved, such as the Office of the United Nations High Commissioner for Refugees, the United Nations Children's Fund, and the World Food Program. The International Committee of the Red Cross plays a major role in armed-conflict situations. Many international nongovernmental organizations, such as CARE and Médecins Sans Frontières, are actively involved. Several countries are major donors of humanitarian assistance, donating both directly and through international governmental and civil society organizations. In the United States, the lead agency is the Bureau for Humanitarian Response, and under it, the Office of Foreign Disaster Assistance, in the U.S. Agency for International Development.

Recent global data on contributions for humanitarian assistance may be found through ReliefWeb's Financial Tracking System (http://www.reliefweb.int/fts).

These data show that the United States is by far the largest donor, contributing about $800 million in 2003, more than a third of the total of just over $2 billion contributed by all donors. About one-fifth of the total assistance that was provided by the United States—about $160 million—came in the form of food commodities (U.S. Department of Agriculture 2003b).

The primary multilateral agency providing food assistance is the World Food Program. Up to October 2003, its donors contributed a total of $2.1 billion for the year, not counting the Oil-for-Food Program operations in Iraq. However, about 16 percent of the projected needs for 2003 remained unmet (World Food Program 2003, 5).

The amount provided by the United States is very generous when compared with the amounts provided by other donors. However, the perspective changes when one compares its contributions with the United States' defense budget of about $400 billion. When foreign aid is measured as a proportion of gross national product, the U.S. contribution is lower than that of many other developed countries. Some say this is misleading because the United States provides large amounts of aid through private, nongovernmental channels (Adelman 2003). However, considerations other than need are more likely to intrude when assistance is private rather than public. Private assistance is more likely to be discriminatory and uneven.

Not all foreign assistance is humanitarian. Humanitarian assistance is defined here as *assistance whose primary motivation is to provide relief for people in situations of extreme need*. It can be provided by individuals, local and national governments, and international governmental and civil society organizations. International humanitarian assistance may be supplied either by private agencies (civil society organizations) or by governmental (public) agencies. Governmental agencies often work with and through civil society organizations, sometimes on a contractual basis.

Frequently, the humanitarian motivation is mixed with other motivations. Humanitarian assistance may be used not only to respond to urgent needs but also to strengthen political alliances or to increase sales of domestic products. Governments may provide international food aid not only to help others but also to provide an outlet for the nation's agricultural surpluses, and thus provide assistance to their agricultural sectors. It may be used to promote particular political or ideological positions. For example, the Food for Progress program under the U.S. Public Law 480 program "is used to support countries that have made commitments to introduce or expand free enterprise elements in their agricultural economies" (U.S. Department of Agriculture 2003b, 1).

In some cases, humanitarian motivations may be claimed to justify actions motivated in other ways. Nevertheless, no matter how difficult it may be to discern in concrete situations, humanitarian assistance is understood here as action driven primarily by compassion, by concern for the well-being of others who are in extreme need.

Foreign assistance agencies sometimes count humanitarian assistance as a subcategory of development assistance, but it is useful to distinguish the two. Humanitarian assistance is mainly about directly meeting extreme human needs, especially (though not exclusively) in the short term. In contrast, development assistance is mainly about economic benefits, usually in the long term, designed to help build economic self-sufficiency. Humanitarian assistance generally is based on delivering immediate benefits in the form of food, medicine, or shelter.

Some analysts suggest that development assistance is humanitarian because "economic growth is bound to trickle down to the poor and the disadvantaged" (Human Rights Council of Australia 1995, 7). However, in many development assistance efforts, economic growth is the primary motivation, and the "trickle down"—if there is any—is incidental. Development assistance projects are assessed primarily in economic terms.

Resources are limited, so choices must be made among different situations in which assistance might be offered. There is little explicit guidance as to where IHA resources should be used. Assistance is now provided in some situations and not in other seemingly comparable situations.

The International Federation of the Red Cross says "relief work is about the 'bottom line' of ensuring basic minimal necessities to keep people alive" (International Federation of Red Cross and Red Crescent Societies 1996b, 47). It might be useful for IHA agencies at all levels to formally adopt the view that *the primary purpose of international humanitarian assistance is saving lives*. If that were to be accepted, we would see that IHA *is potentially needed in any situation in which mortality risks are, or are likely to become, extraordinarily high*. In this approach, all life-threatening situations would be defined as disasters. The Humanitarian Policy Group of the Overseas Development Institute in London suggests a similar definition: "The primary goal of humanitarian action is to protect human life where this is threatened on a wide scale" (Darcy and Hofmann 2003, 13).

With this explicit focus, the effectiveness of any IHA operation would be estimated in terms of the number of lives saved. Where IHA was provided, the actual mortality rate would be compared with an estimate of the mortality rate that would have been likely in the absence of the IHA operation. The cost-effectiveness of such operations would be estimated in terms of the cost per life saved. With experience, it should be possible to make reasonable estimates. Techniques of estimation could be borrowed from specialists who assess the effectiveness of public health interventions.

Most of the guidelines available with regard to IHA now focus on the management of ongoing IHA operations after they are launched. They say little about the selection of situations in which they should be launched. Taking the core purpose of IHA to be saving lives would help in formulating targeting guidelines. Those who call in IHA would have to present the case that lives were at risk, and that assistance could substantially reduce that risk. With experience, guidelines could be formulated to help providers of IHA to more systematically assess and decide which situations to select.

Rights to Assistance

The international community provides humanitarian assistance in many different circumstances, but it is not required to do so. Currently, "international law imposes no obligation on States to respond to requests for assistance or to make offers of contributions for relief operations in other countries.... [And] there is still no international convention setting out obligations of States concerning the donation or acceptance of humanitarian assistance or regulating the coordination of relief in peacetime" (Macalister-Smith 1985, 56, 109–10). The softness of the international community's human rights obligations with regard to refugees in particular was discussed in chapter 15.

Many agree that people should have a right to some kinds of assistance. If, for example, you call your local fire department, they should come. If they do not come, there should be a systematic way in which you can complain and have that situation corrected. You are not supposed to get fire protection service only if and when the fire fighters feel like it. You are—or should be—*entitled* to a designated type and level of service. These rights and obligations should be clearly specified.

Many public assistance (welfare) programs within nations are based on the principle that the needy have specific rights to assistance; they have an *entitlement*. Without such rules, public assistance is likely to be arbitrary and used as a political tool by those in power. International humanitarian assistance will always include an element of ad hoc response to the situations of the moment, but some parts of it should be regularized and made more predictable. People who face extraordinary risks of premature death should be entitled to expect some level of relief.

Some analysts believe that people in need have a right to assistance in armed-conflict situations, under international humanitarian law, but the law is so vague that it cannot be regarded as a real right (Sandoz 1992; Corten and Klein 1992; *International Review of the Red Cross* 1993; Beigbeder 1991; Macalister-Smith 1985). Current international law with regard to the right to adequate food in emergencies is described by Cotula and Vidar (2003). The discourse about the right to assistance under international humanitarian law is mainly about the rights of the donors to have access to the needy so that their goods and services can be delivered without interference. It says needy people have a right to receive assistance *if* other people offer to provide it. It does not say that the needy have a right to receive certain kinds of assistance, and therefore others have an obligation to provide it. Of course, it is not surprising that the donors tend to emphasize their rights rather than their obligations.

The Provider's Motivation

Do the nations of the world really want a stronger global system of humanitarian assistance? It is sometimes suggested that a comprehensive program would be too expensive, but most estimates say the costs would be quite modest, say on the order of $20 or $30 billion a year. There are proposals under which funds on the order of $250 billion a year could be raised with little effort (Tobin Tax Network 2003).

Why should the rich countries of the world agree that the needy have rights to assistance? After all, accepting that the needy have specific rights, and thus that the providers have specific obligations, would reduce the providers' freedom of action. Why should IHA providers agree to a rights-based system? How can granting entitlements to the needy be viewed as advantageous to the providers of assistance?

Consider the broader question: Why would anyone, or any government, want to recognize that others have human rights? The answer is based not on conceptions of narrow self-interest but on some form of enlightened self-interest. We all benefit from social order rather than anarchy. We recognize that in some circumstances we get better results when we limit our freedom. Anyone who joins an organization or signs a contract gives up some freedom in exchange for other kinds of benefits. The argument here is that an IHA system that is at least in part based on entitlements can achieve effectiveness, efficiency, and justice beyond what can be obtained with guidelines that do not include entitlements.

For any single donor nation, however, there would be no reason to agree that the needy in other countries have authoritative claims on its resources. The prospect has been considered and rejected by the U.S. Agency for International Development:

> Some favor an entitlement approach premised on a fundamental U.S. obligation to provide basic human needs to the vulnerable peoples of the world. Universal rights to health and education have become a byword in these circles, the implication being that the U.S., as the world's wealthiest nation, should be the provider of last resort.... Americans like to see progress around the world, but our commitment to doing anything about it falls far short of any consensus on global entitlements to automatic U.S. aid. (U.S. Agency for International Development 1989)

But consider this argument with the words "international community" substituted for "U.S." It does not make sense for the United States alone to shoulder the burden, but a system of entitlements would make sense for the global IHA system taken as a whole, at least for some kinds of circumstances.

The international community should accept the obligation to ensure the well-being of all people, at least up to some minimal level. The world should look after its most vulnerable, just as national governments are expected to look after the most vulnerable within their particular jurisdictions. If we see looking after the weakest among us as a common, shared global responsibility, and not just a U.S. responsibility, the proposal of entitlements becomes more palatable.

In the current global system, emergencies are treated on an ad hoc basis, as if they were not expected. Rather than stationing substantial standby resources "at the ready" throughout the world, new resources must be solicited with each incident. The rules of engagement are being standardized, but slowly (Sphere Project 2000). The IHA donor countries as a group could adopt a collective, self-imposed obligation to provide assistance to the most needy under specific conditions. This would be comparable to creating a global rescue squad that would operate under specific guidelines. Regularizing assistance in this way would help to depoliticize it.

The global IHA system evolves slowly because some national participants want to maintain their own control and do not want to be subjected to a centralized, authoritative command structure. This difficult political problem might be resolved partly by working out a clear division of areas of responsibility and authority for different aspects of IHA. There already exists some informal partitioning of responsibility, with some providers concentrating on disasters in certain geographic areas or in countries with particular cultural affinities.

Implementation

Some needs for international assistance are highly predictable. Chapter 15 suggested ways of regularizing international assistance to refugees. Comparable approaches should be adopted for dealing with other challenges, such as the need to reduce children's mortality worldwide. UNICEF policy already allocates its program budget partly on the basis of the children's mortality rates in the countries it serves (UNICEF 1998, 81). Donor countries could allocate their contributions on the basis of similar considerations.

Even if donors allocated amounts to each country on the basis of clear measures of need, the receiving countries would not be able to claim they were entitled to these sums. They would have no legal recourse if they should receive less than they feel is due to them, and the amounts would vary from year to year because the contributions made by national governments are voluntary. Getting donor countries to make specific commitments about their future contributions could strengthen the system. They could agree on guidelines that say, for example, the countries with the worst child mortality rates have a right to at least a minimal level of assistance. They could commit to providing a specified level of support every year for, say, the twenty countries with the worst child mortality rates in the world.

In chapter 7, it was argued that assistance should not simply reward neediness. For this reason, donor countries could make their commitments not only on the basis of levels of need but also on the extent to which they can effectively use their

assistance to climb out of need. This is the basis of the U.S. Millennium Challenge Account, launched in 2002. President George W. Bush announced that the
United States would increase the amount of development assistance it makes
available, saying, "Greater contributions from developed nations must be linked
to greater responsibility from developing nations" (White House 2002, 1). Under this reasoning, while some countries at times might need unconditional assistance to feed their people, that sort of assistance should be limited. More generous assistance should go to those that can use it to increase their capacity to
provide for themselves.

The global IHA system should be coordinated and centralized more strongly
than it is now. It should be managed through a central agency, with the donors
sitting on its board of directors, participating in the shaping of policy. The rules
under which IHA operations would be undertaken would, in effect, articulate the
rights of needy people to receive assistance under particular circumstances. To
keep the agency on track, there should be a mechanism through which the needy
or their representatives could complain and call for corrective action. The creation of such a global system of humanitarian assistance, operating under explicit, agreed-on rules of engagement, would mark an important step forward in
the governance of the global order.

CHAPTER 17

Global Human Rights

Global Rights and Global Obligations

In 2004, about one-third of Namibia's population, facing a hunger crisis caused by drought, needed food aid. The World Food Program and the United Nations Children's Fund (UNICEF) launched a joint appeal for $5.8 million to help out. After two months, a representative of the World Food Program announced that it had not received so much as a penny (UN Wire 2004). The world's press hardly took notice.

If charity fails, what about rights? The title of a brochure from UNICEF and the UN Center for Human Rights, *Children's Rights Need International Protection*, suggested that the new Convention on the Rights of the Child responded to that need. In what sense do the human rights agreements talk about international human rights?

Human rights are international in the sense that they apply to all persons. However, the obligations are primarily domestic, in the relationships between national governments and their own people. Human rights would be really *international*—in the sense of transcending national borders—only if, upon failure of a national government to do what needed to be done to ensure the realization of those rights, the international community was *obligated* to step in to do what was necessary. There is now no mechanism and no firm commitment to do that with regard to children's rights, the human right to adequate food, and many other kinds of rights. Even for gross violations of human rights such as torture or genocide, the obligations of the international community to act are not well articulated. The International Council on Human Rights Policy describes these as *transnational* obligations, and it analyzes their character under human rights law and principles (International Council on Human Rights Policy 2003).

The right to equality before the law and the corresponding obligation of governments to ensure equity in the treatment of people are ordinarily thought of as applying to people *within* nations. We rarely consider the need to ensure equity among people *across* nations as a human rights obligation. Though equity within nations is a reasonable intermediate target, the ultimate goal ought to be equity across the globe. However, there is now no clearly articulated obligation to pursue global equity in international human rights law.

National governments are the primary duty bearers with regard to the human right to adequate food, and their obligations are mainly to people living under their jurisdictions. However, it should be recognized that the international community also has obligations with regard to food. This derives from its moral responsibilities and its role in the "rings of responsibility." In the rings of responsibility shown in figure 6.1 of this book, the international community is the outer ring, the last resort in looking after people's well-being. The very outermost ring is composed of the international governmental organizations. The international bodies' task is not to deliver services to the needy directly but, to the extent possible, empower agencies in the inner rings. People who do not have adequate food are people of particular nations, but they are also people of the world, and they have rights not only in relation to their own nations but also in relation to the world as a whole. The human right to adequate food would mean very little if obligations to honor that right were limited only to one's own government, one's own nation. Children born in poor countries are not born in a poor world.

This concept applies with regard to all human rights. Though human rights are commonly viewed as claims against states, and thus their national governments, they should be viewed as claims against all humanity. One's own national government carries the primary legal responsibility for the realization of one's human rights, but morally these burdens fall in some measure on all of us. All human rights should be recognized as having global reach.

There is some recognition of this in human rights law. The Universal Declaration of Human Rights says, in article 28, "Everyone is entitled to a social and international order in which the rights and freedoms set forth in this Declaration can be fully realized." Article 22 says that economic, social, and cultural rights should be achieved "through national effort and international cooperation." In the International Covenant on Economic, Social, and Cultural Rights, article 2, paragraph 1, calls on each state party to take steps "individually and through international assistance and co-operation, especially economic and technical, to the maximum of its available resources, with a view to achieving progressively the full realization of the rights recognized in the present Covenant." Article 11 requires states parties individually and through international cooperation to take the measures needed to implement "the fundamental right of everyone to be free from hunger." It says *everyone*, and not just the people of their own countries. *General Comment 12*, on the human right to adequate food, explains the international obligations more fully in paragraphs 36 and 37 (United Nations, Economic and Social Council 1999d).

It is beginning to be recognized that not only states but also international governmental agencies have specific human rights obligations (Kent 1994; Skogly 2001; Skogly and Gibney 2002; Darrow 2003). However, there is still little recognition of the idea that the international community as a whole has such obligations. The idea really is no more ambiguous than the concept that the state has specific obligations. The "international community," like "the state," is a social construct (Soguk 1999).

National governments represent states and act on their behalf. In much the same way, international governmental organizations represent and act on behalf of the collectivity of states. The various specialized organizations at the global level can be viewed as analogous to the specialized ministries at the national level. They are answerable not to some higher-level executive but to the collectivity of states.

The international community should be held accountable not only when it does things that it should not do, but also for failing to do things that it should do. The Committee on Economic, Social, and Cultural Rights has said, "a State party in which any significant number of individuals is deprived of essential food-stuffs, of essential primary health care, of basic shelter and housing, or of the most basic forms of education is, *prima facie*, failing to discharge its obligations under the Covenant (United Nations, Office of the High Commissioner for Human Rights 1990, para. 10)." By analogy, because we know that globally there are many individuals who are deprived of their essential food and other basic needs, we must conclude that the international community is "*prima facie*, failing to discharge its obligations under the Covenant."

Human rights imply democratic global governance and equality not for states but for people throughout the world. The obligations associated with human rights should not be treated as if they end at national borders. Yet in theory, the world still operates under the traditional nation-state system established with the Treaty of Westphalia in 1648. That design has served reasonably well for hundreds of years, but it is now clear that new institutional arrangements are needed. There is a need for stronger global governance.

At its core, the question of governance is: What is it that governments should or should not do? For example, what is it that national governments should do to ensure physical security, to protect and promote people's health, to facilitate commerce, to help the needy? These sorts of questions arise at every level of government. They apply at the global level as well. Although there is no global government as such, there is global governance. Global governance is undertaken by the nations of the world through their international activities, often through international agencies that act on their behalf. Thus we can say that global governance is undertaken by and on behalf of the international community, even if that community is not precisely defined.

International human rights law can be understood as the project of articulating universally accepted standards of governance to protect and promote human dignity. Human rights implies some level of obligation to everyone everywhere, and not only to those individuals under the jurisdiction of one's own national government. The guiding principle should be that the international community is subject to human rights obligations similar to those of states. If a particular action by a national government would be viewed as a human rights violation, then a similar action by, say, the World Bank, probably should be viewed as a human rights violation as well. International governmental agencies are the creations of nation-states and act on their behalf. Thus they are subject to much the same obligations as those states.

What would be the implications of full recognition of the human right to adequate food in a world of democratic global governance? Certainly, we would expect that more of the world community's attention and resources would be devoted to addressing the concerns of weaker nations and weaker persons. The pursuit of global equality would mean that people at risk of malnutrition everywhere would be entitled to the same sort of assistance, at least with regard to that part of their assistance that comes through international governmental agencies. It may be difficult to imagine the achievement of this level of equality in the treatment of needy people, but the concept should be held in mind as the objective, the goal implied by the commitment to the human right to adequate food.

Global Accountability

There is some human rights accountability at the international level, through the United Nations treaty bodies, through nongovernmental organizations, and through the monitoring done by some countries of the human rights performance of other countries. However, most of this activity is concerned with ensuring that states carry out their duties relating to the human rights of people living under their own jurisdiction. Little attention is given to the external obligations of states, that is, their obligations to people living outside their jurisdiction. There is no established mechanism for holding either international agencies or the international community as a whole to account.

Intergovernmental agencies such as the World Bank, International Monetary Fund, and World Trade Organization sometimes act as if they were wholly autonomous, sovereign bodies, answerable to no one. Officials of the International Monetary Fund have claimed that it is not bound by the international human rights agreements (Capdevila 2001). This type of attitude has helped to provoke strong criticisms and sometimes demonstrations against some of these agencies.

These international agencies do have boards of directors to which they are answerable, but often it is those boards that direct the action that needs to be corrected. There are no independent bodies outside these agencies, standing ready to hold them accountable. On the whole, the international agencies function with impunity. According to a major United Nations study, "Impunity can be understood as the absence or inadequacy of penalties and/or compensation for massive and grave violations of the human rights of individuals or groups of individuals" (United Nations, Economic and Social Council 1997, para. 20). The point here is not that the international agencies have committed such violations but that they are capable of doing so, and there is no institutional mechanism for holding them to account if they should violate human rights.

Most of the UN-related agencies are now adopting a human rights approach, primarily because Secretary-General Kofi Annan called upon them to do that in the new United Nations Development Assistance Framework launched in 1997.

However, there is a difference between promoting human rights and acknowledging that one's own agency is subject to human rights obligations. The agencies praise human rights and assert that they are working steadfastly for their realization, but generally they do not acknowledge that they themselves have obligations with regard to human rights. As Sigrun Skogly observes, "Although willing to take part in a dialogue about human rights, the [World] Bank has never accepted any legal obligations in this sphere" (Skogly 2000, 4). The obligations, it appears, are for others.

One major reason why the international agencies and the international community as a whole cannot be held accountable is that their obligations with regard to human rights have not been clearly articulated and accepted. What are—or should be—the obligations of the international community with regard to human rights generally, or with regard to the human right to adequate food in particular? How should the international community act to honor its obligations? Which agencies should have what duties? How can the international community, as a duty bearer, be held accountable?

Strategic Planning

One way to work out the answers to such questions would be to engage the international community, together with national governments, in formulating a solid plan for ending hunger and malnutrition in the world. In chapter 5 we said:

If people have a human right to adequate food, countries must have the goal of assuring that all people have adequate food. That goal should be used as the basis for designing a specific goal-directed strategic program of action.... In this approach, the process of realizing rights is the process of pursuing a strategy to reach a goal.

If we take this to the global level, we would see that the global rights and obligations could be articulated in the commitments entailed in the global plan for achieving the goal.

Planning the ending of hunger and malnutrition would have to begin with setting out a clear vision of how a world without hunger would work. How should future social and economic forces and institutions be reconfigured so that they no longer produce poverty and hunger? The core task is to create *enabling conditions* so that everyone has a decent opportunity to provide for him or herself. Dignity comes not from being fed but from providing for oneself and one's family. Those involved in subsistence agriculture should have the land, the tools, and the seeds they need to be sufficiently productive. Those involved in commercial agriculture should face prices and wage rates that allow their productivity to translate into reasonable incomes. Those who work outside agriculture should be assured of a living wage, adequate to support themselves and their families. The challenges are largely political, having to do with ownership and control of land and other factors of production, and they are largely economic, having to do with the allocation of resources and the determination of prices. The two join together in political economy, in the sense that economic decisions are heavily influenced by political power.

The new arrangements that are envisioned should be based on a clear recognition that free markets have inherent defects and biases. Markets are good at producing wealth and allocating resources efficiently, but (1) they systematically benefit the rich more than the poor, thus producing steadily widening gaps between them; (2) they lead to excessive exploitation and depletion of the environment; and (3) they are gender biased, in the sense that they put more value on what males do and produce.

I see no good alternatives to the market system. Thus, I would advocate a market-based system together with institutional arrangements designed to correct and compensate for its defects. To illustrate, I would insist on transfer payments from the top to the bottom, through taxation and other means, to ensure that the very poor are able to live adequately. I would insist on strong institutional arrangements to ensure that development activities are sustainable and respect the integrity of the environment. And I would insist on the fuller engagement of females, not simply in doing but also in planning and directing the work that needs to be done.

Other kinds of futures without hunger can be imagined and should be discussed. One approach, for example, argues that we should focus on localizing our food supplies (Halweil 2002; Hines 2004; Norberg-Hodge, Merrifield, and Gorelick 2002). The main point here is that strategic planning should begin with formulating the design of the thing that is to be built. We need to envision a world without hunger if we are ever to see it built.

Even before we have the detailed architectural design, we know that achieving its realization would require a detailed plan of action. One would need a clear vision of the end product, and one would also need commitments of resources of many different kinds, and a step-by-step program of action that would transform piles of resources into the thing that is to be built.

That plan could not take the form of a simple list: do A, then B, then C, and so on. Just as in building a bridge or a skyscraper, there would have to be a primary contractor and several subcontractors. The various contracts would have to anticipate that some subcontractors might not perform up to expectations, materials would sometimes arrive late, some workers might go on strike, and so on. Nevertheless, we know that the task is not to deliver excuses but to get the job done, no matter what. We know that we could not simply launch the plan and go away. We would have to stay on it, constantly steering the job toward its completion. Drawing on the analogy of building a bridge, we know that we would need such things as

- a clear vision of what is to be created,
- commitments of the needed resources,

- some way to know when the job is done,
- a plan that will take us to completion,
- a series of steps to ensure the completion of each part of the plan,
- clarity about who needs to do what to get the job done,
- clarity about the incentives that will induce the people who need to act to take the actions required of them, and
- contingency plans to deal with every sort of obstacle.

Of course, the task of ending hunger and malnutrition is not like building a bridge or a tall building. Though our proposed bridge might be new and unique in many ways, the fact is that many other bridges have been built in the past, and there is a lot that can be learned from past successes and failures. However, ending hunger and malnutrition is an entirely new sort of challenge, one that requires tools and approaches that have never before been imagined. In some respects, the challenge is comparable to President John Kennedy's call in the early 1960s to send people to the moon. He had no idea how the job would get done, but he was able to provide the vision.

Although the challenge of ending hunger and malnutrition is analogous to the call to send people to the moon, there are important differences. President Kennedy was able to supply not only the vision but also the resources. And he was able to provide an authority structure through which contractors and subcontractors could be hired and paid and asked to do the bidding of the U.S. government. The task of ending hunger in the world is far more difficult. The vision has to be so compelling and complete that it must include finding ways to muster the required resources, and it must include the creation of an organizational structure adequate to meet the requirements of the job.

There have been many efforts to address hunger and malnutrition at the global level, including:

- the Manifesto of the Special Assembly on Man's Right to Freedom from Hunger, held in Rome in March 1963;
- the International Undertaking on World Food Security and the Universal Declaration on the Eradication of Hunger and Malnutrition, issued by the World Food Conference held in Rome in 1974;
- the Plan of Action on World Food Security of 1979;
- the Agenda for Consultations and Possible Action to deal with Acute and Large-Scale Food Shortages of 1981;
- the World Food Security Compact of 1985;
- the Plan of Action for Implementing the World Declaration on the Survival, Protection, and Development of Children, issued by the World Summit for Children held at the United Nations in New York in September 1990, which included a major section on reducing children's malnutrition;
- the World Declaration and Plan of Action on Nutrition of the International Conference on Nutrition held in Rome in December 1992;

- the Plan of Action that came out of the World Food Summit of 1996, and its follow-up meeting, World Food Summit; five years later; and
- the Millennium Development Program, based on the Millennium Summit of 2000, in which the first goal centers on reducing poverty and hunger.

These initiatives have shared a common weakness: Their focus was mainly on the formulation of national plans of action, not a comprehensive global plan of action. The intergovernmental organizations were viewed mainly as facilitators, not as major actors. These plans did not give adequate attention to the role that the international community must play if hunger and malnutrition are to be sharply reduced.

In the approach envisioned here, the international community would be at center stage, playing major roles in the global program for the realization of the human right to adequate food. The intergovernmental organizations and the national governments, working together, would have to determine the division of responsibilities among them so that each could make its own best contribution to ensuring that people everywhere have adequate food. Of course, it would always have to be recognized that the intergovernmental organizations are not independent agents but are agents of, and accountable to, their member nations.

What role should international agencies have in helping to reduce hunger and malnutrition around the world? Many good food and nutrition programs are already in place. Instead of trying to invent something wholly new, good use should be made of existing institutional arrangements for dealing with the issues. We should see how their methods of work could be adapted so that they help to carry out the obligations of the international community, and thus help to advance the human right to adequate food globally.

The most prominent international governmental organizations concerned with food and nutrition are the Food and Agriculture Organization of the United Nations, the World Food Program, the International Fund for Agricultural Development, the World Health Organization, and UNICEF. They are governed by boards comprised of member states. Responsibility for coordinating food and nutrition activities among these and other intergovernmental organizations in the United Nations system rests with the United Nations System Standing Committee on Nutrition (SCN), formerly known as the United Nations Administrative Committee on Coordination / Subcommittee on Nutrition. Representatives of bilateral donor agencies, such as the Swedish International Development Agency and the U.S. Agency for International Development, also participate in SCN activities. The SCN also includes numerous international civil society organizations concerned with food and nutrition.

The main role of the intergovernmental organizations is not to feed people directly but to help nations use their own resources more effectively. Thus, recognition of the international dimensions of the human right to adequate food would not involve massive international transfers of food. The main function of a new global program for ensuring the realization of the human right to adequate food everywhere would be to press and help national governments address the problem of inadequate food among their own people, using resources within their own nations. There may always be a need for a global emergency food facility to help in emergency situations that are beyond the capacity of individual nations, but a different kind of design is needed for dealing with chronic food insecurity. Moreover, as chronic problems are addressed more effectively, nations would increase their capacity for dealing with emergency situations on their own. Over time, the need for emergency assistance from the outside would decline.

The intergovernmental organizations could use their leverage to press for the realization of the human right to adequate food within the nations they serve. For example, the World Food Program could make it known that in providing food supplies for development it would favor those nations that are working to establish clear and effective entitlements for the most needy in their nations. The intergovernmental organizations could be especially generous in providing assistance to those nations that create national laws and national agencies devoted to implementing the human right to adequate food. If they were relieved of some of the burden of providing material resources, poor nations might be more willing to create programs for recognizing and realizing the right. International agencies could function on the basis of specific rules and principles that could be viewed as precursors to recognition of a genuine international duty to recognize and effectively implement the human right to adequate food.

The intergovernmental organizations are already concerned with hunger and malnutrition, but these are only a part of their broad agendas. For example, the Food and Agriculture Organization gives a great deal of attention to the interests of food producers, and the World Health Organization deals with the full range of health issues. UNICEF addresses a very broad range of subjects related to children. Hunger and malnutrition have not yet gotten the commitment of attention and resources needed to really solve the problems.

Many of the intergovernmental organizations already do good work in addressing hunger and malnutrition. If all the separate pieces were coordinated as part of a large, long-term, goal-directed program, that new alignment of their resources would make their efforts much more effective. Their activities should be reconceived so that they mesh together within a cogent program of action.

The concept of moving progressively toward a global regime of a hard right to adequate food could be the basis for working out a global program of concerted action. The intergovernmental organizations would continue to carry out their other functions; but with regard to the challenge of addressing serious malnutrition, their actions would be coordinated under the new Global Nutrition Action Plan, formulated jointly by the intergovernmental organizations working together with the countries of the world. This plan would spell out the commitments of the various parties that were to play a role, and it would describe the institutional arrangements, the resource commitments, and the program of action.

Rules could be established so that the targets of action would be selected on the basis of clear measures of need, thus reducing the possibilities for making politicized selections. The program could begin with a focus on alleviating hunger and malnutrition in the worst cases, and then as those problems were addressed, move to dealing with less severe situations. Or, instead of targeting simply on the basis of the intensity of the need, the program could initially focus on where it could do the most good. For example, the initial effort could center on ensuring that no child under three years of age goes hungry. A relatively modest and limited goal of that sort could be used as the initial basis for calling forth resource commitments and for designing the institutional arrangements needed to carry out the program.

The new arrangement might include the establishment of a new global body—perhaps described as the Global Nutrition Program Monitor—that had the responsibility for seeing to it that the terms of the plan were carried out. This new body, created by national governments working together with the intergovernmental organizations, would ensure that the agencies making agreements, and thus incurring obligations, in fact carried out their obligations. This monitoring body would not have substantive political power of its own; rather, it would function in a manner comparable to that of the United Nations human rights treaty bodies. Through a process of constructive dialogue, it would call the parties to account for fulfilling the commitments they had agreed to make. The body would also serve in a coordinating role, and it would have the capacity to allocate resources provided to it.

The international community, working through the intergovernmental organizations, would support national governments in dealing with hunger and malnutrition among their own people. Local and international civil society organizations would be a part of the system—in that they would help to identify and report serious cases of hunger and malnutrition, they would help to provide services, and they would monitor to make sure that national and local agencies carried out their work of alleviating hunger and malnutrition.

It might be agreed that where there was serious hunger and malnutrition and national agencies could not or would not solve the problem, the intergovernmental organizations would have the authority and the duty to become directly involved. The nature of that involvement would have to be worked out. Concrete programs of action would have to be designed to fit particular cases, but the planning exercise would establish general procedures and guidelines for action. Consideration would have to be given to issues of consent, costs, logistics, risks, and so on. Intervention would not be automatic and indiscriminate. There would be an agency in place that would be prepared to assess the situation and act under suitable internationally accepted guidelines. Initially, the international community would have a firm duty to assist only where there was consent from govern-ments of the nations receiving assistance.

The major differences between the earlier global efforts to address hunger and malnutrition and the Global Nutrition Action Plan outlined here are:

- The international governmental organizations would have prominent active roles.
- The purpose and program of action would be sharply focused.
- The program of action would be based on clear contractual commitments.
- There would be a serious system of accountability at the global level, based on the establishment of a central agency responsible for ensuring that the commitments were honored.
- The cogency of the entire program would be based on the clear recogni-tion that every individual has the human right to adequate food.

Of course, the idea of ending serious malnutrition in the world through recog-nition of the human right to adequate food everywhere is idealistic. Nevertheless, the idea can be useful in setting the direction of action. We can think of the in-ternational community, acting through the intergovernmental agencies, as hav-ing specific duties with regard to the fulfillment of the human right to adequate food. We can move progressively toward the ideal by inviting the agencies to establish clear rules and procedures that they would follow as if they were firm duties.

The sharp reduction of hunger and malnutrition throughout the world will require clear articulation of the action required to achieve each particular target along the way, and clear commitment by the parties to take the actions that are required. If those parties are serious about sharply reducing the levels of hunger and malnutrition in the world, they should be willing to create a body that would hold them to account for keeping those commitments.

They may not be serious. It would be good to challenge them in order to find out if they are.

The human right to adequate food is just one of many possible points of en-try to the interlocking complex of concerns about human rights, democracy, de-velopment, and governance at every level. It has been presented in this book not as something apart but as one entryway into this larger agenda. Human rights work helps to illuminate the path, throwing light onto the darker sides of indi-vidual and governmental behavior, and clarifying what is right and what is wrong. It contributes to empowering the weak and making the world a bit fairer. Like medicine, its quest is to make itself unnecessary. Human rights are tools to be used along with many other instruments deployed in the pursuit of good gov-ernance, both within nations and internationally. Human rights work is un-ashamedly utopian. Yet in showing us the right direction, human rights work is also eminently practical.

Sources

This is a guide to source materials on the human right to adequate food.

Human Rights Generally

Many useful websites deal with human rights. The most important is the site maintained by the Office of the United Nations High Commissioner for Human Rights, http://www.ohchr.org. Regional human rights agreements and bodies may be accessed at http://www.umn.edu/humanrts/regional.htm/. Some regional human rights bodies have their own websites, such as the European Court of Human Rights' site, http://www.echr.coe.int/.

Several civil society organizations have created websites that provide an overview of, and links to, the many human rights sources on the web. The *Concise Guide to Human Rights on the Internet*, http://www.derechos.org/human-rights/manual.htm?manual#first_hit, prepared by Derechos Human Rights, identifies many other useful websites, offers guidance on finding national materials, provides references to useful search engines, and also offers sections on mailing lists, newsgroups, and chat rooms.

Other sites that provide links to a broad array of human rights-related information include:

- Derechos Human Rights, http://www.derechos.net
- Human Rights First (formerly Lawyers Committee for Human Rights), http://www.humanrightsfirst.org/
- Minnesota Human Rights Library, http://www1.umn.edu/humanrts/ and
- essays on current issues in the field may be found in Human Rights Dialogue, http://www.cceia.org/themes/hrd.html.

Most of the information about human rights on websites is international in its orientation. However, a great deal of useful information can be obtained from the websites of national and other human rights commissions. For example, it would be useful to consult the websites of national human rights commissions, such as those of

- Australia, http://www.hreoc.gov.au
- Canada, http://www.chrc-ccdp.ca
- Guatemala, http://www.ghrc-usa.org
- India, http://nhrc.nic.in
- New Zealand, http://www.hrc.co.nz and
- South Africa, http://www.sahrc.org.za

The common use of the label "human rights commission" should not lead to the belief that there are any great similarities in the character of these organizations. Not all of them are sponsored by national governments. Some, such as the one for Guatemala, are independent bodies that have been set up outside the country.

There are many subnational human rights commissions, such as those in the provinces of Canada and many states of the United States. There is one supranational regional commission, the Asian Human Rights Commission, based in Hong Kong, http://www.ahrchk.net. This is only a sampling. Searches on the World Wide Web would locate the websites of many more human rights commissions.

Civil society organizations (cso's) can be good sources of information about particular countries. Some might be contacted through e-mail. The United Nations Nongovernmental Liaison Service can assist in locating such organizations. It is important to recognize that most human rights cso's (or nongovernmental organizations) tend to focus on civil and political rights rather than economic and social rights. Also, human rights cso's, like other organizations, have their own special agendas, and they may not be well informed about issues outside their areas of specialization.

In addition to its more international information, the website of the Office of the UN High Commissioner for Human Rights provides extensive information on individual countries, including the dates on which they have signed and ratified the major human rights agreements; any reservations, understandings, or declarations they may have issued in connection with these agreements; and their reports to the treaty bodies. Three sources that report on human rights on a country-by-country basis are listed below. They focus on reporting the human rights *situation*, but their reports may nevertheless yield information on the human rights *systems* within these countries. Most of these reports give primary attention to civil and political rights, and less attention to economic, social, and cultural rights:

- Human Rights Watch, http://www.hrw.org. *The Human Rights Watch World Report* is published annually
- Freedom House, http://www.freedomhouse.org/
- U.S. Department of State, *Country Reports on Human Rights Practices*, http://www.state.gov/g/drl/hr/

Newstrawler (http://www.newstrawler.com/nt/nt_home.html) provides means for searching through newspapers of different countries, and thus it may help in finding local stories about human rights.

Websites concerned particularly with food and nutrition are described in the following sections. Some websites focus on other aspects of an adequate standard of living, such as the right to education; see, for example, http://www.right-to-education.org.

Food and Nutrition Generally

The following websites provide useful information about food and nutrition issues from a global perspective. They are not specifically focused on the human rights aspect of those issues. The major international governmental organizations concerned with food are:

- United Nations System Standing Committee on Nutrition (formerly the United Nations Administrative Committee on Coordination / Sub-Committee on Nutrition, http://www.unsystem.org/scn
- Food and Agriculture Organization of the United Nations (FAO), http://www.fao.org
- International Fund for Agricultural Development, http://www.ifad.org
- Integrated Regional Information Network, operated by the UN Office for the Coordination of Humanitarian Affairs, provides regularly updated information on food security, human rights, and related issues; http://www.irinnews.org
- United Nations Children's Fund, http://www.unicef.org/
- United Nations Development Program, http://www.undp.org
- U.S. Department of Agriculture (USDA), http://www.usda.gov
- World Food Program at http://www.wfp.org
- World Health Organization at http://www.who.org

The major international civil society (nongovernmental) organizations concerned with food are:

- World Hunger Year, http://www.worldhungeryear.org
- Bread for the World, http://www.bread.org
- Results, http://results.org/
- Hunger Project, http://www.thp.org/
- Save the Children, http://www.savethechildren.org/
- CARE, http://www.care.org
- World Food Day, http://www.worldfooddayusa.org/

A wide range of useful publications on food and nutrition worldwide may be obtained from the International Food Policy Research Institute, http://www.ifpri.org/. Some websites focus on nutrition problems in a particular country, such as

- USDA National Hunger Clearinghouse, http://www.worldhungeryear.org/nhc
- Food Research and Action Center, http://www.frac.org
- Project Bread, http://www.projectbread.org
- Share Our Strength, http://www.strength.org
- Second Harvest, http://secondharvest.org

Some organizations focus on nutrition issues in subnational regions, such as

- Greater Boston Food Bank, http://www.gbfb.org
- Hawaii Foodbank, http://www.hawaiifoodbank.org/

The Human Right to Adequate Food

The Office of the Special Rapporteur for the Right to Food has a website, http://www.rightofood.org. Its reports also may be accessed at http://www .unhchr.ch/html/menu2/7/b/mfood.htm. The FAO has a website on the right to food, http://www.fao.org/Legal/rtf/rtf-e.htm. Foodfirst Information and Action Network, a civil society organization, has a website concerned specifically with the right to food, http://www.fian.org. The website of the International Indian Treaty Council has a page devoted specifically to the right to food, http://www .treatycouncil.org/new_page_5241.htm.

References

Abila, Richard O. 2003. Case study: Kenyan fish exports. In *Food safety in food security and food trade*, ed. Laurian J. Unnevehr. 2020 Vision, Focus 10. Washington, D.C.: International Food Policy Research Institute. http://www.ifpri.org/2020/focus/focus10/focus10.pdf

Abramovitz, Janet. 2001. *Unnatural disasters*. Washington, D.C.: Worldwatch Institute. http://www.worldwatch.org/pubs/paper/158facts.html

Adelman, Carol C. 2003. The privatization of foreign aid: Reassessing national largesse. *Foreign Affairs* 82, no. 6 (November–December). http://www.foreign affairs.org/20031101facomment82602/carole-c-adelman/theprivatization-of-foreign-aid-reassessing-national-largesse.html

Ad Hoc Group on Infant Feeding in Emergencies. 1998. *Infant feeding emergencies: Policy, strategy & practice*. Dublin: Emergency Nutrition Network, Department of Community Health and General Practice.

Advisory Council on International Affairs. 1998. *Universality of human rights and cultural diversity*. The Hague: Advisory Council on International Affairs.

African Charter on Human and Peoples' Rights. 1981. http://www1.umn.edu/human-rts/instree/ratz1afchar.htm

Aid appeal for Namibia fails to garner any funds, U.N. says. 2004. UN Wire, May 4. http://www.unwire.org/UNWire/20040504/449_23438.asp

Alston, Philip. 1992a. Appraising the United Nations human rights regime. In *The United Nations and human rights: A critical appraisal*, ed. Philip Alston. Oxford: Clarendon Press.

———. 1992b. The Committee on Economic, Social and Cultural Rights. In *The United Nations and human rights: A critical appraisal*, ed. Philip Alston. Oxford: Clarendon Press.

———, ed. 1994. *The best interests of the child: Reconciling culture and human rights*. Oxford: Oxford University Press.

Alston, Philip, and Katarina Tomaševski, eds. 1984. *The right to food*. Dordrecht, the Netherlands: Martinus Nijhoff.

Altman, Lawrence K. 1998. AIDS brings shift in UN messages on breast-feeding. *New York Times*, July 26, 1.

America's Second Harvest. 2001. *Hunger in America 2001*. Chicago: America's Second Harvest. http://www.secondharvest.org/

Amnesty International. 2003. Human right to water. Public Statement, March 24. http://web.amnesty.org/library/index/ENGIOR100022003

———. 2004. *Zimbabwe: Power and hunger—violations of the right to food*. October 15. http://www.amnestyusa.org/countries/zimbabwe/document.do?id=535F524A07527C6C80256F0E0042747E

Andrews, Margaret, Mark Nord, Gary Bickel, and Steven Carlson. 1999. *Household food security in the United States, 1999*. Washington, D.C.: U.S. Department of Agriculture. http://www.ers.usda.gov/publications/fanrr8/fanrr8.pdf

Asian Legal Resource Centre. 2003. *The permanent people's tribunal on the right to food and the rule of law in Asia.* Hong Kong: Asian Legal Resource Centre. http://www.foodjustice.net/modules.php?name=Content&pa=showpage&pid=5&cid=4

Audley, John, Sandra Polaski, Demetrios G. Papademetriou, and Scott Vaughan. 2003. *NAFTA's promise and reality: Lessons from Mexico for the hemisphere.* Washington, D.C.: Carnegie Endowment for International Peace. http://www.ceip.org/files/publications/NAFTA_Report_full.asp

Banik, Dan. 1998. India's freedom from famine: The case of Kalahandi. *Contemporary South Asia* 7, no. 3: 265–81.

Bar-Yam, Naomi Bromberg. 2003. Breastfeeding and human rights: Is there a right to breastfeed? Is there a right to be breastfed? *Journal of Human Lactation* 19, no. 4 (November): 357–61.

Beaton, G. H., and H. Ghassemi. 1982. Supplementary feeding programs for young children in developing countries. *American Journal of Clinical Nutrition* 35: 864–916.

Beck, Ernest. 1999. Popular Perrier? Nestlé pitches bottled water to world's poor. *Wall Street Journal,* June 18.

Beigbeder, Yves. 1991. *The role and status of international humanitarian volunteers and organizations: The right and duty to humanitarian assistance.* Dordrecht, the Netherlands: Martinus Nijhoff.

Bernstein, Nina. 2002. Suit to seek food stamps for thousands wrongly denied them. *New York Times,* March 31. http://www.nytimes.com/2002/03/31/nyregion/31-FOOD.html

Bertolli J., D. J. Hu, P. Nieburg, A. Macalalad, and R. J. Simonds. 2003. Decision analysis to guide choice of interventions to reduce mother-to-child transmission of HIV. *AIDS* 17, no. 14 (September 26): 2089–98.

Brown, J. Larry. 1987. Hunger in the U.S. *Scientific American* 256, no. 2 (February): 36–41.

Brown, J. Larry, and H. F. Pizer. 1987. *Living hungry in America.* New York: Macmillan.

Brundtland, Gro Harlem. 2000. *Nutrition, health and human rights: ACC/SCN Symposium on the substance and politics of a human rights approach to food and nutrition policies and programmes.* Updated September 15. Geneva: World Health Organization. http://www.who.int/director-general/speeches/1999/english/1999-0412_nutrition.html

Bunzl, John. 2002. *Lula: Snatching defeat from the jaws of victory.* Montreal: Center for Research on Globalization. http://www.globalresearch.ca/articles/BUN210A.html

Burden of Disease Unit. 1996. *The global burden of disease and injury series. Executive Summary. Volume 1.* Cambridge, Mass.: Burden of Disease Unit, Harvard University. http://www.hsph.harvard.edu/organizations/bdu/gbdsum/gbdsum5.pdf

Burmese Border Consortium. 2003. *Reclaiming the right to rice: Food security and internal displacement in Eastern Burma.* Bangkok: Burmese Border Consortium. http://www.ibiblio.org/obl/docs/BBC-Reclaiming_the_Right_to_Rice.pdf

Butcher, Goler Teal. 1987. The relationship of law to the hunger problem. *Howard Law Journal* 30: 193–203.

Capdevila, Gustavo. 2001. *Rights: IMF deems itself above certain values, say UN experts.* Geneva: World Bunk Group. http://www.worldbunk.org/Rights.htm

Carnegie Task Force on Meeting the Needs of Young Children. 1994. *Starting points: Meeting the needs of young children.* New York: Carnegie Corporation of New York.

Center for Public Integrity. 2004. *The water barons.* Washington, D.C.: Center for Public Integrity. http://www.publicintegrity.org/water

Chen, Aimin, and Walter J. Rogan. 2004. Breastfeeding and the risk of postneonatal death in the United States. *Pediatrics* 113, no. 5 (May): 435–39.

Christensen, Cheryl. 1978. *The right to food: How to guarantee.* Working Paper 6, World Order Models Project. New York:, Institute for World Order.

Citizens' Board of Inquiry into Hunger and Malnutrition in the United States. 1968. *Hunger, U.S.A.: A report.* Boston: Beacon Press.

Clark, Sandra. 2002. *A summary of issues in making WIC an individual entitlement.* Washington, D.C.: Center on Budget and Policy Priorities. http://www.cbpp.org/4-2-02wic.pdf

Coitinho, Denise. 1999. Understanding human rights approaches to food and nutritional security in Brazil. *SCN News,* no. 18: 50–53, 59–62.

Committee on Military Nutrition Research. 1999. *Military strategies for sustainment of nutrition and immune function in the field.* Washington, D.C.: National Academy Press.

Cook, John T., and J. Larry Brown. 1996. Children's rights to adequate nutritious foods in the two Americas. *Food Policy* 21, no. 1 (March): 11–16.

Coovadia, H. M., and A. Coutsoudis. 2001. Problems and advances in reducing transmission of HIV-1 through breastfeeding in developing countries. *AIDScience* 1, no. 4 (July). http://www.aidscience.com/Articles/aidscience004.asp

Corten, Olivier, and Pierre Klein. 1992. *Droit d'ingérence ou obligation de réaction? Les possibilités d'action visant à assurer le respect des droits del la personne face au principe de non-intervention.* Brussels: Emile Bruylant.

Cotula, Lorenzo, and Margret Vidar. 2003. *The right to adequate food in emergencies.* Rome: Food and Agriculture Organization of the United Nations. http://www.fao.org/DOCREP/005/Y4430E/Y4430E00.HTM

Coutsoudis, Anna, Kubendran Pillay, Hoosen M. Coovadia, L. Pembrey, and M.-L. Newell. 2003. Morbidity in children born to women infected with human immunodeficiency virus in South Africa: Does mode of feeding matter? *Acta Pediatrica* 92, no. 9.

Coutsoudis, Anna, Kubendran Pillay, Elizabeth Spooner, Louise Kuhn, and Hoosen M. Coovadia. 1999. Influence of infant-feeding patterns on early mother-to-child transmission of HIV-1 in Durban, South Africa: A prospective cohort study. *The Lancet* 354, no. 9177 (August 7).

Dahinten, Jan. 2001. Natural disasters kill 25,000 worldwide in 2001. Reuters, December 31.

Dankwa, Victor, Cees Flinterman, and Scott Leckie. 1998. Commentary to the *Maastricht Guidelines on Violations of Economic, Social and Cultural Rights. Human Rights Quarterly* 20, no. 3: 705–30.

Darcy, James, and Charles-Antoine Hofmann. 2003. *According to need? Needs assessment and decision-making in the humanitarian sector.* London: Humanitarian Policy Group, Overseas Development Institute. http://www.odi.org.uk/hpg/papers/hpg report15.pdf

Darrow, Mac. 2003. *Between light and shadow: The World Bank, the International Monetary Fund and international human rights law.* Portland, Ore.: Hart Publishing.

De Cock, Kevin M., Dorothy Mbori-Ngacha, and Elizabeth Marum. 2002. Shadow on the continent: Public health and HIV/AIDS in Africa in the 21st century. *The Lancet* 360: 67–72.

Dennis, Michael J., and David P. Stewart. 2004. Justiciability of economic, social and cultural rights: Should there be an international complaints mechanism to adjudicate the rights to food, water, housing, and health? *American Journal of International Law* 98, no. 3 (July): 462–515.

De Soto, Hernando. 2000. *The mystery of capital: Why capitalism triumphs in the West and fails everywhere else.* London: Black Swan.

Dev, S. Mahendra. 2003. *Right to Food in India.* Hyderabad: Centre for Economic and Social Studies. http://www.cess.ac.in/cesshome/wp/wp_50.pdf

Donnelly, Jack. 1989. *Universal human rights in theory and practice.* Ithaca, N.Y.: Cornell University Press.

Dreyfuss, Michele L., and Wafaie W. Fawzi. 2002. Micronutrients and vertical transmission of HIV-1. *American Journal of Clinical Nutrition* 75: 959–70.

Drèze, Jean, and Amartya Sen. 1989. *Hunger and public action.* Oxford: Clarendon Press.

Dunn, D. T., M. L. Newell, A. E. Ades, and C. S. Peckham. 1992. Risk of human immunodeficiency virus type 1 transmission through breastfeeding. *The Lancet* 340 (September 5): 585–88.

Edkins, Jenny. 2000. *Whose hunger? Concepts of famine, practices of aid.* Minneapolis: University of Minnesota Press.

Eide, Asbjørn. 1989. *The right to adequate food as a human right.* Human Rights Study Series 1. New York: United Nations.

———. 1995. The right to an adequate standard of living including the right to food. In *Economic, social and cultural rights: A textbook,* 2nd ed. Asbjørn Eide, Catarina Krause, and Allan Rosas. Dordrecht, The Netherlands: Martinus Nijhoff.

———. 2001. The right to an adequate standard of living including the right to food. In *Economic, social and cultural rights: A textbook,* 2nd ed. Asbjørn Eide, Catarina Krause, and Allan Rosas. Dordrecht, The Netherlands: Martinus Nijhoff.

Eide, Asbjørn, Catarina Krause, and Allan Rosas, eds. 2001. *Economic, social and cultural rights: A textbook,* 2nd ed. Dordrecht, The Netherlands: Martinus Nijhoff.

Eisinger, Peter K. 1998. *Toward an end to hunger in America.* Washington, D.C.: Brookings Institution Press.

Elhance, Arun P. 1999. *Hydropolitics in the third world: Conflict and cooperation in international river basins.* Washington, D.C.: U.S. Institute of Peace Press.

Embassy of India. 2002. *Agriculture & rural developments.* Embassy of India, Washington. http://www.indianembassy.org/dydemo/agriculture.htm

Engle, Patrice L., Purnima Menon, and Lawrence Haddad. 1999. Care and nutrition: Concepts and measurement. *World Development* 27, no. 8 (July): 1309–37.

European Collaborative Study. 2002. Level and pattern of HIV-1-RNA viral load over age: Differences between girls and boys? AIDS 16, no. 1 (January 4): 97–104.

Ezzati, Majid, Alan D. Lopez, Anthony Rodgers, Stephen Vander Hoorn, Christopher, J. L. Murray, and the Comparative Risk Assessment Collaborating Group. 2002. Selected major risk factors and global regional burden of disease. *The Lancet* 360 (November 2): 1347–60. http://pdf.thelancet.com/pdfdownload?uid=llan.360 .9343.original_research.22978.1&x=x.pdf

Ezzati, Majid, Stephen Vander Hoorn, Anthony Rodgers, Alan D. Lopez, Colin Mathers, Christopher, J. L. Murray, and the Comparative Risk Assessment Collaborating Group. 2003. Estimates of global and regional potential health gains from reducing multiple risk factors. *The Lancet* 362 (July 26): 271–80. http://pdf.thelancet.com/pdfdownload?uid=llan.362.9380.original_research.26678.1&x=x.pdf

Falk, Richard. 1992. Theoretical foundations of human rights. In *Human rights in the world community: Issues and action,* 2nd edition, ed. Richard P. Claude and Burns H. Weston. Philadelphia: University of Pennsylvania Press.

Feinberg, Joel. 1980. *Rights, justice, and the bounds of liberty.* Princeton, N.J.: Princeton University Press.

Fields, A. Belden. 2003. *Rethinking human rights for the new millennium.* New York: Palgrave Macmillan.

FIVIMS. 2002. Website of Food Insecurity and Vulnerability Information and Mapping Systems, Food and Agriculture Organization of the United Nations. http://www.fivims.net/index.jsp

———. 2004. Definition of food security. In *FIVIMS glossary.* http://www.fivims .net/static.jspx?lang=en&page=overview

Fomon, Samuel. 2004. Assessment of growth of formula-fed infants: Evolutionary considerations. *Pediatrics* 113, no. 2 (February): 389–93.

FoodFirst Information and Action Network. 1997. *The right to adequate food (art. 11) and violations of this right in the Russian Federation.* Heidelberg: FIAN. http:// www.infoe.de/report.html

Food and Agriculture Organization of the United Nations. 1996. *Rome declaration on world food security and world food summit plan of action.* Rome: Food and Agriculture Organization. http://www.fao.org/wfs/final/rd-e.htm

———. 1997. *The sixth world food survey.* Rome: Food and Agriculture Organization.

———. 1998. *The right to food in theory and practice.* Rome: Food and Agriculture Organization.

———. 1999a. *Extracts from international and regional instruments and declarations, and other authoritative texts addressing the right to food.* Legislative Study 69.

Rome: Food and Agriculture Organization. http://www.fao.org/Legal/Rtf/legst68
.pdf

———. 1999b. *The state of food insecurity in the world: 1999*. Rome: Food and Agriculture Organization. http://www.fao.org/news/1999/img/SOFI99-E.PDF

———. 2000. *Agriculture trade and food security: Issues and options in the WTO negotiations—country case studies*. Commodities and Trade Division. Rome: Food and
Agriculture Organization. http://www.fao.org/DOCREP/003/X8731e/x8731e00
.htm

———. 2002a. *Declaration of the World Food Summit: five years later*. Rome: Food
and Agriculture Organization. http://www.fao.org/DOCREP/MEETING/005/
Y7106E/Y7106E09.htm#TopOfPage

———. 2002b. *Explanatory notes/reservation to the declaration of the World Food Summit: five years later*. Rome: Food and Agriculture Organization. http://www.fao
.org/DOCREP/MEETING/005/Y7106E/Y7106E03.htm#TopOfPage

———. 2002c. *Fisheries and food security*. Rome: Food and Agriculture Organization.
http://www.fao.org/focus/e/fisheries/intro.htm

———. 2002d. *The state of food insecurity in the world*. Rome: Food and Agriculture
Organization. ftp://ftp.fao.org/docrep/fao/005/y7352e/y7250e.pdf

———. 2003. *The state of food insecurity in the world 2003*. Rome: Food and Agriculture Organization. http://www.fao.org/docrep/006/j0083e/j0083e00.htm

———. 2004. *Committee on World Food Security adopts right to food guidelines*.
http://www.fao.org/newsroom/en/news/2004/50821/index.html

Forsythe, David P. 1991. *The internationalization of human rights*. Lexington, Mass:
Lexington Books.

FOSENET. 2003. *Community assessment of the food situation in Zimbabwe, September 2003*. Harare, Zimbabwe: FOSENET. http://www.kubatana.net/html/sectors/
fos001.asp

Frankenberger, Timothy R., and M. Katherine McCaston. 1999. Rapid food and livelihood security assessments: A comprehensive approach for diagnosing nutrition
insecurity. In *Scaling up, scaling down: Overcoming malnutrition in developing countries*, ed. Thomas J. Marchione. Amsterdam: Gordon and Breach / Overseas Pub-
lishers Association.

Friis, Henrik, ed. 2002. *Micronutrients and HIV infection*. Boca Raton, Fla.: CRC Press.

Galtung, Johan. 1994. *Human rights in another key*. Cambridge: Polity Press.

Garza, Cutberto, and Mercedes De Onis. 1999. A new international growth reference
for young children. *American Journal of Clinical Nutrition* 70, no.1 (July): 169S–
172S. http://www.ajcn.org/cgi/content/full/70/1/169S?maxtoshow=&HITS=10-
&hits=10&RESULTFORMA

Gibb, D. M., T. Duong, P. A. Tookey, M. Sharland, G. Tudor-Williams, V. Novelli, K.
Butler, A. Riordan, L. Farrelly, J. Masters, C. S. Peckham, D. T. Dunn, and National
Study of HIV in Pregnancy and Childhood (NSHPC), Collaborative HIV Paediatric
Study (CHIPS). 2003. Decline in mortality, AIDS and hospital admissions in peri-
natally HIV-1 infected children in the United Kingdom and Ireland. *British Medical*

Journal 327 (November 1): 1019–25. http://bmj.bmjjournals.com/cgi/reprint/327/7422/1019

Gillespie, Stuart, and John Mason. 1990. *Nutrition-relevant actions: Some experiences from the eighties and lessons for the nineties.* Geneva: Sub-Committee on Coordination, United Nations Administrative Committee on Coordination.

Glendon, Mary Ann. 1991. *Rights talk: The impoverishment of political discourse.* New York: Free Press.

———. 2001. *A world made new: Eleanor Roosevelt and the Universal Declaration of Human Rights.* New York: Random House.

Goldman, Armond S., Sadhana Chheda, and Roberto Garofalo. 1998. Evolution of immunologic functions of the mammary gland and the postnatal development of immunity. *Pediatric Research* 43, no. 2 (February): 155–62.

Goldsmith, Jack. 1998. International human rights law and the United States double standard. *The Green Bag* (summer): 365, 372.

Gonzalez, Justo. 1986. Of fishes and wishes. *Seeds (Sprouts Edition)*, November: 1–2.

Good, Martha H. 1984. Freedom from want: The failure of United States courts to protect subsistence rights. *Human Rights Quarterly* 6, no. 3 (August): 335–65.

Greenhouse, Linda. 2000. The Supreme Court: The foreign policy issue; Justices overturn a state law on Myanmar. *New York Times*, June 20, 23.

Haddad, Lawrence, Eileen Kennedy, and Joan Sullivan. 1994. Choice of indicators for food security and nutrition monitoring. *Food Policy* 19, no. 3: 329–43.

Haddad, Lawrence, and Arne Oshaug. 1999. How does the human rights perspective help to shape the food and nutrition policy research agenda? *Food Policy* 23, no. 5: 329–45.

Hall, David. 2003a. *Water multinationals: No longer business as usual.* London: Public Services International Research Unit. http://www.psiru.org/reports/2003-03-W-MNCs.doc

———. 2003b. *Water multinationals in retreat: Suez withdraws investment.* London: Public Services International Research Unit. http://www.psiru.org/reports/2003-01-W-Suez.doc

Halweil, Brian. 2002. *Home grown: The case for local food in a global market.* Washington, D.C.: Worldwatch Institute. http://www.worldwatch.org/pubs/paper/163/

Hines, Colin. 2004. *A global look to the local: Replacing economic globalisation with democratic localisation.* London: International Institute for Environment and Development. http://www.iied.org/docs/sarl/GlobaltoLocal_Hines.pdf

HIV Paediatric Prognostic Markers Collaborative Study Group. 2003. Short-term risk of disease progression in HIV-1 infected children receiving no antiretroviral therapy or zidovudine monotherapy: A meta-analysis. *The Lancet* 362, no. 9396 (November 15): 1605–11.

Holmes, Stephen, and Cass R. Sunstein. 1999. *The cost of rights: Why liberty depends on taxes.* New York: W. W. Norton.

Howard Law Journal. 1987. Special issue on World Food Day Symposium held at Howard University in 1986.

Human Rights Council of Australia. 1995. *The rights way to development: A human rights approach to development assistance.* Marricksville, NSW, Australia: Human Rights Council of Australia.

Human Rights Quarterly. 1998. Maastricht guidelines on violations of economic, social and cultural rights. *Human Rights Quarterly* 20, no. 3: 691–704. http://www1 .umn.edu/humanrts/instree/Maastrichtguidelines.html

Human Rights Watch. 2003. *Not eligible: The politicization of food in Zimbabwe.* New York: Human Rights Watch. http://www.hrw.org/reports/2003/zimbabwe1003/

Humana, Charles. 1992. *World human rights guide,* 3rd ed. New York: Oxford University Press.

Hunt, Paul. 1998. State obligations, indicators, benchmarks, and the right to education. *Human Rights Law and Practice,* no. 4 (September): 109–15.

Hussain, Athar. 1995. Introduction. In *The political economy of hunger: Selected essays,* ed. Jean Drèze, Amartya Sen, and Athar Hussain. Oxford: Clarendon Press.

Insight. 1988. 4, no. 26 (June 27). Includes several articles disputing claims about widespread hunger in the U.S.

International Committee of the Red Cross. 1999. *War and water.* Geneva: International Committee of the Red Cross.

———. 2001. *The right to food: Official statement to the Commission on Human Rights.* Geneva: International Committee of the Red Cross. http://www.icrc.org/Web/ eng/siteengo.nsf/iwpList78/3FB7E0D8B82A07DEC1256B66005FD4ED

International Council on Human Rights Policy. 2003. *Duties sans frontières: Human rights and global social justice.* Geneva: International Committee of the Red Cross. http://www.ichrp.org/

International Federation of Red Cross and Red Crescent Societies. 1994. *Code of conduct for the International Red Cross and Red Crescent Movement and NGOs in disaster relief.* http://www.ifrc.org/publicat/conduct/index.asp

———. 1996a. *The fundamental principles of the International Red Cross and Red Crescent movement.* http://www.ifrc.org/what/values/principles/index.asp

———. 1996b. *World disasters report 1996.* New York: Oxford University Press.

International Indian Treaty Council. 2002. *An analysis of United States international policy on indigenous peoples, the human right to food and food security.* Palmer, Alaska: International Indian Treaty Council. http://www.treatycouncil.org/International%20Indigenous%20Food%20Policy%20Issues.pdf

International Review of the Red Cross. 1993. Guiding principles on the right to humanitarian assistance. *International Review of the Red Cross,* no. 297 (November–December): 519–25.

Jabine, Thomas B., and Richard P. Claude, eds. 1992. *Human rights and statistics: Getting the record straight.* Philadelphia: University of Pennsylvania Press.

Jawara, Fatoumata, and Aileen Kwa. 2003. *Behind the scenes at the WTO: The real world of international trade negotiations.* London: Zed Books.

Jessen-Petersen, Søren. 1999. Food as an integral part of international protection. *SCN News* (newsletter of UN System Standing Committee on Nutrition), no. 18 (July): 32–33. http://www.unsystem.org/scn

Jonsson, Urban. 1994. Millions lost to wrong strategies. *The progress of nations 1994.* New York: UNICEF.

————. 1997. An approach to assess and analyze the health and nutrition situation of children in the perspective of the *Convention on the Rights of the Child. International Journal of Children's Rights* 5, no. 4: 367–81.

Kent, George. 1982. Food trade: The poor feed the rich. *Food and Nutrition Bulletin* 4, no. 4 (October): 33. http://www.unu.edu/unupress/food/8F044e/8F044E05 .htm

————. 1984. *The political economy of hunger: The silent holocaust.* New York: Praeger.

————. 1994. The roles of international organizations in advancing nutrition rights. *Food Policy* 19, no. 4 (July): 357–66.

————. 1995. *Children in the international political economy.* New York: St. Martin's Press.

————. 1999. The United States' targeting of international humanitarian assistance. In *The United States and human rights: Looking inward and outward,* ed. David Forsythe. Lincoln: University of Nebraska Press.

————. 2001. Breastfeeding: A human rights issue? *Development* 44, no. 2.

————. 2002. Food trade and food rights. *United Nations Chronicle* 39: 1. http://www .un.org/Pubs/chronicle/2002/issue1/0102p27.html

————. 2004. Response to 'Breastfeeding and human rights.' *Journal of Human Lactation* 20, no. 2: 146–47.

Kornblum, Elisabeth. 1995. A comparison of self-evaluating state reporting systems. *International Review of the Red Cross,* no. 304 (January–February): 39–68.

Kothari, Rajni. 1997. Globalization in a world adrift. *Alternatives* 22, no. 2: 227–68.

Kourtis, Athena P., Salvatore Butera, Chris Ibegbu, Laurent Beled, and Ann Duerr. 2003. Breast milk and HIV-1: Vector of transmission or vehicle of protection? *The Lancet: Infectious Diseases* 3, no. 12 (December 1). http://infection.thelancet.com/ journal/vol3/iss12/full/laid.3.12.review_and_opinion.27839.1

Krishnaswamy, S., ed. 1963. *Man's right to freedom from hunger: A report of a special assembly held at the headquarters of the Food and Agriculture Organization of the United Nations, Rome, Italy, 14 March.* Rome: Food and Agriculture Organization of the United Nations.

Künnemann, Rolf. 2002. The right to adequate food: Violations related to its minimum core content. In *Core obligations: Building a framework for economic, social and cultural rights,* ed. Audrey Chapman and Sage Russell. Antwerp: Intersentia.

The Lancet. 1999. Slow drip of progress on safe water for all. *The Lancet* 353, no. 9171, June 26.

Latham, Michael C., and Ted Greiner. 1998. Breastfeeding versus formula feeding in HIV infection. *The Lancet* 352, no. 9129 (August 29).

Lawrence, Ruth A., and Robert M. Lawrence. 1998. Making an informed decision about infant feeding. In *Breastfeeding: A guide for the medical profession,* 5th ed. Linn, Mo.: Mosby.

Leary, Virginia. 1994. The right to health in international human rights law. *Health and Human Rights* 1, no. 1 (fall).

Leckie, Scott. 1989. The UN Committee on Economic, Social and Cultural Rights and the right to adequate housing: Towards an appropriate approach. *Human Rights Quarterly* 11, no. 4: 522–60.

Lehman, Stan. 2002. Ending hunger tops new leader's agenda. *Honolulu Advertiser*, October 29, A5.

Longhurst, Richard, and Andrew Tomkins. 1995. The role of care in nutrition: A neglected essential ingredient. *SCN News* (newsletter of UN System Standing Committee on Nutrition), no.12: 1–5. http://www.unsystem.org/scn

Macalister-Smith, Peter. 1985. *International humanitarian assistance: Disaster relief actions in international law and organization.* Dordrecht, The Netherlands: Martinus Nijhoff.

Madeley, John. 2000a. *Hungry for trade: How the poor pay for free trade.* London: Zed Books.

———. 2000b. *Trade and hunger: An overview of case studies on the impact of trade liberalisation on food security.* Stockholm: Forum Syd. http://online.forumsyd.se/web/FS_Globala%20studier/002B5F94-000F6CFB-002B5FB1.0/T&Hunger.pdf

March, James G., and Johan P. Olsen. 1989. *Rediscovering institutions: The organizational basis of politics.* New York: Free Press.

Massing, Michael. 2003. Does democracy avert famine? *New York Times*, March 1.

Maxwell, Simon. 1996. Food security: A postmodern perspective. *Food Policy* 21, no. 2: 155–70.

McGovern, George. 2001. *The third freedom: Ending hunger in our time.* New York: Simon & Schuster.

McLaren, D. S. The great protein fiasco. 1974. *The Lancet* 2: 93–96.

Mears, Catherine, and Helen Young. 1998. *Acceptability and use of cereal-based foods in refugee camps: Case studies from Nepal, Ethiopia, and Tanzania.* Oxfam Working Paper. Oxford: Oxfam.

Medeiros-Neto, Geraldo. 2000. The salt iodization program in Brazil: A medical and political conundrum. *IDD Newsletter* (International Council for Control of Iodine Deficiency Disorders), May, 31–32. http://www.iccidd.org

Mendoza, Miguel Rodriguez. 2002. World Food Summit: Trade liberalization and food security. *WTO News* (World Trade Organization), June 11. http://www.wto.org/wto/english/news_e/news02_e/speech_rodriguez_mendoza_11june02_e.htm

Merrills, J. G., and Arthur Henry Robertson. 2001. *Human rights in Europe: A study of the European Convention on Human Rights,* 4th ed. Manchester: Manchester University Press.

Mestrallet, Gérard. 2002. Bridging the water divide. *Development Outreach* (World Bank), fall. http://www1.worldbank.org/devoutreach/fall02/article.asp?id=179

Miller, T. Christian, and Ann Simmons. 1999. Relief camps for Africans, Kosovars worlds apart. *Los Angeles Times*, May 21. http://www.transnational.org/features/contrasts.html

Morbidity & Mortality Weekly Report. 2000. Self-reported concern about food security: Eight states, 1996–1998. *Morbidity & Mortality Weekly Report* 49, no. 41: 933–36.

Morrison, Pamela. 1999. HIV and infant feeding: To breastfeed or not to breast-feed: The dilemma of competing risks. Parts I and II. *Breastfeeding Review* 7, no. 2: 513.

Murray, Christopher J. L., and Alan D. Lopez, eds. 1996. *The global burden of disease: A comprehensive assessment of mortality and disability from diseases, injuries, and risk factors in 1990 and projected to 2020.* Boston, Geneva, and Washington: Harvard University School of Public Health, World Health Organization, and World Bank.

Nagy, Thomas J. 2001. The secret behind the sanctions: How the U.S. intentionally destroyed Iraq's water supply. *The Progressive* 65, no. 9 (September). http://www.progressive.org/0801issue/nagy0901.html

National WIC Association. 2002. *Monday Morning Report*, February 4.

Nduati, Ruth, Grace John, Dorothy Mbori-Ngacha, Barbara Richardson, Julie Overbaugh, Anthony Mwatha, Jeckoniah Ndinya-Achola, Job Bwayo, Francis E. Onyango, James Hughes, and Joan Kreiss. 2000. Effect of breastfeeding and formula feeding on transmission of HIV-1: A randomized clinical trial. *Journal of the American Medical Association* 283, no. 8 (March 1): 1167–74.

New Mexico Breastfeeding Task Force. 2003. *Breastfeeding and the law: The legal history of breastfeeding.* http://www.breastfeedingnewmexico.org/law_page.html

New York City Welfare Reform and Human Rights Documentation Project. 2000. *Hunger is no accident: New York and federal welfare policies violate the human right to food.* New York: Urban Justice Center's Human Rights Project.

Norberg-Hodge, Helena, Todd Merrifield, and Steven Gorelick. 2002. *Bringing the food economy home: Local alternatives to global agribusiness.* Bloomfield, Conn.: Kumarian Press.

Oddy, Wendy H. 2002. The impact of breastmilk on infant and child health. *Breastfeeding Review* 10, no. 3: 5–18.

Owens, Edgar. 1987. *The future of freedom in the developing world: Economic development as political reform.* New York: Pergamon Press.

Oxfam. 2002. *Rigged rules and double standards: Trade, globalisation, and the fight against poverty.* London: Oxfam. http://www.maketradefair.com/assets/english/Report_English.pdf

———. 2003. *Dumping without borders: How US agricultural policies are destroying the livelihoods of Mexican corn farmers.* Washington, D.C.: Oxfam International. http://www.oxfamamerica.org/publications/art5912.html

Pasour, E. C., Jr. 1976. The right to food. *The Freeman* 26, no. 4 (April). Reprinted at website of Liberty Haven, http://www.libertyhaven.com/noneoftheabove/humororsatire/righttofood.html

Pejic, Jelena. 2001. The right to food in situations of armed conflict: The legal framework. *International Review of the Red Cross* 83, no. 844: 1097–1110. http://www.icrc.org/Web/eng/siteeng0.nsf/htmlall/57JRLG/$FILE/1097-1110_Pejic.pdf

Pelletier, D. L., E. A. Frongillo, Jr., D. G. Schroeder, and J.-P. Habicht. 1995. The effects of malnutrition on child mortality in developing countries. *Bulletin of the World Health Organization* 73, no. 4: 443–48.

Phadke, Mridula, B. Gadgil, K. E. Bharucha, A. N. Shrotri, J. Sastry, N. A. Gupte, R. Brookmeyer, R. S. Paranjape, P. M. Bulakh, H. Pisal, N. Suryavanshi, A. V. Shankar, L. Propper, P. L. Joshi, and R. C. Bollinger. 2003. Replacement-fed infants born to HIV-infected mothers in India have a high early postpartum rate of hospitalization. *Journal of Nutrition* 133: 3153–57.

Phillips, Wendy. 2001. *Why children stay hungry: Agricultural trade, food security and the WTO.* Mississauga, Ontario, Canada: World Vision. http://www.worldvision.org/worldvision/wvususfo.nsf/f7b30c7d9156f79b8525646000810b4b/e09c6c3bb6 4c2b8b88256b65005b15ba/$FILE/Why%20Children%20Stay%20Hungry%20- %20Final.pdf

Physicians Task Force on Hunger in America. 1985. *Hunger in America: The growing epidemic.* Boston: Harvard University School of Public Health.

Poppendieck, Janet. 1998. *Sweet charity: Emergency food and the end of entitlement.* New York: Penguin Books.

———. 1999. Hunger in the land of plenty. In *America Needs Human Rights*, ed. Anuradha Mittal and Peter Rosset. Oakland, Calif.: Institute for Food and Development Policy.

Postel, Sandra. 1999. *Pillar of sand: Can the irrigation miracle last?* Washington, D.C.: Worldwatch Institute.

Rao, A. R. 1977. Human breast milk as a commercial infant food. *Environmental Child Health* (December): 286–88.

Regalado, Aurora A. 2000. State's failure to fulfill and defend its citizens' right to food: The Philippine experience. Paper delivered at the Asian Consultation on Economic, Social and Cultural Rights, Quezon City, Philippines, January 27–28. http://www.philsol.nl/A00a/NCOS-FoodSecurity-janoo-main.htm

Right to Education Project. 2003. *Whither education? Human rights law versus trade law.* 2003. http://www.right-to-education.org/content/strategy/whiter_education.html

Ritchie, Mark. 1999. *The World Trade Organization and the human right to food security.* Minneapolis: Institute for Agriculture and Trade Policy. http://www.agricoop.org/activities/mark_ritche.PDF

Robinson, Mary. 1999. *The human right to food and nutrition.* Geneva: Office of the UN High Commissioner for Human Rights. http://www.unhchr.ch/huricane/huricane.nsf/view01/183FBDBB9C91E434802567520031D24C?opendocument

Rohter, Larry. 2003. Brazil's war on hunger off to a slow start. *New York Times,* March 30.

Roosevelt, Franklin Delano. 1941. The four freedoms. http://www.libertynet.org/ffiedcivic/fdr.html

Rosset, Peter. 2002. *U.S. opposes right to food at world summit.* Oakland, Calif.: Food First and Institute for Food and Development Policy. http://www.foodfirst.org/media/opeds/2002/usopposes.html

Roth, Kenneth. 2004. Defending economic, social and cultural rights: Practical issues faced by an international human rights organization. *Human Rights Quarterly* 26 (February): 63–73.

Sandoz, Yves. 1992. "Droit" or "devoir d'ingerence" and the right to assistance: The issues involved. *International Review of the Red Cross*, no. 288 (May–June): 215–27.

Sanghvi, Tina, and John Murray. 1997. *Improving child health through nutrition: The nutrition minimum package.* Arlington, Va.: Basic Support for Institutionalizing Child Survival (BASICS) Project, for U.S. Agency for International Development. http://www.basics.org/publications

Save the Children Fund UK. 1997. *Household food economy analysis: Kakuma Refugee Camp, Kenya.* Nairobi: Food Economy Assessment Team, Save the Children Fund UK.

Sen, Amartya. 1981. *Poverty and famines: An essay on entitlements.* New York: Oxford University Press.

———. 1999. *Development as freedom.* New York: Alfred A. Knopf.

Shue, Henry. 1996. *Basic rights: Subsistence, affluence, and U.S. foreign policy*, 2nd ed. Princeton, N.J.: Princeton University Press.

Skogly, Sigrun. 2000. Inspecting the World Bank's responsibilities. *Hungry for What Is Right*, no. 18 (April): 4–5.

———. 2001. *The human rights obligations of the World Bank and the IMF.* London: Cavendish.

Skogly, Sigrun, and Mark Gibney. 2002. Transnational human rights obligations. *Human Rights Quarterly* 23, no. 3.

Soguk, Nevzat. 1999. *States and strangers: Refugees and displacements of statecraft.* Minneapolis: University of Minnesota Press.

South African Human Rights Commission.1999. *International Consultative Conference on Food Security and Nutrition as Human Rights: Conference proceedings report.* Johannesburg: South African Human Rights Commission. http://www.sahrc.org.za/food_security_report_final_with_cover.PDF

———. 2002. *3rd economic and social rights report.* Johannesburg: South African Human Rights Commission. http://www.sahrc.org.za/esr_report_1999_2000.htm

———. 2003. *4th economic and social rights report.* Johannesburg: South African Human Rights Commission. http://www.sahrc.org.za/esr_report_2000_2002.htm

Special Report on Infant Feeding, SidAfrique. 1997. *SidAfrique*, nos. 11–12 (September–October).

Sphere Project. 2000. *Sphere Project: Humanitarian charter and minimum standards in disaster response.* Geneva: Sphere Project. http://www.sphereproject.org/

Spirer, Herbert F., and Louise Spirer. 1993. *Data analysis for monitoring human rights.* Washington, D.C.: American Association for the Advancement of Science.

Stammers, Neil. 1999. Social movements and the social construction of human rights. *Human Rights Quarterly* 21, no. 4 (November): 980–1008.

Steiner, Henry J., and Philip Alston, eds. 2000. *International human rights in context: Law, politics, morals*, 2nd ed. Oxford: Oxford University Press.

Sturm, Roland. 2003. Increases in clinically severe obesity in the United States, 1986–2000. *Archives of Internal Medicine* 163: 2146–48.

Thurston, Robert H. 1878. *A history of the growth of the steam engine.* New York: D. Appleton and Co. Reprinted at http://www.history.rochester.edu/steam/thurston/1878

Timberlake, Lloyd, and Laura Thomas. 1990. *When the bough breaks ... Our children, our environment.* London: Earthscan Publications.

Tobin Tax Network. 2003. http://www.waronwant.org/?lid=2

Toebes, Brigit C. A. 1998. *The right to health as a human right in international law.* Antwerp: Intersentia-Hart.

Tyson, Kathleen. 1999. In the eye of the storm. *Mothering,* no. 94 (May–June): 68–69. Also see http://www.televar.com/ffitysn

UNICEF. 1998. *The state of the world's children.* Oxford: Oxford University Press.

UNIFEM. 2004. *Women and Water.* At-a-glance: UNIFEM: Working for women's empowerment and gender equality. http://www.unifem.org/filesconfirmed/2/351_at_a_glance_water_rights.pdf

United Nations. 1986. *The Limburg principles on the implementation of the International Covenant on Economic, Social, and Cultural Rights, 1986.* UN Doc. E/CN.4/1987/17, Annex. New York: United Nations. Reprinted in *Human Rights Quarterly* 9, no. 2 (1987): 122–35; and in *International Court of Justice Review* 37 (December 1986): 43–55. http://www2.uu.nl/english/sim/instr/limburg.asp

———. 2004. *Commission adopts eight resolutions on economic, social, cultural rights, as well as text condemning neo-Nazism.* Press Release HR/CN/1088, 16/04/2004. New York: United Nations. http://www.un.org/News/Press/docs/2004/hrcn-1088.doc.htm

United Nations, Economic and Social Council. 1977. *Standard minimum rules for the treatment of prisoners. Adopted by the First United Nations Congress on the Prevention of Crime and the Treatment of Offenders, held at Geneva in 1955, and approved by the Economic and Social Council by its resolution 663 C (XXIV) of 31 July 1957 and 2076 (LXII) of 13 May 1977.* Geneva: United Nations. http://www.unhchr.ch/html/menu3/b/h_comp34.htm

———. 1995. *Third periodic report: Russian Federation. 10/08/95. E/1994/104/Add.8. (State Party report), Substantive session of 1996.* August 10. Geneva: United Nations. http://www.unhchr.ch/tbs/doc.nsf/c12561460043cb8a41256110445ea9/7c52c1f6ab98f701c12563f0003bf419?OpenDocument

———. 1997. *The realization of economic, social and cultural rights: Final report on the question of the impunity of perpetrators of human rights violations (economic, social and cultural rights), prepared by Mr. El Hadji Guissé, special rapporteur, pursuant to Sub-Commission Resolution 1996/24.* E/CN.4/Sub.2/1997/8, June 27. Geneva: United Nations. http://www.derechos.org/nizkor/impu/guissee.html

———. 1998. *Extradjudicial, summary or arbitrary executions: Report of the special rapporteur on extrajudicial, summary or arbitrary executions, Mr. Bacre Waly Ndiaye, submitted pursuant to Commission resolution 1997/61, addendum, mission to the United States of America.* E/CN.4/1998/68/Add.3, January 22. Geneva: United Nations.

http://www.unhchr.ch/Huridocda/Huridoca.nsf/TestFrame/ce9d6cdd9353d632
c125661300459b39?Opendocument#CONTENTS?Opendocument.

———. 1999a. *Human rights as the primary objective of international trade, investment and finance policy and practice: Working paper submitted by J. Oloka-Onyango and Deepika Udagama, in accordance with Sub-Commission resolution 1998/12.* E/CN.4/Sub.2/1999/11, June 17. Geneva: United Nations. http://www.unhchr.ch/Huridocda/Huridoca.nsf/TestFrame/414357dfe8c9ce76802567c9002f6dec?Opendocument.

———. 1999b. *Intergovernmental meeting on the draft Protocol on Water and Health to the 1992 Convention on the Protection and Use of Transboundary Watercourses and International Lakes, for submission to the Third Ministerial Conference on Environment and Health (London, 16–18 June 1999) for adoption.* MP.WAT/AC.1/199/1, EHCO 020102P, March 24. Geneva: United Nations.

———. 1999c. *The right to adequate food and to be free from hunger. Updated study on the right to food, submitted by Mr. Asbjørn Eide in accordance with Sub-Commission decision 198/106.* ECOSOC E/CN.4/Sub.2/1999/12. Geneva: United Nations. http://ods-dds-ny.un.org/doc/UNDOC/GEN/G99/138/13/PDF/G9913813.pdf?OpenElement

———. 1999d. *Substantive issues arising in the implementation of the International Covenant on Economic, Social and Cultural Rights: General Comment 12 (twentieth session, 1999), the right to adequate food (art. 11).* ECOSOC E/C.12/1999/5. Geneva: United Nations. http://www.unhchr.ch/tbs/doc.nsf/MasterFrameView/3d02758-c707031d58025677f003b73b9?Opendocument

———. 2000. *Substantive issues arising in the implementation of the International Covenant on Economic, Social and Cultural Rights: General Comment no. 14 (2000): The right to the highest attainable standard of health (article 12 of the International Covenant on Economic, Social and Cultural Rights).* ECOSOC E/C.12/2000/4, August 11. Geneva: United Nations. http://www.unhchr.ch/tbs/doc.nsf/385c2add1632f4a-8c12565a9004dc311/40d009901358b0e2c125691500509obe?OpenDocument

———. 2002a. *Economic, social and cultural rights; The right to food; report by the special rapporteur on the right to food, Mr. Jean Ziegler, submitted in accordance with Commission on Human Rights Resolution 2000/25.* UNECOSOC E/CN.4/2002/558, January 10. Geneva: United Nations. http://www.unhchr.ch/Huridocda/Huridoca.nsf/TestFrame/832c9dd3b2f32e68c1256b970054dc89?Opendocument

———. 2002b. *Substantive issues arising in the implementation of the International Covenant on Economic, Social and Cultural Rights: General Comment 15 (2002), the right to water (articles 11 and 12 of the International Covenant on Economic, Social and Cultural Rights.* ECOSOC E/C.12/2002/11. Geneva: United Nations. http://www.unhchr.ch/tbs/doc.nsf/385c2add1632f4a8c12565a9004dc311/a5458d1d1bbd713fc1256cc400389e94?OpenDocument

———. 2003a. *Economic, social and cultural rights: The right to food—report of the special rapporteur, Jean Ziegler, addendum, mission to Bangladesh.* UNECOSOC E/CN

.4/2004/10/Add.1, October 19. Geneva: United Nations. http://www.unhchr.ch/pdf/chr60/10add1AV.pdf

————. 2003b. *Economic, social and cultural rights: The right to food—report by the special rapporteur, Jean Ziegler, addendum, mission to the Occupied Palestinian Territories.* Geneva: UNECOSOC E/CN.4/2004/10/Add.2, October 31. Geneva: United Nations. http://www.unhchr.ch/pdf/chr60/10add2AV.pdf

United Nations, General Assembly. 1999. *Declaration on the Right and Responsibility of Individuals, Groups, and Organs of Society to Promote and Protect Universally Recognized Human Rights and Fundamental Freedoms.* General Assembly Resolution 53/144 of 9 December 1998, A/RES/53/144, March 8. Geneva: United Nations. http://www.unhchr.ch/Huridocda/Huridoca.nsf/(Symbol)/A.RES.53.144.En?Opendocument

————. 2002. *Third committee recommends continuation of office of high commissioner for refugees through end of 2008.* Press Release GA/SHC/3728, November 20. Geneva: United Nations.

————. 2003. *The right to food: Note by the secretary general.* A/58/330, August 28. Geneva: United Nations. http://www.unhchr.ch/Huridocda/Huridoca.nsf/TestFrame/a0abf6e040272ce7c1256dc000371f47?Opendocument

United Nations, International Human Rights Instruments. 2003. *Compilation of general comments and general recommendations adopted by human rights treaty bodies.* HRI/GEN/1/Rev.6, May 12. Geneva: United Nations. http://www.unhchr.ch/tbs/doc.nsf/898586b1dc7b4043c1256a450044f331/ca12c3a4ea8d6c53c1256d500056e56f/$FILE/G0341703.pdf

United Nations, Office of the High Commissioner for Human Rights. 1990. *CESCR General Comment 3: The nature of states parties obligations.* Geneva: United Nations. http://www.unhchr.ch/tbs/doc.nsf/385c2add1632f4a8c12565a9004dc311/94bdbaf59b43a424c12563ed0052b664?OpenDocument

————. 1993. *Vienna Declaration and Program of Action.* World Conference on Human Rights, Vienna (UN Document A/Conf.157/23). Geneva: United Nations. http://www.unhchr.ch/huridocda/huridoca.nsf/(Symbol)/A.CONF.157.23.En?OpenDocument

————. 2001. *Human rights: A basic handbook for UN staff.* Geneva: United Nations.

————. 2002. *Office of the high commissioner for human rights.* Geneva: United Nations. http://www.unhchr.ch/html/menu6/2/OHCHR.pdf

————. 2003. *Human rights and trade.* Geneva: United Nations. http://www.unhchr.ch/html/hchr/cancunfinal.doc

United Nations Conference on Trade and Development. 2001. *Handbook of Statistics 2001.* New York: United Nations.

United Nations Development Program. 1997. *Reconceptualising governance.* New York: United Nations Development Program.

————. 1998. *Integrating human rights with sustainable development.* New York: United Nations Development Program. http://magnet.undp.org/Docs/policy5.html

———. 1999. The invisible heart: Care and the global economy. In *Human development report 1999*. New York: United Nations Development Program.

———. 2002. *Human development report 2002: Deepening democracy in a fragmented world*. New York: Oxford University Press. http://hdr.undp.org/reports/global/2002/en/

United Nations System Standing Committee on Nutrition. 2000. Commission on the Nutrition Challenge of the 21st Century. *Ending malnutrition by 2020: An agenda for change in the millennium*. Geneva: United Nations. http://www.unsystem.org/scn

———. 2004. *5th report on the world nutrition situation: Nutrition for improved development outcomes*. Geneva: United Nations. http://www.unsystem.org/scn

UN Wire. 2004. Aid appeal for Namibia fails to garner any funds, U.N. says. UN Wire, May 4. http://www.unwire.org/UNWire/20040504/449_23438.asp

U.S. Agency for International Development. 1989. *Development and the national interest: U.S. Economic Assistance into the 21st Century*. Washington, D.C.: U.S. Agency for International Development.

U.S. Department of Agriculture. 1996. *World Food Summit: Interpretive statements*. Washington, D.C.: U.S. Department of Agriculture. http://www.fas.usda.gov/icd/summit/interpre.html

———. 1999. *U.S. action plan on food security: Solutions to hunger*. Washington, D.C.: U.S. Department of Agriculture. http://www.fas.usda.gov/icd/summit/usactplan.pdf

———. 2000a. *Food security assessment*. Washington, D.C.: U.S. Department of Agriculture. http://www.ers.usda.gov/publications/gfa12/gfa12.pdf

———. 2000b. *Reaching those in need: Food stamp participation rates in the states*. Washington, D.C.: U.S. Department of Agriculture. http://www.fns.usda.gov/oane/menu/Published/fsp/FILES/Reaching.pdf

———. 2001. *Trends in food stamp participation rates: 1994–1990*. Washington, D.C.: U.S. Department of Agriculture. http://www.fns.usda.gov/oane/MENU/Published/FSP/FILES/Participation/1999TrendsReport.pdf

———. 2003a. *Household food security in the United States, 2002*. Washington, D.C.: U.S. Department of Agriculture. http://www.ers.usda.gov/publications/fanrr35/

———. 2003b. *USDA announces P.L. 480, Title I, Country Allocations for Fiscal 2003*. FAS Online, Foreign Agricultural Service. http://www.fas.usda.gov/scriptsw/PressRelease/pressrel_dout.asp?PrNum=0045-03.

———. 2004. *Household food security in the United States, 2003*. Washington, D.C.: U.S. Department of Agriculture. http://www.ers.usda.gov/publications/fanrr42/

U.S. Department of State. 1998. *Mexico country report on human rights practices for 1998*. Bureau of Democracy, Human Rights, and Labor. Washington, D.C.: U.S. Department of State. http://www.state.gov/www/global/human_rights/1998_hrp_report/mexico.html

———. 1999. *Country reports on human rights practices: 1999*. Bureau of Democracy, Human Rights, and Labor. Washington, D.C.: U.S. Department of State. http://www.state.gov/www/global/human_rights/1999_hrp_report/japan.html

Valente, Flavio. 2000. *Recent developments on the operationalization of the human right to food and nutrition in Brazil.* Oslo: International Project on the Right to Food in Development. http://www.nutrition.uio.no/iprfd/Encounterdocuments/DocO2-G28.html

Valente, Flavio, Luiz Schieck, Nathalie Beghin, Martin Immick, Denise Costa Coitinho, Denise Shrimpton, Milton Rondo, and Kátia Chagas Lúcio Valente. 1999. *Understanding human rights approaches to food and nutritional security in Brazil: Lessons learned.* Brasilia: UNICEF.

Weiss, Thomas G., David P. Forsythe, and Roger A. Coate. 1994. *The United Nations and changing world politics.* Boulder, Colo.: Westview Press.

White House. 2002. *The Millennium Challenge Account.* http://www.whitehouse.gov/infocus/developingnations/millennium.html

Winstanley, Gerrard. 1941. A declaration from the poor oppressed people of England. In *The works of Gerrard Winstanley,* ed. George A. Sabine. Ithaca, N.Y.: Cornell University Press.

Wiseberg, Laurie. 1996. Introductory essay. In *Encyclopedia of human rights,* 2nd edition, ed. Edward Lawson. Washington, D.C.: Taylor & Francis.

Wolf, Leslie E., Bernard Lo, Karen P. Beckerman, Alejandro Dorenbaum, Sarah J. Kilpatrick, and Peggy S. Weintrub. 2001. When parents reject interventions to reduce postnatal human immunodeficiency virus transmission. *Archives of Pediatrics and Adolescent Medicine* 155 (August): 927–33.

World Alliance for Breastfeeding Action. 1998. *Quezón City Declaration: World Alliance for Breastfeeding Action international workshop, June 1–5, 1998, Philippines.* Penang, Malaysia: World Alliance for Breastfeeding Action.

———. 2004. *Nurturing the future: Challenges to breastfeeding in the 21st century. WABA Global Forum II, 23–27 September 2002, Arusha, Tanzania.* Penang, Malaysia. World Alliance for Breastfeeding Action.

World Food Program. 2003. *Estimated food needs and shortfalls for WFP operational activities.* Geneva: World Food Program. http://www.wfp.org/YellowPages

World Food Program and UN High Commissioner for Refugees. 1999. *Guidelines for calculating food rations for refugees.* Geneva: World Food Program. http://www.wfp.org/OP/guide/rations.html

World Health Assembly. 2001. *Infant and young child nutrition.* WHA54.2, May 18. Geneva: World Health Organization.

World Health Organization. 1981. *International Code of Marketing of Breastmilk Substitutes.* Geneva: World Health Organization. http://www.who.int/nut/documents/code_english.PDF; also find subsequent related World Health Assembly Resolutions at http://www.ibfan.org/english/resource/who/fullcode

———. 1998. HIV *and infant feeding: Guidelines for decision-makers;* HIV *and infant feeding: A guide for health care managers and supervisors; and* HIV *and infant feeding: A review of* HIV *transmission through breastfeeding.* Geneva: World Health Organization.

———. 1999a. *Management of severe malnutrition: A manual for physicians and other senior health workers.* Geneva: World Health Organization.

————. 1999b. *World health report.* Geneva: World Health Organization.

————. 2001. *New data on the prevention of mother-to-child transmission of HIV and their policy implications: Conclusions and recommendations—WHO technical consultation on behalf of the UNFPA/UNICEF/WHO/UNAIDS Inter-Agency Task Team on mother-to-child transmission of HIV, Geneva, 11–13 October 2000.* WHO/RHR/ 01.28.2001. Geneva: World Health Organization. http://www.who.int/reproductive-health/rtis/MTCT/mtct_consultation_october_2000/consultation_documents/new_data_on_mtct_conclusions/table_of_contents_en.html

————. 2002. *World health report 2002: Reducing risks, promoting healthy life.* Geneva: World Health Organization. http://www.who.int/whr/2002/en/

————. 2003a. *Global strategy for infant and young child feeding.* Geneva: World Health Organization. http://www.who.int/nut/documents/gs_infant_feeding_text_eng.pdf

————. 2003b. *HIV and infant feeding: Framework for priority action.* Geneva: World Health Organization. http://www.who.int/child-adolescent-health/publications/NUTRITION/HIV_IF_Framework.htm

World Health Organization and World Trade Organization. 2002. *WTO agreements and public health: A joint study by the WHO and the WTO secretariat.* Geneva: Geneva: World Health Organization. and World Trade Organization. http://www.who.int/mediacentre/releases/who64/en/

World Trade Organization. 1996. *Marrakech Agreement Establishing the World Trade Organization.* http://www.wto.org/english/docs_e/legal_e/04-wto_e.htm

————. 2001. *Ministerial declaration.* WT/MIN(01)/DEC/1. Geneva: World Trade Organization. http://www.wto.org/english/thewto_e/minist_e/min01_e/mindecl_e.htm

————. 2003. *Understanding the WTO.* Geneva: World Trade Organization. http://www.wto.org/english/thewto_e/whatis_e/tif_e/tif_e.htm

Yourow, Howard C. 1996. *The margin of appreciation doctrine in the dynamics of European human rights jurisprudence.* The Hague: Martinus Nijhoff.

Index

food production, 193, 195; and food security, 57, 193, 194, 197, 200; and food sovereignty, 199–200; food trade patterns, 194–95; government obligations regarding, 57, 196, 200; and the human right to adequate food, 196–97; and international human rights law, 196; and national sovereignty, 198; and power differentials, 199; reconciling human rights and trade policy frameworks, 197–99; and special rapporteur on the right to food, 57
Treaty of Westphalia (1648), 25, 77, 78, 199, 223
Tyson, Kathleen, 180–82, 184

UN Commission on Sustainable Development, 191
UN Committee on Natural Resources, 191
UN Declaration on the Rights of Indigenous Peoples, 31
UN Declaration on the Right to Development, 31
UN Declaration on the Right to Peace, 29–31
undernourishment, 21
undernutrition, 7, 8, 21. See also malnutrition
UN General Assembly: adoption of children's rights agreements, 32; adoption of Universal Declaration of Human Rights, 26, 28; and drafting/ratification of international human rights agreements, 78; and ECOSOC, 38; and human rights responsibilities, 37; Third Committee, 37, 39, 160
UN High Commissioner for Refugees (UNHCR), 120, 202, 205–6, 207
UNICEF (United Nations Children's Fund), 9, 35, 48, 214, 221, 228;

budget allocations, 219; and Committee on the Rights of the Child, 33; and Innocenti Declaration, 51, 166; and NGO's/CSO's, 42; obligations as nonstate actor, 118; and world mortality, 15, 16, 19, 146
UNICEF Executive Board, 51, 166
Union of International Associations, 42
United Kingdom, 135–36
United Nations Administrative Committee on Coordination/Sub-Committee on Coordination (ACC/SCN). See United Nations System Standing Committee on Nutrition (SCN)
United Nations agencies and human rights, 35–36
United Nations Charter, 26, 28, 29, 38
United Nations charter bodies, 37–40
United Nations Conference on Environment and Development (1990), 52
United Nations Council for Namibia, 37
United Nations Development Assistance Framework, 118, 224–25
United Nations Development Program, 35, 138–39
United Nations Environmental Program, 113
United Nations Fund for Population Activities, 35
United Nations Office for Coordination of Humanitarian Assistance, 214
United Nations' special rapporteur on the right to food, 7, 56–57, 155
United Nations System Standing Committee on Nutrition (SCN), 7, 15, 53, 74, 201, 228
United Nations treaty bodies: central functions of, 40, 41; and complaints from individuals, 29, 30, 40–41, 132
United States, 156–62; charity emphasis in, 123–25; data on food inse-